HN
385.5
.W515
1990

Williamson, Bill,
  1944-

The temper of the
  times.

$39.95

The Temper of the Times

For Diane

The Temper of the Times

Times

British Society since World War II

Bill Williamson

Basil Blackwell

Copyright © Bill Williamson 1990

First published 1990

Basil Blackwell Ltd
108 Cowley Road, Oxford, OX4 1JF, UK

Basil Blackwell, Inc.
3 Cambridge Center
Cambridge, Massachusetts 02142, USA

British Library Cataloguing in Publication Data
A CIP catalogue record for this book is available from the British Library.

Library of Congress Cataloging in Publication Data
Williamson, Bill, 1944–
    The temper of the times: British society since World War II/
Bill Williamson.
        p.   cm.
    Includes bibliographical references.
    ISBN 0–631–15919–3
        1. Great Britain–Social conditions–1945–   2. Great Britain–
    Politics and government–1945–   I. Title.
    HN385.5.W515   1990
    306′.0941–dc20   89–77330
                                                        CIP

Typeset in 11½ on 13½ pt Garamond
by Wearside Tradespools, Sunderland
Printed in Great Britain by
T.J. Press Ltd, Padstow

Contents

Preface

There is a self indulgence in writing, which it is best to acknowledge. I have written this book to clarify what I have come to understand about British society in the post-war period. It is now half a century since Hitler invaded Poland and World War II began. The madness of Fascism left the Europe into which I was born a poor, politically divided, shattered place strewn with corpses; millions of people had died and at least 6 million of those deaths were the result of systematic genocide in death camps. That was the legacy. The country into which I was born had fought against Fascism, and by the time I got here, the battle was almost over. Many of the hopes for a better world which my parents' generation had, and for which they fought, have been realized. Many others have not.

In a nutshell, that is the context of this book. I have tried to understand and explain what has happened in Britain since the war. A balance has been struck for each post-war generation between their hopes for a better world and the practical possibilities of realizing them. I want to know how that balance is arrived at. I want to know why some people can look back on the past forty years with quiet satisfaction and why others do so with regret. This book is an attempt to understand these matters.

Now that it is finished, I can see many ways in which it might have been different. Above all, of course, as I knew full well when I began it, the book has opened up for me many new questions to which I will now search for answers. My treatment of those questions I knew I was dealing with is, of course, incomplete and, certainly, in many ways flawed. Nevertheless, despite its weaknesses, I remain convinced about one essential element of its approach: the way the book seeks to engage the reader in a debate, not only about what people in British society have done, or thought, but also about how they have felt. I hope, too, to persuade those who read this book that the business of writing history is something saturated with the assumptions, beliefs, prejudices and interpretations of historians. There is no historian-free history or interpretation-free social science. There is only good and bad history, good and bad social science.

To my mind, the worst of both are studies which strain towards a false objectivity, guided by the erroneous view that the evidence of history in some way speaks for itself and somehow exists apart from the historians who work with it. In such a view, the aim of history is thought to be that of reconstructing the past as it was. Historical facts, however, as the great historian E.H. Carr once pointed out, are always interpreted facts. They have no meaning apart from the interpretations which lend them significance. This does not mean that history can be made into whatever we want it to be. On the contrary. It means that those who quarry in the past have an obligation to present their evidence clearly and in ways which make it accessible to others to interpret. It means that there has to be an open acknowledgement that historical interpretation involves dialogue between the researcher and the evidence and between the concerns of people today and those of yesterday.

Approached this way, the value of any well-constructed and well-researched historical interpretation has to be judged by its credibility. Whether an argument fits the evidence is only one, albeit a major, part of the test. Interpretations must square, too, with experience and with the way in which people in the past made sense of their world. Whether a particular interpretation of the past meets these requirements is something to be tested in public, in a wide-ranging and open way.

I hope what I have written is accessible to people and will be approached in a critical and constructive way. I am more concerned that there should be debate and dialogue about what I have written than there should be agreement about it. The world I started out in was dangerous and, in the end, destructive, precisely because too many people were prepared to accept glibly what their leaders or their teachers believed to be the truth about history. I look forward to discussions in which the approach, the claims and the evidence of this book are all inspected and evaluated. I expect from those discussions that my own experience of the period I have written about will be broadened and deepened. If I provoke a similar response in those who read the book I shall be well pleased. In this way we can all arrive at an understanding of the past and come to a sane view of why some accounts are flawed. The more people who are involved in those discussions, the better. For unless we understand the past in a critical way, there can be no clear view of what the future should be.

Ideas do not just emerge. Those developed in this book grew out of my teaching and my efforts, as an ordinary citizen of my country, to understand its politics. The ideas have been tested out on colleagues and students. The book was conceived when I taught in the Department of Sociology and Social Policy in the University of Durham. That was a good setting in which to brood on what is actually involved in interpreting the world. Work with students pursuing their studies extramurally reinforced my conviction that, however well I myself might be able to bring it off, the discussion of sentiment and feeling was an important part of history. I am grateful for the opportunities those colleagues and students gave me to test out my ideas.

I wish to record my thanks to the staff of the Mass Observation Archive at the University of Sussex for the help they gave me in using that rich resource. My friend and former colleague, Professor John Veit-Wilson of Newcastle Polytechnic, read parts of the manuscript and discussed with me my interpretation of aspects of the development of the welfare state. Our views have differed but I learned much from his comments. The staff of the university libraries in Durham and Newcastle, as well as of the library in Newcastle Polytechnic, were always helpful and well organized. Once more, I wish to thank them for the quietly efficient way in which they make work of this kind possible.

The manuscript of this book was checked by my daughter, Joanna Williamson, and by her equally literate friend, Bridget Rendell. They detected more errors of grammar than I imagined possible and I shall try hard in future to improve my use of commas. Beryl Parker, of the Department of Adult and Continuing Education of the University of Durham, typed large sections of the manuscript and did a great deal to help me prepare the rest on the word-processor. I am grateful for the work she has done. Dennis Doran, from the same department, led me through the intricacies of word-processing better than anyone has been able to in the past. I remain suspicious of computers but feel much less inadequate about using them. Finally, a grant from the Staff Research Fund, and a term's leave granted to me by the University of Durham, made it possible for me to carry out some of the work for this book free of normal teaching duties. I am very grateful for that opportunity and hope, despite the straitened times, the university will continue to make it possible for its staff to take research leave. It is a most productive way to support the research which is so central to the life of any university worthy of the name.

I could not end without thanks to my wife, Diane, and my son, Johnny, who have put up with grumbles, absences and, from time to time, meals ruined by my almost manic enthusiasm for talking about what I was writing. Their comments, though, have been much more valuable to me than I am sure either of them imagines. I hope they feel the effort of putting up with me was worth the result. It goes without saying that responsibility for all the errors, weaknesses and distortions of the book is mine alone.

Bill Williamson
Durham 1989

Acknowledgements

I wish to acknowledge gratefully the permission given by the publishers, Faber and Faber, to reproduce quotations from John Osborne's play, *Look Back in Anger*, and from Philip Larkin's poems, '*Annus Mirabilis*' and '*Homage to a Government*,' from the collection, *High Windows* (Faber and Faber 1974). I wish to thank the poet, Tony Harrison, for his permission to quote extracts from his *Selected Poems* (Penguin, 1984) and from *V* (Bloodaxe Books, 1985). Bloodaxe Books have kindly allowed me to reproduce a quotation from George Charlton's poem '*Nightshift Workers*' (in *Poetry With an Edge* edited by Neil Astley, Bloodaxe Books, 1988).

Introduction

The period of time with which this book is concerned corresponds almost exactly with that of my own life. I was born in 1944, just a year, almost to the day, before the end of the war in Europe. My parents lived on a council estate on Tyneside and during the war my father worked in Vickers-Armstrong's factories building armaments for the Royal Navy. In addition to twelve-hour shifts in the factory he was obliged to do auxiliary fire service duty. My mother was not drafted to war work on the account of looking after my brother, who was born in 1939. I came along at a time when the end of the war was in view, but my mother's memories of the time were less of the war itself and much more of the relentless busyness of looking after the children.

Theirs was not a heroic war. They kept themselves informed of its military developments from Sir John Hamilton's publication, *War Illustrated*, which they took on subscription, but they were largely unaffected by military violence. Tyneside was not badly bombed although its strategic importance to the war effort was great. Distance from European airfields, good coastal defences and industrial smog protected the Tyne from *Luftwaffe* attack. Their war was mundane. Like millions of others they coped the best they could with shortages, shift work and uncertainty, and muddled through finding their pleasures where they could.

By the time I arrived the Allied armies were driving their way north through Italy, preparations for the Normandy landings were almost complete and Stalin's armies were advancing steadily in their long sweep through eastern Europe. The bombing offensive against Germany was relentless and carried on right into 1945. Dresden was destroyed on the nights of 13 and 14 February with deaths estimated to be between 30,000 and 130,000. The death that mattered most to my mother was that of my twin brother. He died of pneumonia, which newer drugs might have cured, on 11 February, the last day but one of the Yalta Conference where Churchill, Stalin and Roosevelt agreed among themselves the political outlines of Europe and the Far East after the war was over.

Conventional military force, especially on the eastern fronts, destroyed Hitler; Japan was defeated with the atom bomb in the August of 1945. Each outcome, in different ways, was a triumph of military organization, political planning and the mobilization of science and technology for political ends. The ultimate irony, of course, is that the ramified outcomes of total war, particularly the nuclear weaponry it threw up, have been unamenable to control in ways which could secure the promise of that better world for which millions had died.

Not all the babies born in Europe in the last year of the war were planned; war disrupts that sort of thing. But we were a generation for which much was planned. Hitler had had his grand schemes to build for us a *Reich* in a racially pure Europe, which was to last for a thousand years and be free of democracy, Jews, Communists, gypsies, homosexuals and those who were mentally handicapped. The war itself, at least for some, was fought to ensure that we would have a different future. And while it was being fought, plans were being laid in Britain for a future which would guarantee us decent health care, education and the right of employment in a world in which disagreements between nations would be resolved peacefully in a framework of law and collective security.

These were high hopes and widely shared. No one, of course, could have known then precisely how the new world would be built or, indeed, if it could be built. And there were some whose highest hopes were to retrieve and restore as much from the pre-war world as possible and who looked on the new with a sense of doom. My parents were hopeful of a better world and trusted a Labour government under Attlee to help build it. Their hopes were fixed on educational opportunities for their sons, hopes which by then reflected a much clearer sense of what they themselves had been denied.

Hindsight allows us now to see that some of their hopes for a better world were naive to the point of innocence and that they lacked a precise vision of the ways in which it had to be different from the past. The trust which men like my father placed in the capacity of the country's leaders to make old institutions work in new ways was misplaced, yet entirely understandable. But that trust was part of a broad movement of opinion and feeling, with popular memory of the 1930s on its side, that the opportunity and the mandate was there to build a better, more decent world. For us young ones it was like coming in on the crest of a wave.

And in truth, by the tests most people apply to measure progress, many of those early post-war hopes were, in fact, realized. Living standards steadily improved during the 1950s; the welfare state was put in place; colonies were transformed into Commonwealth. New structures for international co-operation, particularly the United Nations, have kept hopes alive that collective security can be based on negotiation. But if that fails Europeans have known for the last thirty-five years that American commitments to our security would match up to any Soviet threat.

The world remains, however, a dangerous and divided place. The forty years which have passed have been precariously peaceful in Europe. But the price of that has been to shift the theatres of great power-conflict to other areas of the globe and for all of us to have to live under the ominous shadow of nuclear annihilation. Within this framework, which is itself unstable and fast changing, people in Britain and the rest of Europe, and indeed all over the world, have experienced quite profound transformations in their societies and their personal lives.

It is the principal aim of this book to explore these changes, to trace against this background changes in British society in what Raymond Williams has called 'structures of feeling' (1977). A typically difficult concept, it refers to social experience and practical consciousness, to what he calls the 'affective elements of consciousness and relationships' (1977:132). Williams is, of course, particularly interested to examine how changes in structures of feeling are traceable in art, and in particular literary art, and how those changes themselves are part of larger moments of change in the class structures of capitalism. My concern is with a much shorter period and with how change is expressed in personal relations, in social perceptions, in modes of self recognition, in social values as part of lived and living experience and in social actions of various kinds.

The book has its origins, unashamedly, in personal bio-graphical reflection. The disconnected memories of my early childhood are of a world of ration books, tram cars, corner shops, women with their hair tucked into triangular head-scarves. They include playing with old gas masks and ARP tin hats left over from the war. They are of regular visits to local cinemas with their gold braid decor and sickly smells of mingled sweat, smoke and perfume spray. And I have a particularly vivid memory of laughing at my mother painting black lines on her legs to simulate nylon stockings. These are memory traces of a 1940s life-style, and a further elaboration of their setting (an inter-war council estate, free of cars or a park to play in, the municipal wash house, the swimming baths, the public library and the houses with their doors painted all the same colour) would spell out vividly both the austerity of the period and, at least in that Labour stronghold, the confident optimism that the local authority could provide us with what we needed. Certainly, the memories cannot be properly understood by me or anyone else apart from the setting which gave them shape.

Austerity and municipal socialism are part of these memories. So, too, is what I could only recognize much later as the distinctive characteristics of the class system of this society. Class relationships are part of the structure of a society; they are built into its history, its economic arrangements, its culture and its life-styles and are encountered directly in how we experience other people. Visits to the doctor's surgery were for me, even as a pre-school child, uncomfortable. The panelled silence of the place, the supercilious receptionist and the doctor himself, whose accent, voice and whole demeanour set him apart from all his patients, all conspired to make me wonder whether people like us had any right to be there at all. The surgery always prompted in my mother an attitude which I now recognize as one of deferential defensiveness, and her unease was so out of character that she communicated it to me.

Those aspects of class relations which translate into some people feeling convinced of their social superiority, and others feeling that they are in some ways inferior or less important or inadequate, will be given a central place in this book. For class is not just a matter of the distribution of wealth or power; it concerns, too, the distribution of self respect and of moral worth. Sennet and Cobb were so right to place the study of 'the hidden injuries of class' on the agendas of sociological research (1972).

Deference and feelings of inferiority are facets of how class is experienced. So, too, is ambition. My father was a factory worker all his working life. Prior to World War II he had attempted, through a correspondence course, to gain some of the educational qualifications he had by then come to understand he had been denied. The war foiled his ambitions but the 1944 Education Act enabled him to refocus them on his children. I have a particularly clear memory of being carried on his shoulder past my primary school on the day we had received the news that my brother had passed his 'grading exam' and would be starting the grammar school. My father told my brother: 'Now you'll have to put "ing" on the end of your words. You'll have to say "running" and not "runnin", "swimming" and not "swimmin".' I nearly fell off laughing. Why anyone should talk like that was beyond me.

This small episode on a dreary wet night early in the year 1950 can only be understood in terms of the distinctiveness of class relations in British society at that time; it is a little moral tale of ambition, of how social differences are constructed and of naive hope. I am sure my father wanted the best for his son: he could not have anticipated then just what that would subsequently mean for his son, or for his relationship with him, or for the ways in which his son would come subsequently to understand his own past and define his own values. But the differences which did emerge between father and son, between one generation and the next, are tightly enmeshed in the longer-term transformations of class which themselves are part of the post-war reconstruction of British society. The ambivalence which the scholarship boy felt towards his class of origin, his sense of what his own highest ambitions were, are part of this as well. The idea that we grammar school boys should get on and do well in the world and carry forward some of the hopes of our parents is part of a new 'structure of feeling', which eroded the more austere collectivism of the immediate post-war years and helped usher in the affluent society.

Education was the means through which some of us achieved social mobility. In addition to that, thousands moved further up in the world by moving house and buying their own homes. The Conservative Party was astute enough in the 1950s to sense that their idea of a property-owning democracy would be electorally appealing to working class people. In the case of my own family this happened in 1955, although we moved from our council house in 1950 to a tied flat above the shop my mother managed. That move to a home we owned was an escape for us and a turning point. It corresponded with my brother starting the grammar school and with an uncle who was too ill to drive giving us his car, which made it easy to have family camping holidays and weekend trips to the country. What we experienced privately as good fortune was, in fact, part of a more widely diffused improvement in living standards which some people, but by no means all, began to enjoy in the early 1950s.

It was, however, a precarious peace we were all enjoying, and fighting in Korea threatened to destroy it altogether. I remember being curious about what Communists were. My father explained that if there were lots of people all wanting bread or sweets and there was not enough to go around, then the Communist was the man who would try and share them out so that people got a fair share. I thought that was a good idea but I knew I should not think like that because somehow Communists were bad and to be feared.

My parents were not then or later particularly interested in politics, although they were aware of the news and discussed it. In many ways the past and the future mattered to them much more than the present, and the private world of their family, although not just their own immediate family, was much more compelling in its demands and interests than the public world of politics. How they drew that line between the public and the private is, of course, not just a matter of their personal inclinations; it is also an aspect of the political culture of the society. When my brother, late in the 1950s as a student at Durham University, took an active interest in the politics of nuclear disarmament, my parents were quite worried lest he neglected his studies. Politics for them was best left to others, a kind of indulgence which the likes of us could not afford.

They voted Labour; my father attended branch meetings of his union, the AEU, but the realm of politics as a field of action or personal commitment was not something that really concerned them. Even uncle Fred, railway guard, Labour Party member, *Reynold's News* reader who had every argument that could be levelled at the Tories precisely prepared, though he was valued as a member of the family, had his political inclinations either ignored or laughed at. But it was uncle Fred who explained to me one afternoon, when the death of Stalin was announced, that Stalin had been a very great man.

These are just memories, experiences sifted from the flow of total experience to be regarded later as being in some way significant. I can even remember the 1951 general election, because uncle Fred pinned a rosette on me and sent me round the street singing:

> Vote vote vote for Mr Popplewell
> Who's that knocking at the door?
> If it's Labour let him in,
> If it's Tory kick his shin
> And he won't come a'knocking any more.

For the period of the early 1950s before, I, too, went to the grammar school, I can recall lurid news items about the Mau Mau rebellion in Kenya; the announcement of the death of King George VI is very vivid and so, too, are the courage of Captain Carlson on the *Flying Enterprise*, burning candles to boil his tea, the Festival of Britain – remembered for the mug I was given at school – and, of course, the conquest of Everest. I found that far more interesting than the Coronation.

Vivid, too, are the Remembrance Day parades beside the war memorial at the top of our street after we left Scotswood, although it was only years afterwards that I could begin to appreciate their significance for the older generation whose memories encompassed the war itself and perhaps, too, World War I. No one in my family had any direct military connections: their memories, at this time, were marked by the industrial struggles of the coalfields in the 1920s and the depression years of the 1930s. Some of their stories from these times were told to us often enough in our childhood for us always to remember that in some way we, too, were connected with those difficult times.

The hopes my parents had for us were part of their memory of their own pre-war experiences and of the hopes they had nurtured during the war. My point for the moment is that memory, too, is part of political culture and of how values are shaped. And it is simply wrong to treat memory as if it was something uniquely individual. For what memory sifts out from that total set of experiences and images which make up everyday life are those episodes or feelings which are framed in some way as being significant. Sometimes that framing is personal, like the birth or death of a baby; but the public events which stand out have already been framed by others, by government or the mass media or political or social movements of various kinds, to give a definite shape and meaning to the the way in which events should be interpreted and to identify which ones should be seen as significant. How the past is perceived and valued is an aspect of prevailing structures of feeling, a facet, too, of the ideological structuring of history itself which can become formalized and framed as institutions.

My mother used to say that she was never any good at history: she could not remember the names and dates of kings and queens. And years later she could not take seriously the concern I showed for the ordinary details of her life in a mining village. She could not see her own past as something in which anyone could show a genuine historical interest. Lacking such an interest herself, she was in effect debarred from seeking to understand what social forces had given shape to her life and to the opportunities and experience it had offered her.

Lacking also the resources with which to explore the past in an active way, it was almost inevitable that people in circumstances like those of my parents would come to rely on historical interpretations framed by others. But I am not thinking here of how they understood the Magna Carta or King Canute; I am thinking of the Dunkirk spirit or the people's war or the Communist threat or the actions of rebels or terrorists in the far-flung theatres of colonial war which continued to engage British forces in the 1960s. I am not suggesting that ordinary people are merely victims of someone else's propaganda. There is too deep a well of common sense and too healthy a disrespect for received opinions for that to be the case. But it is necessary, again to use Williams's terms, to distinguish between structures of feeling which are dominant and those which are residual or emergent (1977).

For cultures and modes of perception and feeling are never static. They change through time: new forms of understanding emerge, sometimes to be incorporated into the old, sometimes to replace it. In post-war Britain, in contrast certainly to France or the Federal Republic of Germany, an older dominant culture, with the structures of feeling which were part of it and the perception of the national past on which it fed, retained strong institutional support. It was ritually endorsed in the ceremony of monarchy, in civic rituals of all kinds from, for example, the Festival of Britain to local summer pageants, and in the routine operation of the country's political system, its educational system, its courts and its media of mass communication. Here was a framework of perception and understanding and emotional feeling which the traumas of Hitler's war had strengthened and vindicated, and which needed strenuous defence against potential enemies from the East.

It was not a setting from which a radical alternative interpretation of the past or of the present could emerge. The despair of the New Left in Britain in the 1950s at the political behaviour of the working class is a reflection of this fact. But so, too, is the nostalgia for the past of writers like Waugh or Eliot whose elitism and cultural pessimism could not be squared with the materialism, the planning and populism of the early post-war period.

By the mid 1950s significant breaks did begin to open up in the dominant culture. John Osborne's play, *Look Back in Anger*, shocked its audiences. Jimmy Porter's comment that 'people of our generation aren't able to die for good causes any longer. We had that done for us, in the thirties and forties, when we were still kids' was profoundly disturbing to an older generation committed to Empire and fighting the Cold War. Jimmy went on:

There aren't any good, brave causes left. If the big bang does come, and we all get killed off, it won't be in aid of the old-fashioned, grand design. It'll be for the Brave New-nothing-very-much-thank-you. About as pointless and inglorious as stepping in front of a bus. (Osborne 1956:84–5)

Osborne was later to refer to royalty as 'the national swill' and 'the gold filling in a mouthful of decay' (1958:65). What he was railing at was the Establishment – a word which became popular in the 1950s; the class system, the BBC with its staff, as he put it, of 'highly trained palace lackeys with graveyard voices and a ponderous language stuffed with Shakespearian and semi-Biblical echoes' (1958:65). But there was yet more: he was angry about South Africa, the H-bomb and the debacle of Suez.

The Suez affair can be rightly regarded as a turning point. The Russian invasion of Hungary, which followed shortly after the British, French and Israeli attack on Egypt, may have confirmed many of the worst Cold War presuppositions about the Soviet threat, but Suez took away from Britain any moral superiority it might claim over the Eastern bloc.

I knew about Suez but recall being more concerned about Hungary. The Pathe News films that I saw twice weekly at least during this period – we lived three doors away from the local cinema – were filled with images of Hungarian refugees. But it did not really matter to me. It was far more important to my brother who was hoping he would do sufficiently well at school to defer his national service. I think both he and my parents were worried that a deteriorating political situation might lead to a general call-up to the forces which would involve my brother.

I can claim no real interest in politics until the Cuban missile crisis of 1962 when, as a student in London, I listened to Kennedy's broadcast insisting that the Russians should turn back from Cuba, and wondered whether there would be a world to wake up to the next day. For the period between Hungary and the Bay of Pigs I was far too preoccupied with adolescence to take much notice of the world beyond my immediate circle of friends.

The world we lived in was full of girls, rock'n'roll, illicit drinking, youth clubs, dance halls and, in my case, school, although not for any reasons connected with its academic purpose; school meant simply more friends, girls, football and fun. My education was not spoiled by the thought that it was important for a career. Everybody got jobs then: we could pick and choose. And my parents were by then not so enamoured of the effects of the grammar school on my brother, so that they consciously, so I found out later, lifted some of the pressure from me to do well at school.

My awareness of a larger world of politics and international affairs was, of course, steadily expanding, although it was not a world for which I felt any particular responsibility. My brother was a great influence here; he imported into the home his interest in CND – the Campaign for Nuclear Disarmament. He came back from university for weekends with books none of us had ever heard of and, playing the missionary role, particularly towards me, got me to read some Orwell, Kafka, Huxley and Lawrence. When *Lady Chatterley's Lover* became legal he bought it as a present for my mother. She disappeared off into the sitting room for two days and came out, slightly blushing since she knew my brother was looking closely at her to see what she would say about the book. She gave it back to him with a knowing look and said, 'It's good; just like real life.'

It is only much later, of course, that personal experience can be reinterpreted in the light of commentary about what was going on in this period. The emergence of youth culture, the affluent society, the Americanization of popular culture and the growth of mass society are among the ideas which were both then and later deployed to make sense of this period of time.

Visual images are central to my recall of even my personal past and since, unlike millions of others, we did not have a television set until 1958, the images which stand out come from cinema newsreels. In the later 1950s and early 1960s they were often of ceremonies in Africa with colonial governors in their funny hats helping one of the royal family lower the Union Jack to give some new nation its independence. Black people in such film reports were always portrayed as tribesmen locked in their traditions while we obliged them with their freedom. Decolonization was never, however, a gift, although that is how it was presented. It was something wrung from a declining world power and it corresponded in Britain with immigration from the West Indies and the first 'racial' disturbances in Nottingham and in Notting Hill.

Between 1960 and 1962, the time I spent in the sixth form of the grammar school, there was much discussion about Britain and the Common Market. Uncle Fred was dead against it if it meant having to drink 'all that pissy wine wor Clive brings back from France', and I felt, following a visit to Germany in 1960, that it would be a good idea to join. I remember writing an essay on the Common Market as part of a selection interview at a teacher training college. It ended in a rhetorical flourish echoing President Kennedy's words during his trip to Berlin after Ulbricht had built the Berlin Wall; Kennedy had said 'I am a Berliner.' I wrote, 'I am a European.'

In truth, I was intensely bored by the Common Market. What intrigued me more was the trial of Adolf Eichmann and the earth orbit of Yuri Gagarin. I made two pencil drawings of each man and set them out alongside one another. They symbolized for me, rather too obviously in retrospect, two quite different human potentialities. Science, imagination and economic achievement on the one hand and absolute evil on the other vied with one another for the future of the human race. The gap between possibility and performance could not, it seemed to me then, be wider.

Sputniks and decolonization and the cap-in-hand approach to

both the Americans and the Common Market all mark the early 1960s out as a time when people in this country became clearly aware of the country's loss of status as a world power. But as was the case with thousands of other families, what we experienced at the time was something my parents certainly understood as progress. We acquired a brand-new Mini car in 1960; my brother and I spent a holiday abroad that year; our school moved to a new building and quadrupled its annual intake of pupils. My brother was at university, part of that first generation of working class kids who had had a crack at education after the age of fourteen. The welfare state and economic growth had delivered their goods in abundance.

My brother had by this time discovered revolutionary socialism and was developing an understanding of post-war politics radically at odds with that of my parents, who felt quite deeply alienated from his views and attitudes. My view now of what my brother was experiencing then is that he was resolving the inadequacies he felt in himself, and which were prompted by his encounter with a bourgeois culture at university, by a thoroughgoing identification with the class from which he came. It was not, however, the class of his parents; it was the historic working class with its mission to transform capitalism.

For a long time we could not have a serious conversation with one another. By sheer good luck – it was certainly undeserved – I became a student of sociology at a London polytechnic. It was for me, although not at first – I was far too homesick and appalled at my own intellectual inadequacies – a liberating experience. What I read put my own experience and that of my parents and brother into an entirely new light, but it led to an understanding of this society sharply at odds with that which my brother approved of. And because it did not lead me into revolutionary politics I think my brother thought of me for a while as something of a class traitor.

My reading at the time did, however, strengthen a sense that there was much deeply wrong with this society, although I felt then somewhat overawed by the complexity of the task of understanding it. The Profumo scandal which broke in 1963 confirmed my sense of its corruption. It was really exciting and

I read the papers avidly. The Establishment was in disarray, or so it seemed; real change was in prospect.

And the pace of change seemed to accelerate during the 1960s. Labour governments, new technology, Mary Quant, the Beatles, 'Swinging London', abortion law reform and much, much more have left a residue in the historical imagination of British society of a period of time when quite profound changes occurred. The symbol of it is 1968. The historian, Arthur Marwick, has described it all as the end of Victorianism (1982). Others have written of an 'expressive revolution' although it is one which, in retrospect, was not as profoundly transformative of society as many of its adherents felt at the time (Martin 1981). Ever present, of course, was the Vietnam War and the appalling scenes of burning children suffering for the defence of a democracy which many believed had become indefensible. In the confusion and complexity of the sixties only this is clear: that nothing any longer was clear, that the political moods of the young were international in character and that new forms of radical consciousness were certain to shape the agendas of politics.

What for some was a sense of confident optimism gave way in the early 1970s to a sense of crisis and despair about the future of the society. But throughout the 1970s new structures of feeling did emerge. The women's movement challenged the society in quite fundamental ways but did not replace a preoccupation with the economics of decline as the key issue on most political agendas. And the 1980s has seen in the peace movements and the ecology movement new resources for what Raymond Williams has called 'a journey of hope' (1983). The danger, though, as he saw it, is that the political institutions of British society and particularly those of the labour movement are not really geared up to translating the nurtured hopes for peace, for respect and equality between men and women and for care for the environment into practical plans to build a different society.

And what militates against change is the fact that most of the ordinary people of British society, preoccupied as they necessarily are with the 'decisive pressures' of family and work or unemployment, and lacking access to extended learning or information, are locked into a 'practical and limited set of interests', and are unable to share fully in what Williams called the 'affordable dissent' of sections of the middle class (1983:254).

The prospects of realizing a different future rest, in Williams's view, in challenging what he called the 'nameable agencies of power and capital, distraction and disinformation and all these interlocking with the embedded short-term pressures and the interwoven subordinations of an adaptive commonsense' (1983:268). The promise is of a world where new kinds of human relationship are possible, where intelligence is not contrasted with emotion and where society is concerned with livelihood rather than merely production.

The task of defining more precisely the elements of the emergent structure of feeling Williams was concerned with and of defending new political structures appropriate to their realization is an enormous one. It is one which will require changes in social perception and in attitudes and feelings towards ourselves and other peoples. It is one of the ironies which prompted me in the end to try to write this book, that the framework of co-operation and care which focused post-war aspirations for a better world is now a set of structures which inhibit the realization of the kind of sensibility a decent society presupposes.

Michael Ignatieff captured this for me when he noted that we have needs above those of income and food and clothing; we need, too, love, respect, honour, dignity, solidarity with others and social arrangements appropriate to the realization of all these:

the bureaucratised transfer of income among strangers has freed each of us from the enslavement of gift relations. Yet if the welfare state does serve the needs of freedom, it does not serve the needs of solidarity. We remain a society of strangers. (1984:18)

Whether this can change depends ultimately on how we comprehend the society in which we live and the feelings and attitudes it sustains. It has been a source of great concern to me that social science has a great responsibility to provide such an understanding but has not matched up to it. There are, of course, exceptions, but in the main social science has been too insensitive to history to grasp the extent and pace of change which has overtaken us. It has been too preoccupied with ideas and structures and groups to understand the potency of feelings, relationships and personal change.

Historians, too, however, have their faults. Theodore Zeldin organized his history of France during the nineteenth and twentieth centuries around a discussion of six passions: ambition, love, anger, pride, taste and anxiety, and made the individual Frenchman his starting point (1978). 'Historians', he wrote, 'have by custom concerned themselves with public lives, with issues and movements. So they have left private lives, the emotions of the individual, to the novelists' (1978:preface). His concern, in contrast, was to focus on how people feel about themselves 'without taking it for granted that their behaviour is determined principally by their economic situation'.

This is an argument for taking seriously how people respond emotionally to experience, for trying to see how feelings are part of how people think and act. Some historians have grasped the truth of this and of these, perhaps, Sir Lewis Namier is the most well known in Britain. In his essay 'Human Nature in Politics' he insisted that political ideas are inseparable from their underlying emotions. They are, as he put it, 'the music, to which ideas are a mere libretto, often of a very inferior quality' (1955:4).

In the course of my lifetime Britain has become a very divided society. It is a society in which a whole series of cultural, ideological and economic fractures detach people from one another and blunt their sensitivities to an understanding of each other's needs. Behind a thin democratic veil it is a society which relies on apathy and self interest and ignorance as the conditions for its political stability. Its economic metabolism is catalysed by the takeover bid, the amalgamation and redundancy, and the complexity of all this is concealed in simple formulae which a politically ill-informed electorate can grasp. It is a society which transfers the costs of social change to those least able to bear them and is blind to the unintended consequences of its social policies.

The social diversity of British society is unlikely ever to crystallize around the great nineteenth-century solidarities of class, and class conflict is not the mode through which the society's dissolution is likely to take place. Between those who are unemployed and employed, decently housed and badly housed, between those who are young and those already well-entrenched in jobs, between those who are sick and those who are well, those who are black and those who are white, between men and women, there are the driven wedges of mutual misrecognition and self interest which undermine their capacity for collective action for common ends.

It is not, however, the society which spawned Fascism in the inter-war period: its foundations are not yet at least in fear and violence supporting an authoritarian state. There is no well-organized movement of the Left to crack down; there is little prospect in sight of any political group being able to cash in on an ideology of one nation united against some common enemy.

But the society is still in crisis and vulnerable to the instabilities of international politics, the consequences of its own relative economic decline and widening inequalities. The microchip and the multinational have set in motion changes whose full implications are impossible to predict but which are transforming the structures of economic and social life in profound ways. Aristotle once noted that 'when looms weave by themselves, men will be free'; the technological prospect he alluded to has arrived. The political question remains a puzzle; how should that freedom be organized?

I think of this book as a contribution to a discussion of that question, not an answer to it. I see it as a tentative and partial attempt to provide the outlines of an answer to the question often asked by people from my parents' generation, when they look around what to many of them has become a violent, uncaring society – 'What went wrong?'.

My aim is to understand the past and its constraints so that we can have a future. I am not so clear in my own mind what that future should be. All that I am clear about is that it cannot be defined in a simple way; its outlines have to come clear from discussions involving as many people as possible, and for that discussion to take place there is an urgent need for people to be better informed and to have more opportunities to join the debate. Social science and history have a central role to play here and an obligation; it is to provide not blueprints for the future but resources for analysis. And to be adequate, those resources of analysis and interpretation must sustain an imaginative grasp of change which recognizes, as Barraclough once put it, that 'contemporary history is world history' (1967).

I have attempted in this book to provide an account of social change in Britain since World War II which focuses on changes in attitudes and sentiment against the background of Britain's changing role as a world power. My aim has been to connect change in the public realms of politics with alteration in the private realms of feeling, attitude and personal relations. In a society as complex and diverse as modern Britain, it is necessary to explore these changes as they are experienced by different generations, social classes, nationalities, ethnic groups and, of course, by men and women.

At the core of it is a concern with feelings and commitments and with the ideas and policies people will give their support to. It is about how people in British society construe their obligations to one another, and not just to those in their immediate circle of family and friends, but also to those ever-widening circles of the strangers with whom, both in Britain and abroad, they are intricately connected.

The book is organized into eight main chapters. Chapters 1, 2 and 3 are concerned with the period of World War II and post-war reconstruction. Chapters 4, 5 and 6 deal with the 1950s and the development of the 'affluent society', taking the account through to the end of the 1960s and on up to the first oil price rise of 1973. Chapter 7 deals largely with the rest of the 1970s and up to the end of 1981. Chapter 8 covers the 'Thatcher years' from the Falklands War to the present day.

1
British Society and World War II

Modern British society did not just evolve to its post-war forms: it was reconstructed. There was much left over from the past and the difference between Britain and, say, France, and certainly Germany, was that the social institutions and values of the society had in many ways been strengthened and vindicated by the war. Not all of them, of course; throughout the war hopes were nurtured of a future which would be different from and better than what had prevailed before it, and many people felt the difference would have to be of revolutionary proportions.

A sense of revulsion against the past was not uncommon. And for those who had joined in the defeat of Hitler that revulsion was something experienced all over Europe. There prevailed a strong sense that the conditions from which Fascism and Nazism had flourished should never again be allowed to develop. Andrew Davies has summed it up this way:

The war – the anti-fascist war – had brought in its wake seismic change ... the common struggle – despite many divisions and disagreements – had engendered collective responses on egalitarian lines, and these impulses lived on in the hopes of a fair system of post-war reconstruction. Politically, many of the traditional institutions of authority – landowner, industrialist and Church – were heavily weakened by their somewhat accommodating attitude to Fascism. (1984:65)

He quotes de Gaulle on his return to France in 1944: 'Their [the people's] aversion for the structure of the past was exacerbated by poverty, concentrated by the Resistance and exalted by the Liberation.' (Davies 1984:66).

The problems that had to be overcome were, however, enormous. And the special problems which Britain had to face have themselves to be appreciated against the darker backcloth of a shattered Europe, of a new world order balanced precariously between the United States and the Soviet Union, and of the unimaginable destructive potential of nuclear bombs.

More than 50 million people had been killed; 20 million of these were Soviet dead, 8 million were Polish. Some had died on battlefields but strictly military deaths were only half the total; millions of civilians lost their lives through bombing, starvation or murder; 6 million Jews died in German concentration camps, victims of Nazism. The thought of those deaths in particular induced in some a deep despair and pessimism. Walter Laqueur has tried to capture the mood this way: 'The prevailing mood as the last gun fell silent was one of anguish and helplessness. Human nature had been revealed in its basest aspects, and there was no certainty that there would not be an even more murderous repeat performance' (1982:280). Adorno's remark, 'Is it not barbarous to write poems after Auschwitz?', reflects a deep cultural pessimism among some intellectuals after the war.

Others, like T.S. Eliot, feared that wartime controls and loss of freedoms were likely to undermine the values for which the war itself was fought. His fear was that the idea of the unity of European culture and the idea of peace likely to prevail after the war would be associated with the ideas of nationalism and efficiency. And as he expressed it in his *Horizon* essay, 'The Man of Letters and the Future of Europe', the idea of a culturally unified nation was menacing, and he feared that solutions to problems of life based on engineering and planning would strengthen that mechanization of the mind which for him had been the root of totalitarianism (Eliot 1944).

For others, of course, the experience of war was one which nurtured a vision of an entirely new kind of society in Europe, which could express in its institutions those values of sacrifice for common ends, equality and decency which they believed the war itself had strengthened. George Orwell anticipated as early as 1941, in *The Lion and the Unicorn*, that the war would sweep away the old class system and lay the basis for a practical socialism. 'The war', he wrote, 'and the revolution are inseparable' (quoted Morgan 1985:18).

The visions of a new society were shaped by perceptions of the old one and by the priorities set by the experience of war. The war set the constraints on what it was possible to achieve in the new society. It left a legacy of destruction which was different in its forms for each of the states of Europe, and the political frameworks within which reconstruction had to take place were settled more by military violence than by plans and policies for the future.

And the opportunities open to the different states of Europe at that time reflect their different experiences of total war, of the different ways in which civilian populations had been mobilized to the war effort, of how the war had been made legitimate and how it had been organized and experienced. The experience, for example, of German occupation was different for the people of France and for the people of Russia, Poland or Czechoslovakia. In France the Germans respected French culture; but the people of the East were regarded, like the Jews, as *Unmensch*, and the SS divisions which organized Nazi terror in the East were under different orders to the armies in the West. It was on the eastern fronts and in eastern Europe that the worst atrocities of the war were committed.

This should not be forgotten, because those atrocities are part of the memory of the peoples of eastern Europe and the Soviet Union. They have become part of the social institutions and military alliances of the Eastern bloc, and frame the prevailing understanding of what the threat from capitalism could become. In the case of Soviet *realpolitik*, those memories and experiences of Nazi atrocity explain why no Soviet leadership would willingly dismantle the political orders of eastern Europe, because the countries which the Red Army liberated are a buffer between West and East and perceived in the Soviet Union as an essential part of its security.

Britain experienced no German occupation, although the Channel Islands were overrun. Bombing on a scale which had been expected before the war did not happen; though British cities were, of course, heavily bombed and the experience of London in the Blitz has provided many of those images of forebearance, grit, determination to win through, of a country pulling together, of British pragmatism and cheerfulness and of a nation united with its leadership, which have since become powerful emotional symbols in the popular memory of World War II. Dunkirk and the Blitz dwarf all other symbols in the popular recollection of the war as a nation fighting for its life.

The distinctive Englishness of it all was captured in Orwell's essay, 'England Your England', published in *The Lion and the Unicorn* in 1941. He outlined an idea of a distinctively British brand of patriotism. He wrote: 'One cannot see the modern world as it is unless one recognizes the overwhelming strength of patriotism, national loyalty' (1962:63). The English version of it was not for him comparable to the militaristic patriotism of Hitler and Mussolini. Of the British people he wrote: 'No politician could rise to power by promising them conquests or military "glory", no Hymn of Hate has ever made any appeal to them' (1962:68). 'In England', he added, 'all the boasting and flag-wagging, the "Rule Britannia" stuff, is done by small minorities. The patriotism of the common people is not vocal or even conscious' (1962:68). Orwell tried to portray England in this remarkable essay as a 'family with the wrong members in control': he castigated its decaying and stupid ruling class, its Blimps – 'the half-pay colonel with his bull neck and diminutive brain' – as well as the English left-wing intelligentsia and its querulous attitudes, its tastes in cookery from Paris and its political opinions from Moscow. 'This war,' he wrote, 'unless we are defeated, will wipe out most of the existing class privileges. There are every day fewer people who wish them to continue' (1962:89).

Orwell's mistrust of the 'Old Guard' was echoed by J.B. Priestley in his *Postscript* broadcasts on the wireless, and Mass Observation reported as early as November 1940 a spreading awareness of the war 'even among women . . . as in some way revolutionary or radical' (quoted Calder 1969:160). Whether this mood among women continued beyond the tense days of 1940 is open to question. A Mass Observation report in 1943, *War Factory*, pointed to apathy and lack of interest in the war among female factory workers and a 'complete lack of war feeling' (Mass Observation 1943:47). Reflecting on the results of this study and comparing them to others, Tom Harrisson, Mass Observation's director, commented in his preface on 'the dangerous decline in positive citizenship' (1943:9).

For the very early part of the war there is evidence, not confined to women, of general gloominess and defeatism and fear. The Ministry of Information Home Intelligence reports provide for a short period in 1940 a picture of 'fear, helplessness and resignation, mixed in with very real courage and steadfastness' (Rankin 1973:398). Perhaps more typical of the period after 1940, when the war settled down into the long slog that it became for most non-combatants, is the comment of an old lady from Coventry. Asked by her priest what she did when she heard the sirens, she replied, 'Oh I just reads my Bible a bit and then says "bugger 'em" and I goes to bed' (quoted Rankin 1973:398).

It is old ladies like this who give credence to the idea that this was a people's war. This was the war of rationing and clothing coupons, of the Women's Land Army, the Blitz, Bevin Boys, *Workers' Playtime*, *Music While You Work*, Tommy Handley and ITMA, Air Raid Precautions, Henry Moore's sketches of Londoners sheltering in the underground, Dame Myra Hess's concerts at the National Gallery; it is the war of evacuation of children, the Home Guard, Vera Lynn; it is the war when English circumspection gave way to spontaneous conversation between strangers and when the rich lost their servants; it brought with it works canteens, day nurseries, production committees and twelve-hour shifts; it was a war of blackouts, bombs and death – 60,000 civilians, 35,000 merchant seamen and 300,000 servicemen lost their lives. Its front lines, as Asa Briggs has put it, 'ran through Hull, Bristol, Southampton, Plymouth, Coventry and London itself, deep below ground' (1983:271). And it was the war which nurtured hopes for a future radically at odds with the past. 'This was the "people's war"', writes Asa Briggs,

when J.B. Priestley's Yorkshire voice was almost as influential as that of Churchill. And while he sought consolation in English history and the countryside, as Churchill did, he demanded with equal firmness equality of sacrifice and a new more equal deal when the War was over. 'We're not fighting to restore the past', he exclaimed. 'We must plan and create a noble future'. (Briggs 1983:269)

Underlying the changes in sentiment which Priestley's comments echo were extremely subtle changes in how people became aware of one another, their social contact and their sense of personal worth. Titmuss noted in his widely acclaimed study, *Problems of Social Policy*, that even during the Blitz people experienced great sympathy from others, especially those who had been bombed out; there was less 'social disparagement' than in pre-war days:

The civilian war of 1939–45, with its many opportunities for service in civil defence and other schemes, also helped to satisfy an often inarticulate need; the need to be a wanted member of society. Circumstances were thus favourable to fuller expression, for there was plenty of scope for relieving a sense of inferiority and failure. (Titmuss 1950:347)

This was the essential contrast to the inter-war years. The requirements of total war furnished people, particularly ordinary working class people, with a new sense of their moral worth. The Beveridge report on social security, the Education Act of 1944, the white paper on employment policy, the Barlow report on industrial location, Uthwatt on land use, the whole 'white paper chase' of post-war reconstruction are some of the official forms through which this underlying feeling was expressed.

The civilian experience of war was necessarily different to – if sometimes no less violent than – that of the armed forces or those who, like merchant seamen, were in the front line of battle. For service personnel the war was an experience of long-drawn-out boredom and violent battle and of the daily tedium, which often nurtured amazing ingenuity to meet the ordinary needs of daily life. There were two and a quarter million men in the army in 1941 of whom, as Angus Calder has put it, 'an impressive proportion were "browned off" in camps in Britain' (1969:287). What bothered them, as many observers noted, was what they called 'bullshit' and boredom. Mass Observation studies of conscripts at the beginning of the war reported no enthusiasm for it. One observer wrote: 'The foremost characteristic of their outlook is cynicism about everything. They like democracy but they know damn well that all we are fighting for is British capital. Patriotism, the Flag and the Empire are a lot of tripe – only they don't say tripe' (quoted Calder and Sheridan 1985:114). And another Observer notes some of the reasons which women had given for joining the WAAF; writing to Tom Harrisson, she notes: 'The reasons girls gave for joining up – between ourselves, of course – not to the officers – had very little to do with "doing one's bit". General boredom with life was the keynote' (quoted Calder and Sheridan 1985:131).

Forces personnel were clearly very conscious of the social class hierarchies of the services. Alun Lewis, the poet, touched on this at the beginning of the war, reflecting on his failure to organize a debating society in his unit:

It's odd, the mixture there is in the army . . . Centralised and socialised in distribution and production of goods, monastic in its celibacy and its veto on private property, communal as hell: and yet absolutely crucified by repression, regimentation, precedence and the taboos of hierarchy. (Quoted Calder 1969:286)

The response of soldiers, sailors and airmen to forces life naturally varied according to their specific experience of war itself, the traditions of their regiments, their rank and so on. And while, as Dr Addison has recently pointed out, 'the social history of the armed forces has yet to be explored in depth', a decline in deference and reduced tolerance of class distinction was an undoubted pattern of change. And in contrast to the soldiers of World War I, much attention, often with unexpected consequences, was given to the education and welfare of soldiers. Particularly important in this respect is, of course, the Army Bureau of Current Affairs (ABCA), which organized army education after 1941. ABCA kept soldiers informed of current, social and political events. 'Most of the anecdotes about

Army education', writes Dr Addison, 'confirm that it tended to work in a left-wing direction' (1985:15).

Army education was, however, only a once-a-week event; the really formative experiences were those of muddling through. In the servicemen's songs and in their attitudes to their superiors and to the daily business of war, there is much evidence to confirm this. For many servicemen, particularly in the army, service life was comparable to their civilian experience of being at work. There was the same tedium, the same distinctions of authority and power and the same concern to avoid doing more than was necessary.

Arthur Koestler, reflecting on his experience of army life twenty years after the war in an article on patriotism, noted a prevalent 'Them–Us' attitude among the troops which for him was a uniquely British phenomenon. 'Politics', he wrote, 'hardly entered into this attitude':

instead of the fierce class hatred which had scorched the continent with revolutions and civil wars, there was a kind of stale, resentful fatalism. I learned to conform to our unwritten Rule of Life: Go Slow; it's a mug's game anyway; if you play it you are letting your mates down; if you seek betterment, promotion, you are breaking ranks and will be sent to Coventry. (Koestler 1963)

What was different, of course, was the travel and the broadened experience that it allowed. In his book on Wigton, which was based on long interviews with the residents of that town, Melvyn Bragg quotes one man, Frank Moffat, who spoke of his experience in the Navy as his 'university' (Bragg 1976:283). And others he spoke to convinced him that the war was a chance for many to 'express release' and 'in some way complete themselves' (1976:283). For others the comradeship of service life provided something of a model for the kind of society they envisaged after the war.

J. P. W. Mallalieu wrote in 1963, reflecting on his experience of the Royal Navy during the war, that 'I hadn't much liked the Britain we lived in before the war.' But in the dirt, cold, boredom and danger of war, the men he served with became a community:

Without orders, and certainly without conscious virtue, we found that we had stopped working against each other or for ourselves and had begun to share whatever came of misery or pleasure. I liked this and hoped that when the war was over we would carry some such feeling from service into civilian life. (1963: Special Preface)

Care should be taken, however, not to overgeneralize: servicemen and women experienced terrible suffering in combat, or in prisoner of war camps, and the service experience was one of enormous variety. Perhaps it is safe, though, to say this: the experience of war led them to expect change after it was over. And what is more, understanding their own importance to the defeat of Hitler, they believed they had a *right* to better conditions after the war. Senior British politicians were acutely conscious of this. Ernest Bevin, the Minister of Labour, was moved to tears when, watching troops embark for the Normandy landings at Portsmouth docks, some members of his own union who recognized him shouted, 'Look after the missus and kids, Ernie' (Bullock 1967:318). And in a speech to the House of Commons two days later introducing the white paper on employment policy, he linked the Normandy landings to full employment by reporting that men of the 50th Division had asked him: 'Ernie, when we have done this job for you, are we going back to the dole?' (Bullock 1967:319).

The high expectations which the invasion forces took with them to Normandy were something which gave rise to official concern in Whitehall. Lord Woolton, then Minister of Reconstruction, was fearful that post-war economic conditions would not allow these high expectations to be met. In his memoirs he reinforced this point, quoting a letter he had received from a Mr Howard Marshall of the Public Relations Service who had spent time with the troops before the D-day landings. Marshall wrote:

a good deal was said about reconstruction – indeed, after home leave and mail and Burma, reconstruction in terms of homes and jobs was the main topic . . . There's faith in our ability as a nation to pull through in peace as we have in war, but no faith at all in the present system . . . the movement of men's minds out here is unquestionably left . . . They've been uprooted for years: they've lived hard; they've suffered and seen their best friends killed. They are thinking freshly. (Quoted Woolton 1959:302)

Woolton then makes a connection between the views of soldiers and opinions which came to prevail at home: 'it was not unreasonable', he wrote, 'that the wives of service-men, with these ideals already in their minds, who received from their husbands overseas letters that expressed ideas of the kind about which Howard Marshall wrote to me, should have voted overwhelmingly for the Socialists' (1959:303).

The government had, of course, been aware from almost the beginning of the war of rising expectations. The Controller of Home Publicity at the Ministry of Information reported to the minister that 'There was a widespread feeling that things would never be the same again' (quoted Balfour 1979:295). He noted a declining faith in parties and even in Parliament; the main positive hopes were for an end to unemployment, a levelling of income and equal chances for all children. That was in 1942.

The fear of some in the government was that these expectations could be woven into a larger pattern of class resentment, which would lead to a Communist rising in the country. This was certainly a worry to Brendan Bracken as Minister of Information during the period shortly after Russia's entry into the war. The Director of the Home Division warned in a memorandum that 'the political theory of Communism has now both an audience and an occasion' and that it was necessary to counteract this through the home propaganda (quoted Yass 1983:38). Such comments have to be read against the background of the flow of weekly Home Intelligence reports into the ministry which, throughout the war, noted a resentment of the rich by the poor (Yass 1983:58). On the whole, however, these official fears were unfounded and in retrospect tell us much more about the social perception of British elites than about the political state of the society.

By the end of the war expectations had been built up, among both civilians and soldiers, that a different kind of society had to be built. By 1945, however, both the physical and emotional resources of the society were seriously depleted, and the ideas which could guide the design of a new society were neither precise nor so radically at odds with the reforms of the wartime Coalition that they could constitute a distinct break from the past. In any case, as the leaders of the Labour Party understood, Parliament was in no position to reflect accurately the changed mood of the electorate until a general election had been fought.

And the two streams of opinion which flowed together in 1945, that of the servicemen and that of the civilians, fed demands for a return to normality rather than to something radically different. The contrast between Britain and Germany and France is in this respect stark. In both Germany and France a strong sense of having to bury the past prevailed, coupled with high hopes, especially in France, for a very different kind of society in the future. Britain possessed no Resistance movement: there were few obvious traitors and there was no clear notion of a new Europe to be built.

Orwell's 'London Letter' to the *Partisan Review* in 1945 captures something of the mood of Britain. In his first letter of 1945 he recants his earlier views that the war and the revolution were inseparable. 'Britain', he wrote,

is moving towards a planned economy, and class distinctions tend to dwindle, but there has been no great shift of power and no increase in genuine democracy. (1945:80)

He felt he had overemphasized the anti-Fascist character of the war and underrated the 'enormous strength of the forces of reaction'. In his second letter, written after a trip to France and Germany, he was struck by the sharp contrast between the Continent and Britain. He notes in Britain:

the pacifist habit of mind, respect for freedom of speech and beliefs in legality ... But if I had to say what had struck me most about the British people during the war, i should point to the *lack* of reaction of any kind. In the face of terrifying danger and golden political opportunities, people just keep on keeping on, in a sort of twilight sleep in which they are conscious of nothing except the daily round of work, family life, darts at the pub, exercising the dog, mowing the lawn, bringing home the supper beer etc. etc. (1945:325)

He could not decide whether their 'semi-anaesthesia' was a sign of decadence or of 'instinctive wisdom'.

These articles communicate something, too, of the everyday mood of people in London. He refers to their short temper, shopkeepers who treat their customers like dirt and the shortages of whisky, combs and teats of babies' bottles. Contraceptives, though, were plentiful. There are echoes here of an earlier *Horizon* article by Cyril Connolly, which dealt with the issue of the guilt felt by some civilians that they had not participated as fully in the war as the soldiers, but which comments at the same time on the general 'feel' of London and civilian life (1944). He noted its shabbiness and vulgarity, 'its carious houses, the contraceptives in the squares, the puddles of urine in the telephone boxes, the sulphurous wines and goat stew in the restaurants' and its 'bored, pale, ferrety people milling round the streets ... who grow more disagreeable every day'. He comments, 'Never in the whole war has the lot of the civilian been more abject, or his status so low' (1944:152). This was a letter to an imaginary friend returning from the forces from abroad for further training. Many servicemen felt quite differently and returned home victors with many tales to tell.

They returned home having served alongside comrades from what was called then the Empire: they returned to a country which still possessed a colonial empire in Africa and which maintained imperial possessions in the Far East. They returned as members of armed forces whose traditions, command and attitudes were deeply part of that imperial legacy. And it was a legacy which was lent a new and dignified respectability by victory in war.

That legacy, as Jan Morris has eloquently emphasized, had impregnated the lives of British people; it had become part of their sense of who they were (J. Morris 1979:551). Some it had soured; others felt proud of it; and some were ashamed. What the Empire left, though, among many other things, was 'its long trail of racial arrogance' (Morris 1979:551). The experience of being abroad and fighting for that Empire did little to alter those old attitudes. Since the institutions which were the support of those attitudes did not alter fundamentally, through the war, the attitudes themselves persisted and were in many ways ritually endorsed in the way victory was celebrated. And in the moral afterglow of victory, British world views, coloured and reinforced by the experience of servicemen, remained intact.

Embedded in those world views is what can, in retrospect, be seen as a naive and complacent chauvinism, a belief without foundation that Britain could take its place in a new world and prosper in that world without fundamental changes in its institutions. A full description of the attitudes and expectations of people in Britain in the immediate aftermath of war would have to be qualified to capture differences among people which reflected other differences of age, of class and of gender. It would have to reflect, too, the national and regional diversity of the country and the political and ideological differences, which in their turn reflect the diverse political traditions of the country as a whole. No generalization is therefore safe: in contrast, though, with the countries of continental Europe, there was no widespread sense that the social institutions or central values of the society should change. The expectation was for improvement and there was a tacit trust that existing institutions, if not those who currently led them, could be relied upon to consolidate the gains of victory.

The general election

The presence of leaders of the Labour Party in Churchill's wartime coalition government was one of the factors which ensured the political stability of the society during the war years. By the end of the war in Europe, however, there was a strong body of opinion, particularly on the Left of the Labour Party, that the coalition should end and that a general election should take place. No general election had been held since 1935 and the major parties had maintained an electoral truce throughout the war. Parliament could not any longer claim to be representative of the wishes of the British people.

Churchill had wished the coalition government to carry on longer than it did and certainly at least until victory over Japan was secured. Inevitably, however, the divisions between the parties began to open up as the war ended, and questions of post-war reconstruction began to be discussed. Those discussions were not confined to the home front. Churchill's decision to allow British troops to be used in Greece against the Communists, who had been the strongest anti-Nazi force in the country, embittered the Labour Left against the coalition. And it was only through the organized power of the trades union block vote that Ernest Bevin was able to retain the support of the Labour Party conference in October 1944 for the continuation of the coalition. The Left, and Aneurin Bevan in particular, were enraged about Greece. Bevan told the House of Commons that Churchill's intervention in Greece was on behalf of the rich and the powerful in that country. For him, this episode marked, as much as anything else, the differences between the two parties and underlined the urgent need for Labour leaders to distance themselves from Churchill (Foot 1982).

The general election which took place in 1945 was one in which the Tories relied heavily on the wartime achievements of Winston Churchill as their strongest claim for re-election. And Churchill himself relied on a strategy of tarring socialism with the same brush as Nazism. In his first broadcast of the campaign he claimed that a socialist system could not be run without the apparatus of a Gestapo. He saw socialism as an attack upon 'the right of the ordinary man and woman to breathe freely without having a harsh, clumsy, tyrannical hand clapped across their mouth and nostrils' (quoted Foot 1982:505). For Aneurin Bevan the issue was also about power. In his election address to the voters of Ebbw Vale he wrote: 'What this election is about is a real struggle for power in Britain. It is a struggle between Big Business and the People' (quoted Foot 1982:505).

Churchill's Gestapo speech had provoked distress and disappointment in many people. Attlee had replied to it the next day by distinguishing Churchill the war leader and Churchill the party politician. 'The voice we heard last night', said Attlee, 'was that of Mr Churchill, but the mind was that of Lord Beaverbrook' (quoted Calder 1969:667). It is hard, however, to trace among the electors such a high degree of ideological sensitivity. The paramount issue for them was housing, followed by social security and full employment (McCallum and Readman 1947). But it is without doubt that people did draw a distinction between Churchill the war leader and Churchill the politician, and in that second guise he was closely identified with the old order to be swept away.

The election was not fought out on any of the major international issues like the future of Germany, or relationships among the great powers. Election addresses by Conservative candidates (of whom just over half had served in the armed forces, compared to only 23 per cent of their Labour opponents) showed them to place great trust in their leaders for the management of foreign policy and to be concerned primarily with the great powers. This was in contrast to Labour addresses which followed ideas of collective security (McCallum and Readman 1947). The same analysis of election addresses showed that the Empire was mainly a Conservative subject and that Labour candidates showed a distaste for the word 'Empire', and preferred instead the more modern term 'British Commonwealth of Nations'.

The Labour victory in the 1945 election was to many people a surprise result, and for Labour supporters in Britain the memory of it is still something to provoke a kind of political ecstasy. Michael Foot has written that, 'No Socialist who saw it will ever forget the blissful dawn of July 1945' (1982:13). Aneurin Bevan wrote in *Tribune* that, 'the British people had voted deliberately and consciously for a new world, both at home and abroad' (quoted Foot 1982:14).

This is not the place to recapitulate the arguments which explain the Conservative defeat. Kenneth Morgan has shown convincingly enough that the Labour victory was something to be seen against the circumstances of the war years themselves and the changes in public mood which occurred then (1984:44). What emerged was what he calls a vogue for planning and egalitarianism which a Labour Party, now seen as realistic and respectable, could give direction to. And it was a vote, too, against the past, against the dole, the means test and poor housing.

What the experience of managing the war effort had done, however, among other things, was to have convinced whole sections of the British Establishment that these gains for Labour could indeed be accommodated in the framework of a capitalist society, and that the Labour Party itself had already been tamed. *The Times* greeted Bevan's appointment as Minister of Health as a case of 'the poacher turned gamekeeper' (quoted Howard 1964:22). And it is not too difficult in retrospect to understand why some leaders of business could live easily with the nationalization of wasting assets and the welfare state; one gave them ample compensation and the other social peace.

It is easy, too, in retrospect to see that the Labour Party had not only been tamed; it had tamed itself. Attlee policed his government to guarantee its respectability, and the new Labour members of Parliament adjusted readily to the conventions of the House of Commons and Parliament. In the constituencies from which Labour leaders derived their support, there was considerable loyalty to the Party, but very little evidence of an active commitment to socialism. Hugh Dalton noted in his diary that in his Bishop Auckland constituency, in the heart of the Durham coalfield, the big issues in the election were pensions, housing and a fear of a return to pre-war unemployment. He noted signs of hostility towards the Jewish owners of new factories in the area, and observed that socialism, conceived as either state planning or greater equality, was hardly discussed (Pimlott 1985:409).

Socialism was something which mattered more to various groups among the intellectuals, publishers and journalists in the society than to either the organized labour movement or its rank and file. And while their wartime experience convinced many ordinary people of the importance of planning and of fair shares and of the need for greater opportunities, it was the intellectuals of the Left who refocused those hopes as something realizable through Keynesian economic management and through control of Parliament and of some sectors of the economy. By the end of the war the ideas which defined some of the social contours of a socialist Britain, and which had been associated with men like Sir Richard Acland of the Commonwealth Party, J.B. Priestley and his progressive Establishment committee on reconstruction, Victor Gollancz, the left-wing publisher of New Left Books, and a host of other writers and publicists like Edward Hulton of *Picture Post* or Bill Connor of the *Daily Mirror*, were given precise focus by a Labour leadership whose contact with the progressive intellectuals was much stronger than with the working classes on whom they depended to be elected to Parliament. And men like Herbert Morrison knew, too, that if Labour was to have electoral credibility it had to appeal to a wider constituency, including clerical workers and the new professionals. British socialism had to be tempered by the practicalities of the ballot box, Parliamentary procedures and what many Labour leaders understood as the national interest.

It is hardly surprising in this context that, somewhat startled by being elected, some Labour leaders felt positively euphoric for the future. Hugh Dalton recalls in his memoirs:

That first sensation, tingling and triumphant, was of a new society to be built; and we had power to build it. There was exhilaration among us, joy and hope, determination and confidence. We felt exalted, dedicated, walking on air, walking with destiny. (1962:3)

It is not so clear that ordinary people felt the same way. They had to cope with the difficult circumstances of everyday life in a society still austere and still tightly organized under wartime controls.

Constraints and opportunities

Historians differ considerably in their assessment of the broad impact of World War II on British society. In 1950, Richard Titmuss was struck by the transformation it effected in the role of the government's obligation in society to provide social services (1950). For T.H. Marshall, the war transformed the conditions and meaning of citizenship (1965). And Arthur Marwick has stressed the long-term redistributive effects of the war and the improvement it brought in working class living standards (1968:289).

Other historians are more cautious. Calvocoressi and Wint in their book, *Total War*, have argued that despite government controls and wartime developments in social policy, despite the increased awareness of poverty and inequality through evacuation, mobility and better communications and despite a steady increase in standards of living, the effects of the war on social inequality were not great:

But the gains of the working classes did not greatly disturb the economic gradations of British society. The rich and the very rich, although hard hit by direct taxation, found their compensations – the rich recovering after the war their ease and affluence through expense accounts and capital gains, and the middling and professional classes finding, somewhat to their surprise, that they were the principal beneficiaries of new social services such as subsidised further education. (1974:425)

Angus Calder has argued even more forcibly that the war did little to transform British society. In his *The People's War* he writes:

After 1945, it was for a long time fashionable to talk as if something of a revolution had in fact occurred. But at this distance we see clearly enough that the effect of the war was not to sweep society onto a new course, but to hasten its progress along the old grooves. . . . After the war the forces of wealth, bureaucracy and privilege survived with little inconvenience, recovered from their shock, and began to proceed with their old business of manoeuvre, concession and studied betrayal. (1969:21)

The war, he claims, strengthened tyranny: 'The new capitalism of paternalistic corporation meshed with the state bureaucracy was emerging clearly, along with the managerial ideology which would support it' (1969:22).

Calder is here raising questions about the longer-term significance of the economic changes of war on capitalist society. His account therefore cannot be separated from those debates about capitalism as a form of society and of the ways in which it changes. In his much-acclaimed book, *The Road to 1945*, Addison noted aptly that this is a problem which is largely subjective (1982). 'If capitalism', he wrote, 'is regarded as inherently productive of ruthless exploitation and equality, then by definition the war changed little' (1982:276). His own view, however, echoes that of Keynes: the problem was not whether people should exploit one another but 'how such exploitation should be regulated' (1982:276). By this test, he feels, the war led to genuine improvements in living standards and a 'spirit of parsimony' gave way to a 'spirit of greater welfare and more confident management' (1982:21).

There is no simple way to assess these differing judgements. The challenge is really to look behind the obvious data on living standards, to examine the more complex issue of change in the structures of social relationships, particularly those between different social classes, and to look at what these changes implied for how exploitation was regulated, perceived and, above all, *felt*. The measure of change becomes how far people came to see their society and themselves in different ways and to act on the basis of that new understanding to define new demands of their society and to open up new opportunities for themselves and others. To use Raymond Williams's terms, it is a question of tracing within the society and its institutions the changing relationships between those cultural and political forms and structures of feeling which are dominant, and those which are either residual or emergent (1977).

Britain survived the war. Its government changed in 1945 and that change is evidence of an emergent structure of feeling, focused on the realization of a new kind of social order. The political rhetoric of the emerging society was one rich in the language of planning, efficiency and equality of opportunity. And in 1945 the majority of voters saw the Labour Party as the party most likely to build that society.

The new structure of feeling lacked, however, deep institutional supports. Older dominant cultural forms and institutions in politics, law, the professions and education survived the war. So, too, did many aspects of the patterns and relationships of everyday life, echoing in rural areas the traditions and life-styles of a pre-industrial Britain and in urban areas those of an older industrial working class. And the structure of relations between different social classes, though changed, had not been transformed by the war. Those feelings of superiority and deference and of acceptance of position which were part of it remained, for many, intact. Ernest Bevin wrote to Attlee, just before the 1945 general election, that one thing the war should have done was 'to remove the inferiority complex amongst our people' (quoted Marwick 1980:229). But for many the old reference groups had not changed and nor had their expectations.

Unchanged also were those unspoken principles of inclusion and exclusion which, despite a rhetoric of equal opportunities, helped older Establishment groups retain their monopoly of power and privilege at every level in the society. 1945 may have appeared to some as a political revolution. The apocryphal story of the woman in the Ritz, who reacted to the news of Labour's triumph with the comment 'They've gone and elected a Labour government, the country won't stand for it', states the point humorously. But the social revolution on which a political revolution could feed had not, in the British case, developed and this was a major limitation on what a Labour government could achieve.

Two further sets of constraints placed limits on what the Labour government could do. The economic legacy of the war was one of depleted resources, human exhaustion, severe debt, low productivity, poor management and inadequate investment in science and technology. Correlli Barnett has argued that in the face of all this both labour and capital in Britain put greater priority on building the new Jerusalem of a welfare state than on rebuilding a shattered economy (1986). In addition to limited resources, however, Britain had a place in the new international order that was unalterably different to what it had been before the war. There was little scope for Britain to play a great power role in a world straddled by the United States and the Soviet Union and against the background of a crumbling Empire. And the wartime dependence on American aid meant, in any case, that post-war plans for reconstruction and collective security had to be co-ordinated with those of the United States. The world, as one historian has put it, 'had changed much more than people in England realised' (Lloyd 1979:270). The Labour ministers who took over the great offices of state in 1945 quickly found themselves struggling with both sets of problems; their plans for the future had to be adjusted to the economic and political realities of the present. Hugh Dalton describes in his memoirs how, as the Labour Chancellor of the Exchequer, he became 'worn down' by the intractable unbalance of Britain's external payments and the exhaustion of the Canadian and American loans (1962).

How these constraints limited and gave shape to Britain's post-war economic and social development is something to be traced in more detail in subsequent chapters of this book. What is clear at this point is that an adequate understanding of the course reconstruction took, and, therefore, of the kind of society Britain became, must begin from an appreciation of the legacy of war, of the way in which the social forms of the society gave shape to expectations, and of how the realization of these was constrained by the logic of international *realpolitik*. It is vital, too, to go beyond descriptions of expectations and demands and to talk about feelings and attitudes. The optimism of those who looked to the future was balanced by the pessimism and regret of those who valued the past. The feeling among some people that the community as a whole, as in wartime, had a responsibility for the welfare of those in need was tempered by others, through the belief that individuals should take responsibility for their own well-being. Such differences reflect the diversity of interest and experience of people in a complex, divided society. The image of a community united in war conceals and concealed the way those divisions were manifest in wartime and how quickly they set the agendas of politics afterwards.

2
Rebuilding Britain

Against a growing realization, after Germany's defeat, of the full extent of Nazi barbarity, Britain stood for decency, democracy, tolerance and the rights of individuals. Such values were part of a powerful frame of social and self recognition. Returning from a visit to France where he had met many writers, Sartre among them, who had admired what he called the 'civic consciousness' of British society, Stephen Spender noted:

> It is therefore possible to understand the enthusiasm of the French visitor to England. Despite the shabbiness of dusty London, he sees the English as a people who have retained their sanity, a standard of living which is not on the edge of an abyss, decency, trust in each other, considerateness. (1945:6)

Such values, however, clashed with some older values which had survived the war, which legitimated the social hierarchies of class distinction and endorsed individual achievement above collective improvement. Despite the fact that the war, at least for many, had been fought against Fascism and racism, there remained in Britain a strong undertow of anti-Semitism and a sense of racial superiority. These were not just the values of a reactionary ruling class mesmerized by Empire: they were part of the 'cautious conservatism', as one historian has described it, of British society as a whole, a set of attitudes with deep roots in the political culture of the country (Morgan 1985). The notions of what it meant to be British embedded in that culture need to be clarified, for they gave shape to a prevailing understanding of citizenship with decisive consequences for political life.

Citizenship is a political concept just as much as it is a legal one: it carries particular connotations of national identity as well as those of rights, entitlements and obligations. At the end of the war, there was a strong feeling that the political connotations of citizenship had to acquire new meanings which transcended the limited boundaries of the nation state.

George Orwell, for example, looked forward in 1947 to a federation of western European states transformed into socialist republics without colonial dependencies (1947:348). He was prescient enough, however, to know that much stood in the way of such a development. American and Russian hostility were two powerful forces working against such a possibility and Orwell is here, of course, signalling the Cold War. In addition to this, however, Orwell cited imperialism as an obstacle to a new Europe. The British worker, he noted, 'instead of being told that by world standards, he is living above his income, has been taught to think of himself as an overworked, downtrodden slave' (1947:349). The consequence was that people in Britain failed to understand the structure of economic and political relationships of the modern world, and of the role played in that world by the poor societies – many of which were still colonies, in Africa, the Far East, and the Caribbean – which contributed much to the British economy and shielded it from a full realization of the need to modernize and to develop new markets.

A war had been fought to protect the sovereignty of Britain. After the war, that sovereignty, then thought to be endangered by the Soviet Union, was securely lodged with the Atlantic Alliance and financially underwritten by American capital. It was an arrangement negotiated by Lord Keynes and strongly endorsed by the Labour government. Keynes was fearful that if American dollar loans could not be secured, an even more severe austerity would have to be imposed on Britain than had been imposed during the war. The government's fear was that an isolationist America, freed of its obligations to defend Europe, would give away too much to the Soviet Union and Europe would be under a kind of permanent Soviet threat.

The British perception of the Soviet threat, a perception framed decisively in the Labour government by the Foreign Secretary, Ernest Bevin, was not confined to the theatres of central or western Europe but extended to the Middle East – to Iran in particular – and to the Far East, where Britain maintained a strong military presence. What emerged as foreign policy under Attlee's government was based on a central and very conservative assumption, that Britain remained after the war a great power (K.O. Morgan 1985:278). And in the immediate aftermath of war, there was a strong body of feeling, even among the Left of the Labour Party, that Labour should never again display the weaknesses of the naive pacifism of the 'appeasement era' before the war.

There is, therefore, something of an apparent paradox to be explained about the posture of the Labour government: in foreign and defence affairs, its policies were traditional – pro-American and anti-Soviet – and certainly hardly influenced by discussion among some in the Labour Party of a socialist foreign policy. Even in Europe itself, this paradox appeared; particularly so in Germany, where the British government gave more support to German conservatives than it did to the German Social Democrats. In its domestic policy, however, it presented itself as a radical, socialist government committed to public ownership of industry and the welfare state.

The paradox is, however, only apparent. Against an understanding of Britain's historical commitments as an imperial power, its straitened economic circumstances after the war, the complex international questions with which any government would have had to deal (such as the problems of Palestine or Germany) and, not least, the temper of public opinion in Britain – which, while being primarily concerned with domestic issues and a return to normality, was not at all troubled by the idea that Britain still had a world role to play – it is hardly surprising that the government felt it right to adopt the stance it had taken.

The framework of international relations and of economic problems set constraints on the Labour government and limited its opportunities. So, too, did the attitudes of the people themselves. Their prevailing sense of what they sought to realize in their own lives constrained the government's sense of what policies were politically acceptable.

In the British case such sentiments were given their shape in the context of a class system which the war had not destroyed. It was that structure of social relationships and opportunity, of power and influence and of modes of self recognition and evaluation, which continued to constrain how people in Britain made sense of their world and expressed their demands for the kind of new world that was to be built. It was class which gave shape to the prevailing sense of what it was to be British: it was class which determined the form of the welfare state. And it was class which governed how the changes in policy and society after the war were actually experienced by different groups of people.

The Attlee government left a legacy of reform which has stamped the character of British society to the present day. Kenneth Morgan has described it as 'without doubt the most effective of all Labour governments, perhaps among the most effective of any British government since the passage of the 1832 Reform Act' (1985:503). The changes it brought about should not be underestimated: for working class people there were tangible gains in living standards, the economy was reconstructed and Britain became a more open and more democratic society. It was nonetheless a society cast in an older mould and ill-adapted to meet the competitive challenges which it had later to face, or to respond creatively to the vision some had of a different set of values governing how people would live and relate to one another.

This argument can be developed in many different ways. In this and the next chapter it is examined in relation to three aspects of the meaning of citizenship. The first concerns what it meant after the war to be British. The aim here is to say something about what values and symbols and feelings were woven into the prevailing sense of national identity. The second concerns the obligations of citizenship and the ways in which people construed their responsibilities towards one another, particularly the less well off and those who could not meet their own needs by themselves. Finally, there is the question of equality and of attitudes towards the conditions under which other people live.

The idea essential to a society committed to welfare, that unjustifiable inequalities erode the citizenship rights of everyone, was one which never really caught on in Britain after the war. This is only in part explained by the way in which a capitalist society inevitably works; that is, by generating routinely social inequalities. In the British case it is related, too, to what Tawney, before the war, had called 'the religion of inequality' which in the British case had become a 'morbid obsession' (1964:58). And Tawney was well aware how this morbid obsession breeds in some a superciliousness, in others deference, and in others a pride in what they take to be their own achievements, which becomes an indifference to the plight of others less favoured than themselves. Such feelings, routinely made legitimate by the everyday life-styles of different groups of people, are no basis on which to construct a notion of a common citizenship.

Patriotism and national identity

Gerth and Mills define patriotism as 'love of one's country and people' (1970:198). It does not imply, they say an 'emotional investment' in the political order of the society. It refers more to a pride in the cultural heritage of the nation and is devoid of aspirations to win 'glory' (which they in turn define as the 'prestige of power') in international competition. Nationalism, on the other hand, is a sentiment which does bind the mass of a citizenry to common aspirations in the power competitions between nation states.

At the end of the war there was, of course, a widely diffused and deeply felt sense of national pride at having come through the war successfully and having defeated Hitler. The nation, however, is a symbol and is itself evoked by symbols. In *How We Lived Then*, Norman Longmate quotes a letter from a woman working in the Women's Voluntary Service, which was written to a friend on the day of the end of the war in Europe, and which illustrates this point well (1971). Crowds gathering in Whitehall had sung 'For He's a Jolly Good Fellow' to Winston Churchill and throughout the country street parties echoed to the sounds of 'Land of Hope and Glory', 'There'll Always be an England' and, rather incongruously Longmate felt, 'Knees up

Mother Brown'. The woman from the WVS wrote to her friend about what she did that day:

> We all walked to Buckingham Palace. As we got in front of it the floodlighting flicked on. It was wonderful . . . magnificent and inspiring and it seemed we had never seen so beautiful a building. The crowd was such as I had never seen – I was never so proud of England and our people. It was a crowd of separate individuals. There was never any mass feeling. Everybody spoke quietly or was silent – everybody looked just relieved and glad. We waited. Coloured rockets went up behind us. Then the King and Queen and two princesses came on to the balcony. We yelled and yelled and waved and cheered. They waved back to us. It was wonderful . . . Then we began to walk . . . We went to Big Ben. It was floodlit and looked magnificent. I heard myself say 'Dear Big Ben, Dear Big Ben' . . . What moved us all beyond anything else was the great Union Jack on the Lords. It was just a great, lovely, Union Jack, flying grandly in the sky by itself . . . It was unforgettable. (Longmate 1971:503)

This was a private letter written close to the events she described and can be taken, therefore, as an authentic illustration of how that woman, and perhaps thousands like her, felt. Her sense of pride in her country was clearly evoked by the symbols of the royal family, the Houses of Parliament, the flag, but also by a sense that the people themselves possessed a distinctive quality, an absence of 'mass feeling'.

There is an echo here, of course, of anti-German home front propaganda in which the Nazis were always portrayed as evil and Germany itself as a society ordered from the top, whose people had been easily led to a kind of collective madness and brutality (Balfour 1979). And it is significant, too, that the woman's response was to symbols which evoke for many people in Britain a sense of the past, of tradition. But it was then, and remains, a rather narrowly conceived version of the country's institutions, greatness and achievements and one coloured strongly by the historical awareness of the upper class of the society and not of the ordinary people.

A strong element in the prevailing images of that national past was the Empire. On 25 May 1945 Empire Day celebrations were held, and in the Albert Hall there was a Festival of Empire, described by *The Times* as an 'unofficial victory parade'. Soldiers, sailors and airmen were there: so, too, were representatives of the British Legion, the Chelsea Pensioners, the Home Guard and ordinary men and women who had fought fires in the Blitz, and the Royal Navy marched in to the tune of 'Heart of Oak'. The Dean of St Paul's, speaking at an Empire Day service, said that the Empire was a stabilizing influence in the world:

Our Empire illustrated co-operation without domination for the whole of the world – co-operation between countries, without the domination of one over the other. It was probably the greatest creation of British political genius. (*The Times*, 25 May 1945)

Empire Day was celebrated in schools throughout the country, and although Empire turned into Commonwealth, the civic rituals associated with it always endorsed the British view that the 'mother country' had a leading role to play in fostering the development of colonial dependencies.

Behind the confident facade of a society which had stood alone to fight Hitler and which had fought tirelessly to defend freedom and human dignity there were, of course, many worrying signs that the values Nazi Germany had held and for which it had been opposed – racism, anti-Semitism, authoritarianism – still retained a hold in many parts of British society.

Racism is a thread woven into the tapestry of European culture. In Britain it was given a distinctive twist through the possession of a colonial empire. The subjects of that Empire were never regarded as citizens, so that black people in Britain have always had to cope with the problem of being unwelcome in this society. Kenneth Little's study of race relations in Cardiff in the late 1940s noted that the black community of that city

is segregated with some considerable degree of rigidity from the rest of the city in the geographical, social and psychological senses; in the last respect the existence of strong patterns of colour prejudice among residents of the town is the main causal factor. (1948:161)

One of Little's arguments is that such prejudice had its roots in Britain's colonial history and had been strengthened by members of the 'colonial class' who had returned from overseas. But it was not confined to such people. He notes also that:

Coloured students studying social welfare or methods of teaching in the poorer quarters of London and other cities still complain fairly frequently of attitudes of 'superiority' as well as curiosity towards them on the part of even some of the most down-at-heel and decrepit inhabitants in the districts concerned. (1948:218)

Richmond's study of the experience of 345 West Indians who came to Britain during the war to help with the war effort, and who stayed in Liverpool, confirms this general impression. Richmond writes that: 'The English man found it difficult to throw off altogether his previous notion of the coloured man as inferior' (1954:65). Technicians were asked where they had learned their English, whether they used to wear clothes at home and whether girls in Jamaica wore grass skirts. British workers often expressed astonishment that the West Indian technicians could operate machines. One technician told Richmond:

I remember the first day I started at the factory. I was put on a machine I was quite familiar with because we had used it a lot at home. I began work straight away, but before long I had a crowd of spectators around me all of them wide-eyed. One chap asked 'Where did you learn to do that?' I told him I learned it all in a factory in Kingston. Everyone was very surprised that we knew anything about machines at all: I suppose they thought we did our boring with wood and fire. (1954:60)

The lack of understanding of what colonial societies were really like is a constant theme in accounts both of British attitudes to black people and of the astonishment of black people at the level of ignorance they encountered. Kenneth Little, reporting a survey by the League of Coloured Peoples into *Race Relations and the Schools*, notes that school books were invariably full of misleading stereotypes and that Africans were invariably referred to as 'natives' (1948:220). He quotes

Miss Perham, a writer on colonial affairs, who commented that: 'At school and subsequently I had absorbed the idea that pre-European Africa was a place of complete and anarchic savagery' (Little 1948:221).

What was discussed then as the 'colour bar' was experienced acutely by black people in the fields of housing and employment and in ordinary social intercourse. Many dance halls and pubs excluded black people as a matter of routine. Even during the war the Air Raid Precautions authority in Stepney offered 'colonials' separate shelter accommodation, which was actually inferior in comfort and protection to that offered to whites (Banton 1955:76).

It was during the war, too, of course, particularly after 1943 when large numbers of American troops were stationed in Britain, that more people became aware of problems of discrimination and racial prejudice. The American army segregated its black soldiers from its white ones. White soldiers often provoked hostility among British people for the attitudes and behaviour they showed to black people in Britain. Black American soldiers commented to the US Army Research Branch that white American soldiers poisoned British attitudes towards black people (Richmond 1954). American attitudes were often, however, deeply resented. One lady publican in Britsol told an American serviceman, who had remonstrated with her for serving black customers, 'Their money is as good as yours, and we prefer their company', and one pub in Bristol is reputed to have displayed a sign, 'Only blacks served here' (Little 1948).

In the relationships between men and women, the deep-seated and often violent aspects of racism emerge very clearly. All the evidence points to a deep resentment among white men against white women having any contact with black men. Richmond noted that girls could be quite friendly towards black men in the factory 'but cut them dead on the street' (1954:78). And some pubs would refuse to serve a black man if he was with a white woman. There is evidence, too, that the police often took the initiative in trying to break up relationships between white girls and black men (Banton 1955).

This routine discrimination, which West Indians and West Africans and other groups of black people experienced, led inevitably to a sense of resentment among them. They resented the poor housing, the way they were treated at work and the way they were made to feel unwelcome in pubs and dance halls. The use of the word 'nigger' was bitterly resented. And it is a measure of how deeply implicit the racism of British society then was that even a fairly liberal-minded sociologist like Richmond could note:

The term 'nigger' has been the source of enormous tension and bad feeling. As used in England it is a familiar term for coloured people in general, and rarely has any malicious intent behind it, beyond the *Englishman's usually humorous contempt for the stranger*. (1954:97, my emphasis)

How black people responded to this racism is a theme taken up in subsequent chapters of this book. At this stage in post-war British history black people were not well organized to challenge such racism. The number of black people in Britain was small; they were residentially concentrated in a few big cities in dockland areas, and they were divided among themselves according to country of origin, religion, social status and political attitudes. And at that time, in the 1940s, they had not become the butt of organized political opposition. Kenneth Little has summed up British attitudes at this time as 'for the most part tolerant if somewhat prejudiced' (1948:245).

Anti-Semitism in Britain was not fundamentally challenged by the experience of war and by the knowledge of what Hitler had done to the Jews. Virulent anti-Semitism was not a problem of any political significance in post-war Britain, but there is evidence that as much as 40 per cent of the population, both among middle class and working class people, were capable of anti-Semitic statements when pressed to make them (Sharf 1964:201). Oswald Mosley had made considerable political capital during the 1930s by exploiting anti-Semitism among working class communities in the East End. The British Union of Fascists was not, however, a successful political organization and failed to make any deep electoral impression or to mobilize anti-Semitism into a strong political force.

Anti-Semitism did, however, exist and showed itself in the 1930s in the unwillingness of British authorities to be more helpful to Jewish refugees coming from Nazi Germany, and in the experience of refugees themselves once they had arrived. What stands out in this respect is that public opinion in Britain had failed, on the whole, fully to appreciate the nature of Nazi terror towards the Jews. During the war itself, and afterwards, insufficient attention was given to challenging the latent anti-Semitism of British society. An overall 'Germanophobia' operated, in effect, to blind people in Britain to potentially dangerous anti-Semitism in their own society.

Part of this was a failure to grasp the political importance of anti-Semitism to Nazism. Brigitte Granzow's study of the British press and Nazism led her to conclude that 'decent, liberal minds did not want to realise that members of a civilized nation could regard anti-Semitism as an attractive thing ... They shut their eyes to what they could not understand – for, in a sadly double sense, they did not believe it' (1964:157). Andrew Sharf has made a similar point. A survey of the British press during the period of Nazi rule showed careful and accurate reporting of Nazi action against Jews (1964). What was lacking, he feels, was a full appreciation of it, since it was 'so plainly outside the bounds of sensible analysis beyond the plain declaration of its wickedness' (1964:193).

Bernard Crick, in a preface to Brigitte Granzow's book, attributes the British failure to understand Hitler's totalitarianism to 'a kind of common-sense empiricism in Britain which is blinkered empiricism, a philosophical and political narrowness of imagination about the passions that can move men to politics' (Granzow 1964:21). The prevailing assumption seems to have been, even among the parties of the Left, that anti-Semitism was something which would simply disappear as Fascism itself was destroyed (Lebzelter 1978). One consequence of such an attitude was an inability to appreciate the full seriousness of what was happening to the Jews in Germany. Refugees who came to Britain before the war often encountered disbelief among

English friends at what they told them about Germany (Berg-hahn 1984:138).

Interviews among refugees indicate that they did encounter considerable anti-Semitism. The Association of Jewish Refugees, founded in 1941, saw its main task as one of overcoming prejudice and wrong impressions. A theme which stands out in Berghahn's study of German Jewish refugees is that most of them become more aware of their Jewishness in Britain. In Germany they had thought of themselves first as Germans and had felt fully assimilated into German society (Berghahn 1984).

There is no evidence which connects anti-Semitism clearly with one group or section of British society. And studies in areas like Bethnal Green, where there has been something of a tradition of Fascist activity, reveal that extreme anti-Semitism is something confined to a small and distinctly paranoid group of people. Robb's psychological study of anti-Semitism in Bethnal Green in the late 1940s detected in his sample only 8.7 per cent of respondents who were extremely anti-Semitic (Robb 1954). Most respondents, he felt, were, 'generally speaking, people who will not oppose anti-Semitism rather than those who will make any effort to propagate it' (1954:93). Support for Fascists in Robb's study appeared strongest among older age groups and adolescents; it was the latter who provided most support at Union Movement meetings.

Valuable though psychological studies of prejudice are, they have a fundamental weakness; the focus on individuals tends to obscure the importance of change in their circumstances and also in the broader political context of their lives. Robb, for instance, notes without explaining it that 'There has been a considerable revival of Fascist activities in the borough since early in 1947, chiefly in the shape of open air meetings. There were disturbances at many of these, and for a time they drew crowds of many hundreds' (1954:53). Similar meetings took place in Hackney. The Anglo-Jewish Trades Advisory Council noted in 1946/7 a 'wave of blatant and open anti-Semitism' and the same body noted for 1947/9 that 'anti-Semitism and discrimination are on the increase' (Berghahn 1984:141).

Such phenomena cannot be explained by reference to the psychopathology of individuals. Explanations have to be sought in the social and political history of the period and against the background of the political culture of the society. What stands out in this respect is the failure of British policy in the Middle East to deal with the crisis in Palestine and the demands of the Jewish Agency for increased immigration and, ultimately, for a Jewish state.

The history of British policy in Palestine cannot be recounted here. It is sufficient to note that British delays on reaching a settlement in Palestine, and Ernest Bevin's failure, as the Jewish Agency saw it, to act positively to create a Jewish homeland in Palestine, encouraged Jewish terrorist activity against the British. The explosion at the King David Hotel in July 1946, organized by Menachem Begin for the Irgun Zvai Leumi, and the hanging of two sergeants in retaliation to the actions of the security forces against the Irgun, clearly stimulated anti-Semitic sentiment in Britain. The *Daily Express* published a picture of the sergeants hanging and, in the words of one writer, 'a wave of revulsion against the Jews swept the country' (Leitch 1964:74). There were crowds and rioting in Liverpool and Jewish shops were attacked in both Liverpool and Manchester. Hostile crowds in Bethnal Green prevented a meeting of the Jewish Ex-Servicemen's association from taking place, and scrawled across the entrance to the Canada dock at Merseyside was the slogan 'Death to all Jews' (Leitch 1964:75). An article appeared in the *Morecambe and Heysham Visitor* in which the editor, James Caunt, complained that 'The Jews, indeed, are a plague on Britain.' He was prosecuted for this but found not guilty, and in his summing up in the case Mr Justice Burkett probably helped the verdict of the jury by underlining the importance of the freedom of the press.

The point to be drawn from this is that the very positive and sympathetic attitudes towards the Jews which reporting on the horrors of Belsen and Auschwitz had prompted had not found such deep roots in Britain that anti-Semitism could not raise its ugly head again. Anti-Semitism was still part of the culture of British society, something which could still be mobilized if circumstances offered the opportunity. Popular reactions to the Palestine crisis confirm the point and they reflect, too, the legacy of attitudes connected with Empire and Britain's role as a world power, attitudes which remained chauvinistic and hopelessly at odds with the realistic ability of a much-weakened economy and society to continue playing such a role.

Chauvinism has, since Victorian times, been a pervasive element in the resources of national recognition in Britain and it is hardly surprising, after World War II, that many people could feel a particular pride in being British. The prevailing self perception was that of having been victorious. To many people, Britain stood on the high ground in the moral range of nations. The Germans remained beneath contempt, a nation of militarists who deserved their punishment. That was the view at least until 1948, when the Russian blockade of Berlin induced a shift in popular and official thinking towards a greater sympathy for Germans (Watt 1965). The French were effete: the Italians were cowards. On the horizons of this vision were people who evoked admiration on account of being on 'our side'. Military mythology has a special place for the Gurkhas and some of the Indian regiments: the 'Aussies' and New Zealanders were, of course, 'kith and kin'. The Americans were routinely perceived as brash and big-headed, wallowing in a glory they did not deserve. The Japanese were perceived as essentially wicked and cruel. The Arab world was populated with 'wogs' and most foreigners were thought untrustworthy. Each stereotype reflected back to people in Britain an image of their own most cherished qualities – tolerance, bravery, steadfastness, modesty and decency.

A significant part of this imagery focused on what were taken to be the best qualities of British military traditions, and it is indeed surprising that more has not been made of this in the social histories of post-war Britain. Field Marshal Montgomery was for many years after the war something of a national hero, and he himself took the opportunity often enough to comment on the special qualities of the British 'tommy'. In the films of the post-war period, British military virtues were heavily underlined, and soldiers and ex-soldiers played prominent roles in the society. In the general election of 1945, 52 per cent of Conservative and 23 per cent of Labour candidates had served in the forces (McCallum and Readman 1947). *The Times* noted on 25 May 1946 that the scheme for recruiting teachers 'has fired the imagination of the men and women – and particularly men – who have been serving in the forces or in other forms of national service'. The extent to which such men and women brought their service respect for discipline into the classrooms of the nation's schools is something about which only speculation is possible. For several years after the war, however, military personnel above the rank of captain continued to use their titles. In his diaries, Hugh Gaitskell referred with absolute unselfconsciousness to his colleagues using their military titles (P.M. Williams 1983). Organizations like the British Legion had a high symbolic and political profile, as did other ex-servicemen's associations. Military dress and fashion influenced civilian styles, and the continuation of national service ensured that a large number of young men encountered adulthood in the armed forces, many of them in service overseas.

The evidence is that the experience of war had radicalized many servicemen. For many others, however, it had reinforced a pragmatic acceptance of authority and underlined an unthinking support for the need for discipline as the precondition of an ordered society. For many more, it may be surmised, their experience of military life, especially overseas, confirmed some of the deeply racist stereotypes of foreigners, particularly those with different coloured skins, which have been part of British political culture.

The armed forces reflect the social relation of the society from which they are drawn. In Britain, the class divisions of the society are particularly acute in the military division between commissioned officers and 'other ranks', and prevailing ideas about leadership carried over easily into civilian life in the assumption that army experience was useful for managerial careers in industry. A chemical industry representative told the British Association for Commercial and Industrial Education conference in Birmingham, as late as 1954, that for science graduates 'to enter the Army and take a commission is the best equipment they could have for industry' (Chambers and Landreth 1955:20). Yet Field Marshal Sir Claude Auchinleck commented in his foreword to the book from which this comment is drawn, a book reporting the experience of national service of sixteen recruits, that 'the point that impresses itself upon me most forcibly after reading this book is the apparent lack of contact between the *officer* and the man.'

It was this lack of contact which prompted some people to press for change in patterns of military recruitment. Introducing his army estimates to the House of Commons in 1946 the Minister of War, Jack Lawson, an ex-miner from County Durham, expressed the hope that the 'senior ranks of the army might one day be filled from men who were once "humble workers"' (*The Times*, 15 March 1946). And Mr Rogers, Labour MP for Kensington, complained of the stupidity of some officers. Playing to the sense of humour of his audience, he told of one colonel who put up a notice saying, 'The playing of musical instruments during parade hours is forbidden. The term "musical instruments" includes whistling.' The MP went on to report that within three days five sergeants were up on disciplinary charges for whistling while going about their duties. It was said of the same colonel that he even put his dog on bread and water rations for a week for misbehaviour. What remains seriously true, however, was that the senior ranks of the armed forces were filled routinely by people from the public schools and the upper echelons of the society.

A thorough study of the social history of the armed forces in the post-war world would have to attend, too, to the ways in which forces life confirmed the values and ways of thinking which insist on clear differences in the roles of men and women and bolster an uncritical acceptance of the social status quo. Chambers and Landreth comment that army life was rough and ready. 'Barrack room manners are perfunctory. There is no opportunity for privacy. Bad language is a ritual of soldiers' speech, and sex – the one outside interest certainly common to all of them – is persistently and publicly discussed' (1955:16). And while for thousands their time in the armed forces was a liberating and educative experience, for many others it was an exercise in learning how to cope creatively with boredom. For all, however, it was a powerful experience of socialization into the military realities of a world which was dividing rapidly on the lines of the Cold War, in a society which still clung on to an image of itself at the head of a world-wide, colonial Empire.

The thrust of the argument so far is that while the economic and political circumstances of Britain, both nationally and internationally, had been profoundly altered in the course of World War II, many facets of the society remained relatively unaltered; that Britain remained, despite support given to a Labour government to bring about radical changes, a deeply conservative society, a society whose older institutions and values had been symbolically revalidated by victory. The 'civic culture' of Britain retained a respect for traditional authority, a tacit acceptance of the finely graded social hierarchies unique to the class system of Britain, and a pervasive sense of the need for order and discipline in the society.

This respect for authority and order should not be exaggerated. And in contrast to what had prevailed in continental Europe, the British attitude to authority was in the main pragmatic and could be very irreverent; for some groups, however, it remained deeply tinged with deference. And one historian, Marwick, has pointed to a 'secular Anglicanism' in British society which for him evokes its characteristic tolerance and respect for differences (Marwick 1982). My point for the 1940s is this: most of the most important differences in the society were facets of class inequality. They survived not only the war but the programme of social reforms which followed it. This is a theme taken up in the next chapter.

Cold War

A continuing commitment to maintain a colonial Empire, albeit with the understanding that the countries of that Empire, like India, would eventually achieve their own independence, and the strengthening of the American alliance were two central planks of British foreign policy after the war. The acceptance of

American economic aid and a determination to provide the military resources to maintain the Atlantic Pact were, in Philip Williams's opinion, two features of Labour government policy which reflected the view of the leadership that, had the democracies been better prepared at the time, World War II might have been avoided (1983).

This was the broad consensus at the time, but 'was ripped apart as the implications of resisting Soviet pressure through the American alliance became increasingly distasteful: rapid rearmament with all its repercussions at home, war in the Far East, the restoration of the German army' (P.M. Williams 1983:xii). These are the issues around which political opinion in Britain divided in the late 1940s. What they reflected, and in part, of course, defined, was a shift in public opinion and attitudes towards the Soviet Union and the stabilization of a mentality which E.P. Thompson has aptly called 'Natopolitan' (E.P. Thompson 1978). As he has analysed it, tracing some of its features to the anti-Communism of Auden, Orwell, Koestler and others, it is more than just the affirmation of the virtues of western democracy over Soviet totalitarianism – or vice versa; it is also a prevailing pessimism, which amounts to apathy, that anything can be done about the division between East and West and the drift to nuclear confrontation implied in it. For Thompson, there has been what he calls 'a polarisation of human consciousness which has corresponded to the polarisation of world power' so that across Europe there runs a cultural fault (1978:2).

The form of that fault in the British case must be traced historically to the special circumstances of Britain's adopted role in the international relations of the 1940s. Anti-Soviet attitudes predated, of course, the development of the Cold War: they are, indeed, rooted in reactions to the Russian Revolution of 1917 and the inter-war struggles between Communism and Fascism. During the war, however, following Russia's entry into the fight against Hitler, the Soviet Union became an ally. Anglo-Soviet friendship societies developed, like the Russia Today Society, the Society for Cultural Relations Between the Peoples of the British Commonwealth and the USSR, the

Women's British–Soviet Society Committee and the National
Council for British Soviet Unity, which had committees in over
300 towns and cities (Nemzer 1949).

Evelyn Waugh captured some of this in his evocative image of
the queue waiting to enter Westminster Abbey to see the sword
of Stalingrad. They queued beneath a slogan emblazoned, he
said, by 'a zealous, arthritic communist' which read 'SECOND
FRONT NOW'. 'The people of England', wrote Waugh, 'were
long habituated to queues: some had joined the procession
ignorant of its end – hoping perhaps for cigarettes or shoes – but
most were in a mood of devotion' (Waugh 1984:21). The sword
had been made as a gift to 'the steel-hearted people of Stalingrad' and at a time when newsreels and broadcasts announced
Russian victories on the eastern front, and when the British and
allied advance into Italy was halted, Waugh noted: 'The people
were suffused with gratitude to their remote allies and they
venerated the sword as the symbol of their own generous and
spontaneous emotion' (1984:22). Waugh remarks also on the
'popular enthusiasm for the triumphs of "Joe Stalin", who now
qualified for the name of "uncle"'.

But that was during the war. Afterwards, from several
different quarters and perhaps, too, for many different reasons,
Russia came to be defined, and in public opinion accepted, as an
expansionist threat to freedom, to be resisted at all costs. Ernest
Bevin, for example, Britain's new Foreign Secretary, was, as
Kenneth Morgan has pointed out, 'passionately anti-
communist' (1985:235). He thought of Russia as a more
dangerous threat to western security than that of a revived
Germany and 'was passionately anxious to eliminate the pros-
pect of an isolationist withdrawal by the United States from
European affairs, as had occurred so disastrously after 1919'
(Morgan 1985:263).

From the position of those in power in the United States, the
development most to be guarded against was that of a socialist
or Communist Europe which might, as one writer has analysed
it, simultaneously provide a model for America itself to emulate
and moderate what had come to be construed as the Soviet
threat (M. Cox 1984). The danger in such a moderation is that

the rationale for America's dominance of the western alliance – to protect American capitalism – would have been undermined. And the real American gains from the Cold War, an electorate which expressed its patriotism as anti-Communism, would have been lost.

On this analysis the Cold War, far from being a destabilizing influence in the world, was actually quite the opposite. Rather it became a system of relations and legitimations which was positively functional in justifying America's new world role of tying down the Soviet Union to the most backward parts of Europe.

Such an analysis is quite inconsistent with how some people in Britain construed the Soviet threat in the late 1940s. Denis Healey, then in charge of the International Department of the Labour Party in Transport House and an ardent supporter of Bevin, replied in a pamphlet to criticism from the Left of Britain's pro-American foreign policy. He noted in his *Cards on the Table* that there was a sustained and violent offensive against Britain by Russia. 'They thought they could see the British Empire crumbling and that expansion to fill Britain's place in Europe and the Middle East would be easy' (quoted Bullock 1983:397). This argument was, in Allan Bullock's view, the best exposition of Bevin's foreign policy. It acknowledged that Britain was tied economically, at least for the present, to the United States and could not be otherwise. Whether that link would remain firm was not something left to chance, however. Bevin accepted advice from Christopher Mayhew that an anti-Communist propaganda campaign was needed, and a special office was set up in the Foreign Office to orchestrate it, an office whose existence was not revealed until the 1970s (Leigh 1980).

The press, of course, played its own role in giving shape to the Cold War perceptions of the Soviet Union as an expansionist, totalitarian power with designs on western Europe. So, too, did the major political parties in Britain. The most famous example of this was Winston Churchill's Fulton speech, which depicted the 'iron curtain' from Stettin to Trieste as something which the Soviet Union had imposed on Europe.

Events themselves, however, evoked responses which fuelled the paranoia of Cold War perceptions across the Iron Curtain. In Europe, the problem was Germany and how its future should be organized. In the Middle East, there were problems in Iran and Greece, which raised doubts among western leaders about Soviet intentions. Soviet actions in eastern Europe, particularly in Czechoslovakia but later in Berlin, confirmed western fears that the Soviet Union was entrenching itself. Whether that was the case or not is still a matter for debate. The Red Army was rapidly demobilized after the war and the resources of the country were fully stretched in reconstruction at home. The belief that the Soviet Union intended to dominate Europe was, however, widespread.

By 1950, the belief that the western world was threatened by an international Communist movement gained in credibility with the outbreak of the Korean War. By this time the 'Truman Doctrine', that Communism should be resisted wherever it showed itself, was a firmly established principle of USA foreign policy and one which drew British troops into action in Korea under the auspices of the United Nations.

The developments in international affairs cannot be kept separate from a discussion of what was taking place in domestic policies and in the pace and character of Britain's post-war plans for reconstruction. The international commitments accepted by the Attlee government increased pressure on the defence budget. In doing so, at least in the opinion of many in the Labour Party, particularly those on the Left, they were undermining the realization of Britain's domestic programmes on welfare and the economy. And the acceptance of the idea of a divided Germany, with West Germany rearmed to play a role in the defence of Europe, was deeply offensive to many people on the Left of the Labour Party and was an issue which led to damaging splits in the Party.

Conclusion

The thrust of the argument to this point is this: after the war, Britain's plans for social and economic reconstruction were cast in an international framework which was governed by the logic of Cold War. Hopes for a better world, with a strong international framework of collective security, evaporated to a fear of a new world war between East and West. Britain's role in the new framework of international relations was that of a great power, without the resources to back up the commitments of the role.

The frameworks of understanding, and the rhetoric upon which people in Britain could rely to make sense of their new world, were still entrenched in the institutions of the old. And this is not just an inert historical observation. How a Labour government could, between 1945 and 1951, lead the country into the lap of American foreign policy, into the development of nuclear weapons and into the intellectual and cultural rigidities of Cold War, is a question which for many people, particularly, of course, those on the Left, still requires an urgent answer.

E.P. Thompson's review of Kenneth Morgan's book on the Attlee government is a telling illustration of this (1984). The blighting of hopes, Thompson argues, for a socialist Europe after the war as an alternative to Cold War power blocks threatening one another with nuclear death was something with pervasively stifling effects. 'The Cold War', he writes, 'led the nation into a wasteland of the spirit; it led the Labour movement into a weary epoch of manipulative infighting – the suffocation of block vote rule, the disciplinary expulsions and proscriptions of Transport House, the counter manipulation of communists in pockets like the ETU' (1984:9).

But Thompson's greatest regret, looking back on the hopes of millions after the war, was that the Cold War 'destroyed any socialist vision, dragooned people into flocks of Atlanticist sheep or pro-Soviet goats, and blocked off and "third-way"' (1984). Hindsight, of course, is a very privileged vision, but Thompson is surely right to raise questions about how popular feelings are expressed through institutions and to set the achievements of the Attlee government firmly in the framework of international affairs. The Cold War is one such framework. The experience of war itself was another: so, too was Empire. Each framework gave shape to how people in British society perceived themselves and others and how they construed their priorities.

3
Class and Welfare 1945–1951

The mandate the Labour government received in 1945 was to rebuild the economy on the basis of full employment, provide decent housing and construct the welfare state. What is, however, clearer in retrospect is that the Labour victory at the polls was a reflection of a determination more to bury the past than to open up a radically different future. The legislative programme of the government, seen in this light, was designed more to consolidate wartime gains in welfare and planning than to give expression to a new set of values in a new society.

There was, of course, much talk of a social revolution and excited Labour members of Parliament opened up the new session singing the Red Flag, a parliamentary episode which disturbed Herbert Morrison, who noted that 'these youngsters still had to absorb the atmosphere of the House' (quoted Davies 1984:70). The victory, in strictly electoral terms, was the result of the working class voters of the older industrial areas joining forces with their better-off comrades in the south east and the Midlands and with a significant section of the suburban middle classes (Addison 1982:268). New voters were more likely to vote Labour than those who had voted before. It was not, however, an electoral base on which to construct socialism. Labour received less than half the total votes (47.8 per cent). And the hopes those votes expressed, particularly from skilled workers and lower white collar workers, were for a widening of opportunities rather than for a fundamental transformation in the structure of ownership of industry or of society.

The general mood of the society in 1945 has been described by one historian as conservative and cautious (K.O. Morgan 1985). Britain remained a class-divided society and, in Morgan's view, 'under pressure from middle-class aspirations' with a culture with strong traditional values (1985:326). He writes:

There endured after 1945 a powerful civic culture, a commitment to hierarchical and organic values, to Crown and parliament, to law and order, to authority however it manifested itself, from the policeman to the football referee. It was also a deeply patriotic society, one convinced of its own inner strength. The superiority of Britain was still broadly assumed. (1985:327)

The war had disrupted the everyday life of British society in quite profound ways: five million people had left their normal jobs to be in the armed forces. Thousands of women were mobilized for work in the factories and on the land. Air raids and bombing had forced evacuations and people had to move away to new homes. Near the end of the war, British towns and cities had to accommodate thousands of foreign soldiers. Families were put under the great stress of separation and austerity. Although the role of government was fundamentally different from pre-war days and despite the fact, too, that Britain's whole economic position and international relations were irretrievably altered and unable to sustain the kind of life-styles which had previously existed, the return to everyday life after the war was, in the British case, a return to something familiar and valued. The expectations of people were for a better life and there was widespread support for planning, public ownership and the welfare state.

If this reflected a strongly prevailing mood or structure of feeling about the future, the immediate demands were for a return to a peacetime normality. Soldiers looked forward to demobilization to return to their homes. Eager to ensure that there would be jobs for them when they returned, the government controlled carefully the pace of the demobilization and moved rapidly to return women from the factories back to the family and to domestic work. The point to stress in this chapter is this: the political climate and economic structures of the society had been fundamentally altered by the war, but the social relationships and institutions of the society, the basic values and sentiments and styles of life of which they are a reflection, remained more or less intact.

In addition to the great political problems with which the

post-war Labour government had to cope – the Potsdam negotiations about the future of Germany, Britain's debts, India and so on – there was, in Britain's case, a severe and not clearly recognized, but nonetheless fundamental, problem. The post-war expectations for a better future, particularly with full employment, could not easily be realized, given the way in which the war had drained the resources of the economy.

What was true in the economic realm had its counterpart in the social values of the society. The experience of war had endorsed a set of values which included a commitment to welfare and a just society. Such a society presupposed that people should not only be aware of the manifold ways in which they were interdependent, but that they would also be committed to the obligation to help those who had become dependent and to compensate others for the routine diswelfares which accompany social change in any complex society. War had highlighted for millions of individuals their general obligations to the nation as a whole and it offered endless opportunities for personal sacrifice and for caring for others. It was another matter, however, to transform that sense of interdependence, which wartime emergencies stimulated, into the routine social practice of a reconstructed society after hostilities had ended.

A theme which stands out in the social history of post-war Britain is that of the limited conception of citizenship upon which the social reforms of the period were built. The post-war fortunes of both the concept and the structures of the welfare state illustrate this very well. The vision of a society in which the welfare of people would be expressed as a collective responsibility and in which services and benefits would be provided universally gave way, by the early 1950s, to one in which the well-being of people came to be widely seen as an individual responsibility. The state would be concerned only for those thought to be most in need (Deacon and Bradshaw 1983). And, as the economy faltered, welfare came to be seen by some as a luxury, paid for at the expense of liberty, and no longer a necessary condition of effective citizenship. The debates among politicians and publicists on these matters in the late 1940s and 1950s are expressive of the underlying divisions of wealth, income, power and perception which are part of an unequal society. They have to be seen in that context.

Class inequality

While measurable differences in social inequality decreased during the war and living standards and opportunities for decent health care and education steadily improved afterwards, the structural arrangements, which routinely generated inequalities, were not in any way radically challenged. The attitudes and values, modes of social and self recognition and feelings towards other people, which are also part of the texture of class-divided society, persisted. They were entrenched in the older institutional frames and life-styles of an earlier period which the war had not swept away.

Institutions are living frames of thinking and action, structures of roles and values which give direction to careers and personal commitments. They confirm a sense of the obvious and the normal. The institutions of class-based society confirm, or seek to confirm, the legitimacy and inevitability of its social hierarchies and the principles of inclusion and exclusion on which they rest. Those hierarchies survived the ravages of war and the reforms of Attlee's government; they continued to supply the different sections of British society with ample resources to consolidate the self images of class identity and to provide significant minorities with the grounds for believing that, through their own efforts, their class positions might be improved.

The period of Attlee's government was not, however, a peaceful one. What must stand out in any account of the 1940s is the almost hysterical reaction of middle class people against increased taxation and their sense of their declining standards of living. The reaction of working class people to their new Jerusalem must also be understood against the structured divisions among them, which the war only temporarily suspended. Those divisions, between men and women, north and south, skilled and unskilled, were woven into complex patterns of memory and experience which define the distinctiveness of the British working class. Tom Bottomore has perceptively noted in this respect that, in contrast to the working class of continental Europe, class interests have always been expressed in Britain in sectional and reformist terms (1982). And the reason for this, according to Bottomore, is that the British working class has lacked a *modern* capitalist class with which to do battle; the dominance of British capitalism by mercantile and financial capital – a dominance which the war did not transform and which was itself rooted in Britain's role as an imperial power – facilitated the incorporation of the working class into a national and imperial community.

The dominant class

The account of the structure of those relationships must begin, therefore, with the groups best able to dominate and define them; that is, with the rich and the powerful, the dominant class of British society, a class with a continuing if unobtrusive influence, and a strong symbolic presence in the public sphere.

Class is a matter of the ownership and control of the means of production. It is also a matter of power, life-style, forms of thinking and awareness, organization and communication and leadership. In Britain it is the dominant classes in the society which have always been well organized and possessed of a sense of their own distinctiveness, interests and importance. It is this which explains their success in claiming legitimate right to the positions of leadership and authority, which they have traditionally occupied.

It has always been difficult, however, to describe precisely who they are. The historian, Arthur Marwick, estimated that they made up 2 per cent of the population after 1945 but had a political and cultural importance far exceeding their numbers (1982). He had to acknowledge a difficulty in defining them precisely for, as he writes: 'It was part of the very upper-class ethos that one should be reticient in speaking of class' (1982:40).

In the 1940s, though, there was precious little social research of a kind which charted out their position clearly. When Marwick tried to evoke their life-style and attitude, a relatively simple task in comparison to that of tracing their wealth, he was reduced to the techniques of 'flicking through the diaries of the rich' (1982:44). It is a limited but important method of historical research, but one unfortunately not available to contemporary writers. The result, in part, is that there is no systematic social research about the upper classes of British society for the period after the war. In 1955 G.D.H. Cole, that prolific social critic and historian, even announced with confidence that 'as a social class of really national significance, the upper class has nearly ceased to exist, though much is left of its snob appeal' (1955:68).

It is only later, and still incompletely, that we can build up a picture of how these groups consolidated their position in the post-war world. It can be seen a little more clearly that it is through their monopoly of prestigious positions in the great offices of state, the foreign and diplomatic services, the Civil Service, in the leading industrial and financial institutions of the economy, in the armed forces, the ancient universities and the public schools, that the dominant classes have maintained a cohesiveness and distinctive style of life (Scott 1982). What is more, through that carefully defended monopoly, they have successfully pressed their claims on the valued resources of the society for status, wealth, power and influence.

Essential to their success, however, and something which remains subtly disguised by the more obvious manifestations of their life-style – a life-style centred on the London club, the country house, the City of London, the grouse moor, the Oxbridge high table, the London literary scene, the debutante's ball, the Royal Opera House etc. – something ignored by the social scientists who have ponderously documented their wealth or their family connections, is the way in which the institutions which sustained them were themselves part of a society still being maintained to play a world role as a former imperial power. Peregrine Worsthorne was absolutely right when he commented in 1959: 'The Right is acutely aware that the kind of Britain it wishes to preserve very largely depends on Britain remaining a great power ... Everything about the British class system begins to look foolish and tacky when related to a second-class power on the decline' (quoted Edgar 1976).

Decline, of course, was a major worry for most of the immediate post-war period, and to many Establishment figures high taxation and socialist collectivism were the main symbols of it. So, too, was a sense of regret at the loss of a world role and of Empire. Andrew Gamble has suggested that Empire was one of the pillars of the Conservative concept of nation (1974:167). He quotes Major Ian Fraser, a delegate at the Tory conference of 1948, who said, 'We are not ourselves exclusively a nation of Europe, but a people of the world' (Gamble 1974:167). And Bernard Braine emphasized the point:

Let me proclaim the faith that every man and woman in this hall shares. We are an imperial power or we are nothing . . . Under a spiritless socialism, which has succeeded only in dampening down the fires of our native genius, we have become dependent for our very existence upon foreign aid. (Quoted Gamble 1974:167)

Here is a reflection, of course, of the anti-American feeling which was easily recognizable in Britain at the time. In January 1947, Mass Observation noted that only 21 per cent of their panel reported favourable attitudes towards the Americans. Those, the majority, who at this point objected to them complained of their boastfulness (Mass Observation 1947e). 'Mention the Americans', one respondent said, 'and my tackle is up. They irritate me beyond words.'

Each attitude – the commitment to Empire and anti-Americanism – often combined with a feeling that a whole way of life was under threat from a state-imposed egalitarianism and cultural mediocrity. T.S. Eliot's *Notes Towards a Definition of Culture* (1948) is perhaps the most eloquent and powerful expression of this sense in the cultural field. His defence of high culture and a 'graded society', and his concern that the disintegration of class distinction would breed attitudes of envy to fuel the false dogma of equality of opportunity, was a characteristic feature of much conservative thinking of this time. The same sentiment saturates the thinking of Evelyn Waugh, who regarded the Labour government as a sort of occupying power and who relished the pure snobbery of the upper class company he cultivated.

There was a sense prevalent among members of what later came to be known as the 'Establishment' that they were somehow set apart from the society around them. Harold Nicolson noted, for instance, in his diary for 1951, that he had chaired a BBC discussion on the question, 'Are cliques necessary?' in which Bob Boothby and Kingsley Martin had participated. He wrote: 'I speak about Souls, Kingsley about Bloomsbury and Bob about Cliveden . . . We say that the disappearance of Society means that young men have no opportunity of meeting the great men of their age' (1968:212).

The social contours of their world were narrowly defined. Harold Nicolson, for example, joined the Labour Party in the hope of gaining a peerage; the House of Commons was for him a gentleman's club and Oxford University a particularly precious symbol of the collective identity of his class. Nicolson stood against Auden as a candidate for the Oxford Professorship of poetry and noted in his diary: 'I am always carried away by the mention of Oxford even on a pot of marmalade' (1968:296). His election to the chair would have been a 'great and glamorous honour'.

The Oxford to which he was so deeply attached was not the institution it had been before the war. A Mass Observation survey of undergraduate opinion in Oxford noted that the university was very overcrowded; many of the students were ex-servicemen. Among the political clubs of the students, the strongest was that of the Conservatives. It was a club which was predominantly public school in composition and possessed of a 'feeling that certain of the values of English life are fast passing' (1947b). Mass Observation's observer in Oxford commented that there was a strong Christian revival among undergraduates and that some of the ex-servicemen were beginning to flirt politically with Fascism after a clandestine visit to the university by Oswald Mosley.

Nicolson's diaries strike a chirpy, optimistic note during this period. There were many others, however, from his class background who perceived the world around them in terms that were distinctly gloomy. The political expression of this concern came in the form of opposition – although, in Parliamentary terms, not very vigorous or effective opposition – to aspects of the Labour government's policies in relation to welfare, employment, taxation and nationalization. Whereas at the end of the war some senior Conservatives had feared that full employment and welfare policies would be necessarily inflationary, their opposition came later to centre on fear about the egalitarian ideology they attributed to the government, and their belief that imposed egalitarianism must necessarily entail totalitarianism. Indeed, the word 'ideology' underwent a subtle change of meaning in post-war Britain. Tom Harrisson noted for Mass Observation that the word is 'gradually becoming a xenophobic symbol, a thing no man may presently dare to disclose' (Mass Observation 1947c). The word, he claimed, had changed in meaning from 'visionary speculation' to embrace a fear of Communism and to be contrasted sharply with a much more acceptable idea of common sense.

Theoretical justifications for such a change were cogently set out as early as 1944 in Hayek's *The Road to Serfdom*, and less cogently developed by Conservative propagandists in the 1940s like Aubrey Jones and Bernard Braine. Jones noted in 1946: 'Every society has its division between leaders and the led . . . Such a division is one of the inescapable facts of life. The capacity to guide and inspire is rare; the ability to follow under guidance, to do the humdrum tasks necessary for the realisation of a project inspired by another, is much more common. It is inevitable, therefore, that the rarer quality should be granted a priority status; it is granted by the institution of class' (quoted Eccleshall 1977:74). And Braine, commenting on the inevitability of inequality, argued in 1948 that, even if a socialist government could impose equality, 'Within a very short space of time this new equality will have vanished into the mist. Some men will be rich, some will be poor. Some will be masters, some will be servants. A few will lead. The rest will follow' (quoted Eccleshall 1977:74). Their fear, widely shared by fellow Conservatives, was that the pursuit of equality would lead to economic inefficiency, a stronger state and cultural mediocrity. This perception was elaborated as a matter of straightforward common sense, a view that only the ideologue would wish to contradict.

This way of thinking explains much of the Conservative attitude to the welfare state in the late 1940s and throughout the 1950s. The attitude, shaped by the fact that much of the welfare state legislation had been a continuation of wartime coalition policies and had, in fact, worked to improve the living standards of the poor, can by typified as one of grudging acceptance. There were growing voices, however, on the Right of the Party, which saw the welfare state as something inconsistent with central Party doctrines about property ownership and the 'opportunity state' (Hoffman 1964:213).

It was not until the late 1950s and early 1960s that it became a little clearer that the reforms of the 1940s had not, as critics on the Right had imagined, lessened the built-in inequalities of British society or challenged that subtle power of the dominant groups of society to shape political agendas and social perceptions. Nor had it yet become clear that the welfare state was to benefit well those who were better off and better placed to use the services it provided (Titmuss 1962). It is to this group that we now must turn.

The middle classes

When G.D.H. Cole attempted to define the middle class in 1955 he was struck firstly by the heterogeneity of the group and secondly by the fact that it could only be defined negatively, as a group which was neither *grande bourgeoisie* nor wage earners (1955:96). What could be said with some certainty, however, was that there was a common concern in this heterogeneous group 'with the defence of economic and social inequality against levelling tendencies which threaten either their incomes or their property' (1955:96).

Donald MacRae, writing in 1958 but reflecting on the period of the late 1940s, had an explanation for this concern which lay in what he called the 'psychology of class relations'. It was that the levelling out of some of the obvious symbols of status left an ideological vacuum in the society (1958:267). 'A gnawing discontent is felt', he noted, 'that there are fewer people about whom one can self evidently despise or hate' (1958:267).

The prevailing middle class view of society and of citizenship in post-war Britain had many continuities with the past, and what distinguished this perception during this period was the acuteness of the class consciousness which was so much a part of it. This consciousness is visible in many different ways. A Mass Observation survey of middle class attitudes noted that middle class people look backwards 'sometimes nostalgically' to the nineteenth century, to values like 'stability, initiative, humanitarianism, high moral tone'. They looked forward with some alarm to a society in which they themselves would have no special place (Mass Observation 1948).

A strongly prevailing perception among many middle class people was that high taxation and socialist egalitarianism were threatening the positive role the middle class played in the society. This comes out strikingly in the book by Roy Lewis and Angus Maude, *The English Middle Classes* (1949). This book set out a history of the middle classes and their values. Great stress was laid on how important they were as a buffer between capital and labour and how fundamental their values of hard work and independence were to the welfare of the society as a whole. This book placed high value on their capacity for leadership and public service and insisted strongly that if high taxation and state social services were to blunt middle class ambitions and charity, then the society as a whole would suffer.

Lewis and Maude felt strongly that the middle classes' incentive to seek a relative advantage over their fellows was an admirable quality since they believed it essential to Britain's survival. But:

How grievously these cherished ambitions conflict both with the egalitarian philosophy and with recent political tendencies! The upper-middle classes can scarcely secure (for good and obvious reasons) the comfortable homes they set their hearts on – let alone the weekend cottages which were so passionately sought between the wars. Education other than that provided in State-aided schools becomes more and more costly, while some politicians would abolish it altogether. Medical attention is being 'equalised' and those who wish to obtain it outside the National Health Service must pay twice. Domestic help is as difficult to get as it is expensive when got – and some reformers denounce its very existence. Finally, not only are legacies penally taxed, but keen Socialists broadcast their longing to abolish completely the transmission of wealth in any form. (1949:221)

In a swipe at the social services, they raised the spectre of middle class public service and charity being withdrawn, with a marked loss to the quality of life in the community. 'State social services may free the poor from want', they noted, 'but does the payment of taxes and compulsory insurance contributions spring from the individual's desire to give?' (Lewis and Maude 1949:226). 'On the contrary', they assert, 'may not the whole process tend to dry up the spring of charity?' (1949:226). A Mass Observation report on charity had noted two years previously that while less than one quarter of their panel of informants approved of charity, there were clear social class differences in attitude (1947g). 'Middle class people', it was reported, 'almost invariably discuss the effect of charity on the giver, working class people the effect on the recipient.' A middle class bank official commented: 'Charity provides a useful outlet for generosity which could otherwise be stifled.'

A Mass Observation report of 1946 examined attitudes to 'squatters', people who, on account of housing shortages, occupied empty property. Among the general public more people were opposed to the squatters than in support of them, but 'Feeling was strongest against the squatters among the middle classes and among the old people, in other words among people who were themselves most likely to be ensconced firmly in their own homes' (1946c). There is little evidence of sympathy here for people most affected by post-war housing shortages.

Tones of greater resentment are detectable in middle class voices from this period. Possessed of a strong sense of their moral superiority, especially to working class people, they were confident in their belief that they knew best what was in the best interests of both the country and the working classes. A letter from Mr Buckle of Leicester to *The Times*, commenting on incentives for workers to improve their production, is very telling of this. 'Always realise this', he announced:

at least 75 per cent of these people, at any time, do not like work at all, or do not like the work they are forced to do for economic reasons . . .
The working man's needs are simple; he wants a house to live in, a wife to cook his meals and look after his children; he wants a little to spare for a trip to the pictures with his wife, a pint or so of beer and a few smokes; and he wants money to keep up to this standard. (*The Times*, 21 March 1946)

He urges in his conclusion 'make money the medals for hard and efficient work'. Lying behind this injunction, of course, is the belief that working people are always incipiently idle.

The elements of a structure of feeling among middle class people in post-war Britain begin to stand out; they include a marked resentment against what is taken to be egalitarianism and an intense sense that the social and cultural role of the middle class, and the values it represents, is being eroded. This becomes compounded into a nostalgic image of a world which has gone and fear for the one being built. A further element is a strong sense of a loss of their distinctiveness as a class. Their prevailing image of themselves as a group which had earned their rewards was one they clung to despite being, as Lewis and Maude put it, 'beset with worries' (1949:245).

The working class

The group in society widely thought to be the prime be-neficiaries of post-war planning and the welfare state was, of course, the working class. The Labour government was in one sense their government, though it should not be forgotten that the Conservative Party had considerable working class support. The idea of citizenship embodied in working class support for the Labour government needs to be examined carefully, however, for this gave shape to the kinds of demands working class people articulated through their institutions about the sort of society they wished to see developed in Britain. Those demands reflected, of course, the position of working class people in society, their hopes, experiences and their preoccupations. They reflected, too, the character of the labour movement as a whole.

George Orwell noted in 1945, in his 'London Letter' in the *Partisan Review*, that the general election of that year had been fought largely on domestic issues. He commented on what the British people wanted:

They look to a Labour government to make them more secure and, after a few years, more comfortable, and the chief danger of the situation lies in the fact that the English people have never been made to grasp that the sources of their prosperity lie outside England. The parochial outlook of the Labour Party itself is largely responsible for this. (1945:468)

This was, of course, only partly true. Indeed, the Labour government was in fact motivated by what Jan Morris has called a spirit of 'imperial earnestness'. It possessed a strong and distinctly paternalist sense of 'imperial trusteeship', so that under the government's schemes of renewal, the Empire became an Empire of planners, developers and economic theorists (1979:503). Where the charge begins to ring true is in the prevailing sense of what kind of society the government felt compelled to build and what hopes it responded to. If the Labour Party was parochial, then it reflected accurately the attitudes and values and commitments of its ordinary supporters.

Those ordinary supporters were the beneficiaries of a newly conferred citizenship (T.H. Marshall 1950). The welfare legislation of the period extended to working people the rights to employment, social security, health and education, but there was no strong sense among working people that this was leading to a new kind of society or to any profound change in the class structure of the country. And while the rhetoric of interdependence and of a nation pulling together had a powerful resonance during wartime, no comparable rhetoric describing a peacetime welfare state developed.

The gains to working people of the reforms of the welfare state, though, were obvious. Rowntree and Lavers found evidence in Rowntree's third study of York in 1950 that there had been a dramatic reduction in levels of poverty in that city since the second study in 1936 (Rowntree and Lavers 1951). They detected a reduction from 31.3 per cent of the population in poverty to 2.7 per cent and a remarkable change in poverty's causes. In 1936, it was overwhelmingly associated with unemployment; in 1950 with old age and sickness. Their conclusion was that the welfare measures of the post-war period had considerably alleviated poverty without finally being able to cure it (1951:66).

There was more certainty that some features of pre-war society had been unalterably transformed. The spectre of the detested means test had been removed. The health service proposals, in particular, were widely supported. A Mass Observation report of 1949 commented that the majority of people (with some middle class people dissenting) felt they had benefited from the health service (1949). 'Many of the heartier supporters of the Health Service', the report notes, 'appear still to see it as something magical – an adults' lucky dip with Mr Bevan distributing prizes' (1949:4). The main criticisms of the service were not about its cost, but its slowness. A Liverpool University study of planning in Dudley in the West Midlands in 1950 noted that, 'The new health services have . . . caught the imagination of the people' (The University of Liverpool Department of Social Science 1951:127).

Among older people, those whose memories of insecurity and poverty stretched further back, often into the nineteenth century, there was a sense that much of the insecurity of old age had been removed. The Liverpool University study of Dudley commented that among older people, 'Much of the fear of removal to "the House" has been banished, but there is still a fear in the minds of many old people that as their powers fail and money dwindles, they will be forced into alien surroundings' (1951:133). There are indications that among older people a shift in attitude had taken place; they were much more likely after the war to see their entitlement to a decent pension as a right. A Mass Observation study of the voluntary social services reported a meeting of pensioners in which, following a talk on 'How I became a pauper', the secretary of the association said: 'Friends!! Today they are offering us all sorts of charity. Well, we don't want their charity! We want them to give us enough to get the things we need for ourselves . . . That's what we want, a decent pension, not charity!' (1947g).

Some, of course, could not accept that the new services were theirs as of right. My grandfather, for instance, in his late seventies when the Health Service came into operation, found it very difficult to accept a free service. My cousin Gloria, who lived with him at the time, told me:

I don't think my granda understood the change. Gladys Dailtree came collecting for the Doctor's money and the Labour money. They had a card. If she didn't come Lizzy Storey came. When they changed and health stamps started he didn't click on to that. He didn't click on you could go to the doctors and not pay. He hadn't paid for it so he didn't think you should have it. He didn't like getting two shillings off his prescription. If he had worked and paid for it . . . that would have been a different matter. (B. Williamson 1982:221)

Materially, however, this particular old man was as well off as he had ever been, was part of a system of social security which, before the war, he could only have imagined.

In 1947 Tom Harrisson, reflecting on the recent findings of Mass Observation, noted that there was a good deal of political apathy in Britain; ordinary working class people showed more interest in gambling than politics and displayed an 'uncomplaining acceptance' of the conditions within which they lived (Mass Observation 1947d). Gambling, drink and smoking, Harrisson noted, 'take the largest slice of our national budget', and he went on:

A skilled listener-in might go for days through Britain without hearing a single mention of UNO, USA, USSR, Indian, Atomic bomb or Science. He would collect volumes on the neighbours, shortages, sport, the weather, the land, and perhaps some reference to prices, jobs, Jews, pensions and certainly the latest leading crimes.

Harrisson's comments on gambling are corroborated in a remarkable piece of social reporting by Ferdinand Zweig in his book, *Labour, Life and Poverty*, published in 1948. He regarded gambling as the principal source of secondary poverty in Britain, followed closely by drink. Zweig's interviews with over 400 working men in the pubs and greyhound stadiums of London led him to the view that what the average worker appreciated most of all was excitement. Because of a heightened sense of the insecurities of life and his inclination to live only in the present, the working man was a willing customer of everything that brought excitement (1948:44). Recreation became, Zweig claimed, synonymous with freedom.

In contrast to Harrisson, however, Zweig picked up from his respondents a strong interest in subjects related to social welfare and labour conditions. 'I found in their utterances', he wrote, 'a deeply-felt sense of injustice and grievance for what they regard as wrongs done to them in the past . . . the fear of a recurrence of unemployment, and the memories of the great depression, still haunt their subconscious mind' (1948:62–3).

The social philosophy of the workers can be summarised in a sentence. 'Not rights, but needs, should be the governing factor in social improvement'. They often say, 'The needy should be helped; rights can always be disputed, but needs are clearly seen by everybody'. (1948:63)

Zweig saw a great difference here between middle class and working class attitudes; the middle class were interested in rights, working people put more stress on needs.

The picture he draws of working class life is, however, a complex one; he found a 'ladder-like stratification of the working class with many small rungs' (1948:84). The differences between the labourers and the labour aristocracy of the craftsmen were substantial but they were not as great as those dividing the working class from the middle class. Workers, Zweig noted, disliked middle class people for their perceived snobbery and love of money. But there were other differences, especially those between men and women and between workers from different industries, which made generalizations about the working class unsafe. Zweig himself noted that the 'average worker' did not, in fact, exist except in the social and economic literature.

How then can working class attitudes to welfare and citizenship be characterized? And how had these attitudes changed? The answer has to be built up from an appreciation of the contexts of the daily lives of working class people, though not through this alone. For while much of the pre-war social fabric of Britain remained intact, and while post-war austerity was in some ways more severe than that of wartime and people had to cope with a terrible housing shortage and the strains of overcrowding, there had been a change in the quality of hope and of expectations.

This was probably more true of the skilled working class than of the unskilled. In 1944 Marie Paneth, a social worker in London, writing about her experiences of youth work in the East End in her book, *Branch Street*, typified slum working class life as street based, coarse and always potentially violent. 'There is', she noted, 'an old established and very solid animosity between the streets':

Branch Street takes the lowest place on the social ladder. Many of the inhabitants who have come to live in Branch Street loathe to meet their neighbours from slightly better days, who most probably look down on them. (1944:55)

The children of Branch Street she saw as verminous, with parents who showed no concern for them. They felt themselves to be unjustly treated and behaved like disappointed, unhappy people. Their background and experience, Marie Paneth said, 'had taught them not to trust and not to hope' (1944:123).

Move away from the slums into the respectable working class and the problem is altogether different. Bernice Martin, reflecting on her childhood and youth in Lancashire in the immediate post-war period, recalls an ordered world of home-centred privatism and respectability (1981). Her family and neighbours fought for order and respect in their lives and drew sharp boundaries round the sanctity of their own homes. Their whole culture was one of order and control built up to protect their dignity. Gender roles were rigidly demarcated despite the fact that Lancashire women had had a long tradition of full-time factory work. People 'knew their place and strove to keep it' (1981:69). It was a culture intolerant of outsiders and of those who failed to maintain standards.

For the organized and respectable working class the welfare state was a support for the more effective realization of their private ambitions. A significant number of my own generation were to be direct beneficiaries of such aspirations. In the autobiography I encouraged him to write, my father recalled his views and feelings in 1945:

Louie and I promised each other that if the Labour Party did what they said they would do, we would do everything in our power to give our lads as full an education as possible, by taking every advantage the government could offer, and the family allowances which the twins were entitled to would be put away from them until such times when they would need it for their education. (J. W. Williamson, unpublished:101)

The language is telling: governments offer advantages and guarantee entitlements and there is still the sense, an echo of the pre-war arrangements which had denied him a decent education, that it all might still cost money which he would have to provide. But the full education would be worth it because then we, the children, could better ourselves.

Neither my father and mother nor anyone else at the time could have anticipated accurately what the outcome would be of these hopes being realized. Nor could they have understood then that only a fraction of the children of their class would reap such rewards. That realization was to come later, as we shall see, with profound implications for the whole character of working class life.

One writer has noted that the gradual climb back to prosperity was a long, dispiriting haul 'echoing with pre-war memories

of better days' (S. Cooper 1964:56). But gradual improvements
did come; living standards did rise. New houses, schools and
hospitals were built. It became steadily more credible that
ambitions hardly dreamed of before the war could, in fact, be
realized. What was lacking, of course, was a widely shared
vision of a future which realized ideals other than those of
material improvement and social advancement for individuals.
Put another way, though it is possible to do so only with the
privilege of hindsight, no notion of citizenship or of a common
culture developed with a distinctive rhetoric articulating new
collective ideals. This idea is, of course, most tellingly developed
in the work of Raymond Williams (1958). The thrust of his
argument is that changes in the culture of a society flow from
changes in the structure of the relationships between classes.
This will always be a debatable position to take, but it does
prompt questions about what vision of society the political
representatives of workers clung to and pressed forward.

Here is the clue, I think, to the meaning of citizenship in
post-war Britain; it is to be found in the nature of the
compromise between the labour movement and the class structure of the society. It lies in the distinctive way in which
Labour, in Parliament and town hall, saw its role as delivering
benefits to its supporters. Those benefits, both demanded and
conceded, were largely of a material kind. This is, of course,
understandable given the prevalent historical memory of the
1920s and 1930s, when the privations to be guarded against were
those of poverty and unemployment. Among ordinary people
there prevailed therefore a strong sense of what must be avoided
in the future; there was much less sense of what kind of society
should be built. That came from their leaders.

It is too soon in this account to explore the debates that
subsequently developed in the 1950s and 1960s about the role of
the Labour Party as the party of the working class (for example,
Crosland 1956; Miliband 1961). One historian has suggested
that the Labour Party never had a clear vision of the future and
fudged major issues of policy. His case is that although the
Party received solid support from its members, that support was
unenthusiastic and often cynical and that the Party's leaders

often remained aloof from its ordinary members and even held them in contempt (Cronin 1984:12).

That is certainly too harsh a judgement. What is more certain is that Labour leaders in government were preoccupied with reconstruction, a heavy legislative programme and a complex international situation. Trades union leaders were heavily involved in the politics of nationalization of the major industries. All of this was overlain, particularly from 1948 onwards, with severe economic difficulties in which first Dalton and later, unsuccessfully, Cripps struggled to maintain the value of sterling and boost production and exports.

What it all meant was that social programmes – in housing, education and social services – did not develop as fast as they might otherwise have done. But it was not just a matter of scarce resources; it was a matter, too, of imagination and of the vision of Labour leaders of what form the new services should take. The national assistance measures can now best be seen as attempts to deal with a historical problem, that of the family means test, and to have involved payments below what was needed to keep pace with prices (Deacon and Bradshaw 1983). The Health Service was based on a political compromise between the government and the doctors and was much more concerned with overcoming a backlog of ill health than with defining the policies for a healthier society. Full employment is a key element of the welfare state; the Attlee government achieved this, but encouraged no fundamental review of the meaning of employment in a reconstructed capitalist society. In the newly nationalized industries an opportunity was lost to achieve changes in the way management and work itself were organized.

The failure to define new goals for social policy is very clear in the case of education. Ellen Wilkinson – 'Red Ellen' of the Jarrow March – who became Attlee's Education Minister, fought hard to secure the Labour Party's commitment to raising the school leaving age and to overcome the desperate shortage of teachers the system faced. She was clear in her dislike of public schools and during her time at the ministry the number of direct grant schools fell considerably. Her support for grammar schools and secondary modern schools and her reluctance to put her full weight behind the development of the comprehensive school, or 'multilateral' school as it was known, meant that Labour nurtured a post-war education service that was deeply divided on lines of social class (Addison 1985; History Workshop 1979). The idea that working class children could advance their opportunities through the grammar school was one widely held in the Labour Party and had been so for a very long time, even though the institution itself was not a particularly welcoming one to such children and retained in its pedagogy an institutional style drawn from the older public schools (Barker 1972; Addison 1985:165).

It is not my intention to minimize the extent of change which the programmes of the welfare state brought about. Rather it is to underline that these programmes did not change significantly the structure of class relationships in the society as a whole; the Labour Party was in the end unable to use the institutions of the state to bring about the social transformation many of its supporters had hoped for. This failure, if indeed it was a failure, should not be blamed on the Labour Party. Parties need followers; the Attlee government was not by 1950 an unpopular government. In fact, the Labour Party polled more votes in 1950 that it had done in 1945. In this respect the government gave some expression to the hopes and expectations of ordinary working class people, even if it did not act in advance of their demands to build a different kind of society.

The period after 1948 to the general election of 1950 and the return of the Conservatives under Churchill in 1951 was one of growing economic difficulties for the government and of a worsening international situation. The outbreak of war in Korea marked the beginning of the end of the first phase of Britain's post-war welfare state. The Chancellor, Hugh Gaitskell, insisted on increasing expenditure on rearmament, which the Left of the Labour Party saw as eroding the welfare state. Internecine conflict over the costs of rearmament and over Britain's links with American foreign policy led to the resignation of Bevan, Wilson and Freeman from the government, and the small majority in Parliament became unsustainable.

Kenneth Morgan has summed up Labour's welfare state as a 'mosaic of reform and conservatism' with innovation in health and social security balancing 'relative quiescence' in education. The welfare measures, he says, 'did not, of themselves, produce a more egalitarian or open society' (1985:179–89). He notes, too, that among the prime beneficiaries of the welfare state were the social workers, planners and teachers (1985:187). This claim that the welfare state did not nurture the welfare society, because, in part, its services were dominated by professionals, was taken up tellingly by Richard Crossman in the early 1970s. Following another electoral defeat, he reflected on the failures of the welfare state (1976). The root failure, he believed, was that of the Labour Party to acknowledge and nurture philanthropy and altruism, and in believing instead that the driving force of change in a society was economic self interest. From the 1920s onwards, Crossman noted, 'the normal left wing attitude has been opposed to middle class philanthropy, charity and everything else connected with do-gooding' (1976:278). The building of the new society therefore had to depend on the government allying itself with the professionals and the trades unions to deliver services to the people and on their behalf.

Such a strategy for welfare brought its rewards. What it did not do was challenge the underlying class structure of the society and clearly, as will be seen, in many ways it reinforced it. Nor did it protect the welfare state from the criticism that its services were too expensive for the economy.

For these reasons the idea of the welfare state came to have a restricted meaning in Britain and to rest on a narrow conception of citizenship. Perhaps R.H. Tawney touched on the root of it when, in a 1950 review of Titmuss's book, *Problems of Social Policy*, he noted: 'To share risks is easy; but it is not enough. It is also necessary to share advantages' (1981:156). The problem he detected was that in Britain there was a deeply ingrained idea that 'advantages which are shared are not advantages at all.' This underlying attitude has left profound marks on British social policy. The implication in what he says is that, in the absence of a clear view of what unites people rather than what divides them – and in Britain, then as now, the differences of wealth, power, culture and status which we summarize as class were the principal features of society dividing people off from one another – the values which retain credibility are those which appeal to pride and selfish greed.

Conclusion

What the argument of this chapter points to is this: the conception of citizenship which came to prevail in post-war Britain was a limited one. The society was reconstructed by a Labour government possessed of a much clearer image of what it sought to avoid from the past than what it wished to realize in the future. In this respect it was quite in tune with the attitude and outlook of its main supporters among ordinary working class people. It was a government constrained by the resources of the economy and the world role in which it cast the country. Its failure to bring about a more equal society is balanced by its success in nurturing a more prosperous one, in which the rich and powerful were not really threatened, in which the middle classes experienced, without fully realizing it, great benefits from the new social programmes and in which working people felt largely content that their world was improving. The irony is that the aspirations for which the welfare state laid the foundation were not of a sort likely to sustain support for the kinds of value its institutions were intended to express.

4
From Churchill to Macmillan

Introduction

This chapter covers the period from the election of Winston Churchill's government in 1951 to the replacement of Eden as Prime Minister by Harold Macmillan following the Suez crisis. The parliamentary politics of the period are not, however, the main concern. Such changes themselves have to be seen against the broader undertows of change in attitude and feeling of different groups of British society, adjusting to their altered circumstances and pressing for change in particular ways. It is a period of both consolidation and considerable alteration in British society. With the Suez fiasco, many old certainties about Britain's world role were shattered, but what the future world role should be, no one was really clear. What also stands out is that the post-war assumptions about British society and economy, which put such stress on planning, the welfare state, social harmony and tradition and the preservation of an unmodernized system of industrial relations, were inadequate to meet the challenges of a changed world economy and of rising expectations at home for a better standard of living.

The period of the early fifties is lodged in historical memories as being austere and drab. In *Clinging to the Wreckage*, his tongue-in-cheek autobiographical sketch, John Mortimer writes about 'the bland, forgettable decade that stretched between VJ Day and the Suez adventure' (1982:164). It was, however, a period that gave a distinctive shape to the character of what later became known as the affluent society. Despite the opening up of ideological debates on the fringes of the major political parties, the period is marked above all by a consensus that the purpose of government policy was to achieve 'prosperity'. Indeed, much of the political history of the subsequent two decades could be written around the evolving meaning of that word and its increasingly narrowed reference to private affluence. The consensus extended further to include the assumption that prosperity would be defended in the framework of the NATO Alliance and built on the foundation of Commonwealth trading preferences and a world role for sterling. From within this broad framework British society developed in a distinctive and, as will be seen, essentially depoliticized mode towards the affluent society.

The period can be typified in various ways. There was, firstly, great continuity in what Gerth and Mills once called 'the master symbols of legitimation' of the society (1970). Without many people being aware of the underlying structural weaknesses of the economy there was, secondly, steady growth in living standards, conveying to most people a sense of growing well-being and security.

Britain was not, however, in a stable world. The Cold War was at its height in both Europe and the Far East. British troops remained stationed in Germany, Austria and the canal zone in the Middle East. They were engaged in operations in East Africa to contain what was described in Britain as the Mau Mau rebellion, and were in Malaya fighting 'Communist insurgents'. Nationalism was a potent force in the Middle East and near the end of the period with which this chapter is concerned troops were enmeshed in a violent civil war in Cyprus.

At home the air of confidence which had been generated by the Festival of Britain and the dismantling of rationing controls was tempered in some quarters by the growing realization that, despite the welfare state, Britain remained a society with a weakened and unmodernized economy and a country still sharply demarcated by the contours of class division. I want to show in this chapter that the Establishment vision of Britain's continued world power status – a vision rudely shattered by the Suez fiasco of 1956 – was complemented by a conservatism and materialism among working class people and the institutions of the labour movement, which prevented any radical assessment of the society and its priorities. But it was a time during which some of the first real assessments of the achievements of the welfare state were becoming available in a way which showed the new Jerusalem to be flawed.

Symbols of legitimation

The tacit assumptions about the nature of belonging to a national community and the beliefs which render the institutions of authority of that community legitimate must be regularly re-endorsed. All politically organized communities provide opportunities, often of a ritual kind, to achieve this. In Britain the social and political construction of the people and of the nation as a whole has, for a century and a half, been bound up with the institutions of the monarchy, the Church, Parliament and, from the 1920s onwards, the BBC.

The legitimation of beliefs, values and structures of authority and power is a process, and one which unfolds through the drama and pageantry, both national and local, of political events and cultural occasions. The Festival of Britain in 1951 can be seen in this light. The death of King George VI in the February of 1952 and the coronation of Queen Elizabeth II were, of course, state ceremonial occasions of profound cultural significance whose management reinforced a particular sense of what the essential core of British society really was – something rooted in a timeless tradition.

Of these early opportunities to reassert a traditional view of British national identity and social values, the Festival of Britain is the most ambiguous symbol. Conceived as a centenary to the Great Exhibition and as a celebration of the people's achievements in war and austerity, it was, for many Conservatives, a celebration too closely associated with Labour's achievements in office (Chaney 1983). Nevertheless it became an event widely supported, and the exhibitions on the South Bank of the Thames attracted several million enthusiastic visitors. For the BBC, the Festival was an occasion to project and deploy with great effect the medium of television itself, and the image of the nation those broadcasts sustained was one stressing the rich cultural heritage bestowed by a long and continuous history. But there was an attempt, too, to project an image of a society geared up to a future to exploit science and technology and modern design and to nurture the creative arts (Hewison 1988).

Michael Frayn's essay, 'Festival', touches perceptively and wittily on some of the tacit assumptions of the Festival's organizers, to reveal the underlying tensions of the society as a whole. Far from being a festival of the people as a whole, Frayn saw it as that of the radical middle classes (1964). These were 'the do-gooders; the readers of the News Chronicle, the Guardian, and the Observer; the signers of petitions; the backbone of the BBC. In short, the Herbivores, or gentle ruminants, who look out from the lush pastures which are their natural station in life with eyes full of sorrow for less fortunate creatures, guiltily conscious of their advantages, though not usually ceasing to eat the grass' (p. 331). There were critics of the Festival; Frayn singles out Evelyn Waugh who, as a sort of curator of upper middle class anxiety, articulated that sense that every act of the Labour government had been against their interests and privileges. But this 'carniverous' opposition was muted. The king and queen became patrons of the Festival and on 3 May there was a service of dedication for it in St Paul's. The people and the royal family and the establishment of the arts came together in a celebratory act which underscored their essential unity, and the Festival itself fused the highbrow traditions of art, design and music with the funfair of Battersea park.

Frayn also claims, however, that the Festival was a turning point for the herbivores: the government which had sustained them was exhausted, and the carnivores were ready to replace it and give their support to a very different set of political values. The Labour government fell in two stages in the wake of acrimonious debates in the Labour Party over expenditure cuts and rearmament, and was replaced in 1951 by a Tory government led by Churchill. The facts of political change should not obscure continuities of sentiment and feeling which inclined even Labour supporters to regard the established institutional framework of the society as being basically decent, sound and worthy of respect.

The reaction of people to the death of King George VI on 6 February 1952 is further evidence of that sense of continuity and stability focused on monarchy, which is at the core of a prevailing British sense of national identity. There was a general feeling of sadness and shock at the king's death. In his radio commentary on the lying in state, Richard Dimbleby, it has been claimed, embodied the feelings of his audience in his rich description of the scene (Cannadine 1983). His reference to the 'slow flicker of the candles' touching 'gently the gems of the Imperial Crown, even that ruby Henry wore at Agincourt' linked an imperial-historic symbolism with 'the real tears of those who pass by and see it', creating an atmosphere which was deeply sad and reverential (Cannadine 1983:153).

The coronation of Elizabeth which followed the next year is, however, a much more significant event, revealing structures of feeling saturated with the symbols of Church and state and a popular historiography stressing continuity, order and tradition. The occasion, as Cannadine has pointed out, was still 'avowedly an imperial occasion, with the queen's dress containing embroidered emblems of the dominions, with regiments of Commonwealth and colonial troops marching in procession, with Prime Ministers of the Dominions and India present in the Abbey, and an assortment of heads of state from various exotic colonial protectorates' (1983:153). Richard Dimbleby, the BBC commentator for the occasion, was a man possessed by the idea of royalty and the monarchy as something capturing the essence of British greatness. The Coronation was brought to millions of homes by television and Dimbleby's commentary drew effusively on a reverential rhetoric rooted in a romantic sense of history. Two sociologists, Edward Shils and Michael Young, wrote about the Coronation as a 'national communion' in which, through the pageantry and the symbolism of the ceremony, all relayed in minute detail to millions of homes, the central symbols of monarchy and authority and of family were all fused together (1953).

As a media event the Coronation was a strictly controlled,

indeed contrived, affair, and a very important element of the way in which it was staged had more to do with the technical and political claims of BBC television than with the timeless rituals of the ceremony itself (Chaney 1983). Nevertheless, as a 'civic ritual' it did have deep roots in the ordinary social routines and relationships of the society at large. An interesting paradox about British political culture is then revealed: the 'master symbols of legitimation' of the society may well be imperial, traditional and class-ridden, reflecting the attitudes and interests of national elites, but they are embraced positively in contexts which are essentially local and immediate. The ideological alchemy of it works precisely in that way.

Maurice Broady's study of forty-one Coronation street parties in the Mersey ward of Birkenhead is a piece of urban anthropology which brings this out really well (1956). Stratified into 'roughs' and 'respectacles' – with the roughs thought of as being uncouth and dirty and dependent on national assistance, and the respectables as being hard-working and good neighbours – this ward is a microcosm of the older areas of terraced housing of many of the country's industrial cities. Broady notes a high degree of neighbourliness, with women talking together in the street outside open doorways, and a strong sense of the deprivations of the past. The memory of the hardships of the past sustain a spirit of sympathy and helpfulness among neighbours, and nurture the view that the very best ought to be provided for the children.

At the time of the Coronation, street parties were organized in forty-five streets, catering for between thirty and 140 children each. What Broady discovered was a street-based pattern of social contact with quite precise rules which excluded people from other streets. The implicit rules governing the organization of the street parties prevented those who had organized them from claiming special rewards for doing so, and the overall effect of the parties was to reinforce intensely local patterns of neighbourliness and social identity.

In this way, though this is not a claim Broady himself seeks to make, the ritual of the street party binds a carefully bounded locality to the broader national scene, so that all, roughs and respectables alike, can celebrate a particular version of what ultimately binds them all into a national community. The Coronation was a special event. Royalty touched British people in many other ways; the rough family's visits to great sporting events like Ascot or the FA Cup Final, their presence at the launching of ships, the opening of buildings and their patronage of public institutions of many kinds are all opportunities to link the central symbols of the state to the routines of ordinary, everyday life.

The sense of what that national community is and what values it represents is not a static one; it responds to change and is given different meanings by different groups in society, and in a socially differentiated society the cultural transmission of those meanings and the ways in which they are experienced is always variable. What is interesting about Britain, however, is that there is such a large area of agreement about what their country stands for between the attitudes and values of ordinary working class people and the ruling groups who actually control it. The view, for instance, pervasive among foreign service elites, the military and the leadership of the Tory Party, that Britain still had a major role to play in protecting the free world from Communism and bringing the colonies slowly to the point when their independence could be granted, was one widely endorsed by many working people still emotionally attached to grandiose images of the national past.

But it was not just their education which made this possible; nor were they the mere victims of media propaganda. Their own leaders in the labour movement, with few exceptions, shared such a vision. The Attlee government, for example, had begun the manufacture of Britain's own atomic weapons and Ernest Bevin had been a very traditional British Foreign Secretary in his passionate anti-Communism. The fact that thousands of British families were connected in some way with the armed forces, either directly through their wartime experience of them or through the current arrangements for national service, is also significant. In Korea, East Africa, Malaya and the Middle East, British forces fought and died in conflicts which were part of Britain's world-wide political commitments.

This, too, was the period of the Cold War, of McCarthyism in America, of the trial of Klaus Fuchs, the atomic spy, of the defection of Burgess and Maclean and of the uprising in East Germany in the July of 1953. The political climate was one of great uncertainty and one which justified a high level of military readiness and conscription. Following the outbreak of the Korean War the Labour government had instituted crash measures to build up the army to ten divisions. National service was extended to two years and between 1950 and 1953 an extra 100,000 men were called into the services (Wallace 1970:197). Britain was caught up in a vortex of change in international affairs that was beyond the power of the British government to control. Bertrand Russell, in a broadcast on 17 May 1951, the first in a series on *Living in the Atomic Age*, characterized the mood of the time as one of 'impotent perplexity' (1951:787). 'We see ourselves', he said, 'drifting towards a war that hardly anybody desires – a war that, as we all know, must bring disaster to the whole of mankind. But, like a rabbit fascinated by a snake, we stare at the horror without knowing what to do to avert it' (1951:787).

The following month *The Listener*, in its series *The Changing World*, published a piece by E.H. Carr in which the historian explained: 'The conspicuous fact about the international scene today is the passing of power from Western Europe: for the first time for many centuries Western Europe is no longer the centre of the globe' (1951). Nationalism in Africa, Asia and the Middle East, Communism in the Far East and American domination of the western economy were the broad underlying forces precipitating a lurching sense of crisis and a widespread belief that Britain must be prepared militarily to deal with potential crises across the world.

Throughout this period, say from 1948 to 1953, public opinion was generally supportive of maintaining the manpower levels of the armed forces, extending national service and increasing the defence budget (Marwick 1982:106). Indeed, Marwick suggests that the British public did not really come to a full understanding that Britain was not a major world power until the 1960s.

National servicemen made up 50 per cent of the army's manpower in 1951 (Royle 1986:22). Excepting those who on grounds of conscience or health could legitimately avoid service in the armed forces, all young men at this time faced the prospect of national service. Many of those who experienced it now look back on it as an important and formative period of their lives, though the contributors to one volume of recollections in the main thought it a waste of time (Johnson 1973). Alongside the misery and mindlessness of military discipline, they found comradeship, travel, sex and excitement. It has been claimed, too, that military service helped build bridges of understanding between the younger generation and their elders because they came to have so much in common.

For some, of course, national service was a radicalizing experience and, as will be seen later, the 'anger' of those writers later known as the 'angry young men' – writers like John Osborne, Andrew Sinclair and David Storey – was very much connected with their reaction to national service (Royle 1986:104). Ex-national servicemen took part in the Campaign for Nuclear Disarmament and in the demonstrations against the Suez invasion.

Of greater longer-term signifance, however, though this cannot be demonstrated unequivocally, is the way national service reinforced many aspects of the social divisions of British society. Values like pride and loyalty and *esprit de corps* were generalized from their focus on a particular regiment to the political order of society as a whole. This was particularly true for the ex-public school boys who found in the army the officer jobs they believed were their destiny, as well as a cultural extension of the values of their dormitories and officer corps.

The army tried to build strong local recruitment links and to build up an identity between its regiments and particular counties or towns. When the Gloucestershire regiment returned from Korea, there was a march through Bristol to receive the freedom of the city, and an atmosphere of great public excitement (Royle 1986:64). Passing out parades became family occasions.

The army continued, however, to look for its officers among

the better educated, those from the public schools and the
grammar schools, and the sort of contact young men from
different social class backgrounds had with one another in the
army generally reinforced the prejudices they each brought to
the relationship. On overseas service, particularly in Malaya and
in Kenya, where national servicemen encountered the residues
of the expatriate colonial communities, the result was a confirmation that old social hierarchies were very much intact.
Royle writes:

Although the Japanese had dented the imperial legend in the Far East,
the post-war British colonial caste still had a good conceit of itself. In
Kuala Lumpur, Robinsons was a good substitute for Harrods; cricket
was played on the Padang in Singapore as if it were Lord's; and the
clubs and hill stations still aspired to the manners of pre-war
Anglo-India. (1986:161)

In such a framework servicemen knew their place, and the
regiments maintained such rituals as Guest Nights and dress
uniforms to seal the links between the Mess and the local
'society'.

It was not something the squaddies could question. There
was little in the background of most of them which would have
helped them question it. Writing of his time as a national
serviceman in Egypt, Alan Burns characterized his state of mind
as follows:

My essential state was one of unawareness, sexual, political, social
unawareness. I did not see through the dreary, decadent life around
me, I was ignorant of the imperial set up I was part of, and I had no
comprehension of the real condition of the native Egyptians. (Johnson
1973:86)

More to the point, however, is that political discussion was
actively discouraged. Soldiers did their duty. Only among
officers, it has been claimed, was it safe to talk about politics.
Then, of course, the only expressable opinions were those of a
right-wing Establishment kind. Left-wing thinking of any kind
was seen as the hallmark of the eccentric (Royle 1986). It

amounts to this: national service in Britain in the 1950s was an experience which in manifold ways ritually confirmed structures of authority and hierarchy in the society, as well as the social contours of the class system.

This is not to say that it rendered such divisions legitimate; but it did mark them out and underline their continuity. And the link between the military experience and civvy street was strengthened in the way that companies, in a situation of labour shortage, would enthusiastically recruit ex-servicemen, particularly officers, to positions of authority in management, believing their military experience to be relevant to industry and commerce.

The society to which the soldiers returned in the 1950s still resembled that of the 1940s. Bomb damage still scarred the big cities. Housing shortages were acute and although the planning legislation of the 1940s was beginning to transform the urban landscape of the country with new towns and suburbs and council estates, there was still an atmosphere of urban closeness in the older industrial cities, which is something of a hallmark of British society. Laurie Lee evoked this for London in a broadcast in 1951 when he reflected on why he enjoyed being an 'exile' there. He notes:

The sad, noisy clamour of life lived at close quarters; lovers in doorways, children in back-streets, singing on bus tops Saturday night, whelk stalls, fish shops, cinemas, fairs, chimneys on fire, and the warmth in the winter streets generated by a million fires and a million bodies – it is this mass gregariousness, this feeling that one is at a non-stop party, that I like best of all. (1951:418–19)

Lee is, of course, choosing to ignore the smog, filth and congestion which contributed to a high rate of bronchitic and tubercular illness, and the damage to children which the congested living of the older urban areas allowed.

The non-stop party to which Laurie Lee refers was a celebration of a popular culture banal in its cosiness to a degree which, in retrospect, is barely credible. His lovable Londoners and their counterparts elsewhere went to the pictures twice a week to a diet of Ealing comedies, Hollywood musicals like *Seven Brides for Seven Brothers*, *Oklahoma!* and *South Pacific*. They watched a constant stream of films about the last war, and at home, when they were not watching the growing number of televisions being sold at the time, they listened to the radio; to *Mrs Dale's Diary*, *The Brains Trust*, serials like *Dick Barton, Special Agent*, *Workers' Playtime* and, with a solemnity approaching religious ritual, *Forces Favourites* on a Sunday morning. The presenter of the last of these, Jean Metcalfe, had a way of presenting record requests which quite brilliantly, but in a wholly sentimental way, brought families together and linked them with their soldier sons on the Rhine. The younger members of these families tuned in to the request programmes *Uncle Mac* and *Children's Favourites* on a Saturday morning and to *Top of the Form*, a round-Britain school quiz, through the week.

People took their holidays at the seaside and particularly popular were the holiday camps of Billy Butlin. Communal eating, ballroom dancing, treats for the kids and being looked after by the uniformed 'red coats' was a formula which worked. On Saturday afternoons hundreds of thousands turned out to football matches and, as the historian Asa Briggs has commented, football crowds were as orderly as church meetings (Briggs 1983). On bank holidays whole streets took bus trips to the seaside or the country and a good Saturday night out was a rich mixture of beer and a sing-song. People travelled by train and it was not until 1956 that British Rail, a nationalized industry, abolished third class travel.

The theme of improving living standards is the strongest of the period. But it was an ambiguous achievement. Blackwell and Seabrook have suggested that: 'The significance of the 1950s is this: that it marked the beginnings of the process whereby capitalism succeeded in imposing through its version of prosperity what it had been unable to impose through its version of poverty, deprivation and want' (1985:93). But Arthur Marwick was also right when he noted in British society at the time a complacency and a parochialism and 'the lack of serious structural change' (1982:111). That lack of change is something to be traced not just in the economic management of business enterprises or in the attitudes of the trades unions: it is to be found, too, in the prevailing sentiments of the society and in the priorities, commitments, attitudes and values woven into the fabric of everyday life.

Change did, however, take place. Industrial output rose at a rate of nearly 4 per cent per annum during the 1950s. Substantial growth occurred in those industries manufacturing consumer durables. Consumer expenditure on cars and motorcycles increased from £94 million in 1950 to £325 million in 1957. Expenditure on furniture, electrical goods and other durables rose over the same period from £530 million to £680 million. Neither figure, however, begins to approach the amount spent on alcoholic drink and tobacco. The respective figures are £1,686 million and £1,926 million (Halsey 1972b:88). Unemployment, the social scourge of the 1930s, became a thing of the past. Between 1948 and 1957 the rate of unemployment fluctuated between 1.2 and 2.1 per cent. Indeed, the key problem was one of labour shortage and one which led to a steady increase in the proportion of married women workers and immigrant workers from the West Indies.

Steadily improving living standards were achieved by most groups of workers, but they worked 45 hours each week to achieve them. The percentage of households in owner occupation in England and Wales increased from 27 per cent in 1947 to 42.3 per cent in 1961, and during the whole decade of the 1950s nearly 2.5 million new houses were built (Halsey 1972b:311). Over the same period nearly a million people were moved out of accommodation officially classified as slums. And more and more families, particularly those of ordinary people, realized through their children the better health care and increased educational opportunities which the reforms of the 1940s had promised them.

Much, then, had changed. Closer inspection of the texture and form of social relationships reveals significant continuities in older attitudes and values. At the same time, though, there is in this period a growing sense, particularly among the educated middle classes, of change in the class system and a heightened awareness of the mixed benefits of that.

Consciousness of class

A strong sense of class distinction has always been a feature of middle and upper class social imagery in Britain. Through the social exclusivity of their education and life-styles and a strong sense of their essential superiority, not only in wealth and power but in culture and morality, they have been able to hold on to a view of themselves as being deserving of the privileges they had secured.

In the 1950s this imagery contained an undertow of threat, a fear that their world was being invaded. Trivial but telling indications of this are not difficult to find. The Dean of Balliol College, Oxford, in the 1950s referred disparagingly to 'inky fingered grammar school boys' and sometimes to 'northern chemists', and held firm to the belief that only those with independent means had a right to higher education. Among his undergraduates it was a common form of abuse to describe the grammar school boys as 'troglodytes' (personal communication). Such attitudes were, of course, parodied in Kingsley Amis's novel, *Lucky Jim* (1954). But the sentiments were real enough. Reflecting on her experience in Newnham College, Cambridge, in the 1950s, J. MacNaughton noted, 'The snobbery was absolute – as if they felt now was the last chance to re-establish things as things ought to be and as life had been before the war – now or bust' (Phillips 1979:248).

Sometimes this snobbery was given a theoretical and political justification. Writing in *Encounter* in 1956 Peregrine Worsthorne set out an eloquent defence of traditional inequality. The choice being faced in Britain, he claimed, was not that of deciding between an inegalitarian class structure and a classless society. 'It is between', he said, 'a society dominated by a hereditary governing class which is open to new talents, or a society dominated, at best by an ever-changing succession of elites, at worst by a self-perpetuating elite' (1956:27). Acknowledging that there were a great many individuals 'of no social value who enjoy privileges they have done nothing to deserve', Worsthorne nevertheless went on to favour this system of society over something based on merit alone, since such a system would be rigid and unfraternal. His conclusion is a telling one:

A recognisable and secure upper class, accepting public responsibility in return for undisguised privilege, represents a far lesser danger than would-be elites in an 'egalitarian' society, whose privileges would be hidden and therefore uncontrolled and/or socially barren. (1956:321)

This was the time when half-serious and sometimes deadly serious attempts were made to identify clearly the characteristics of the upper classes, their life-style and their speech. Once again, the magazine *Encounter* was the vehicle. Nancy Mitford published an article in 1955 on the English aristocracy which argued that, although they may seem to be 'on the verge of decadence', they remained the only real aristocracy left in the world (1955:5). In this article she set out the terms of the debate later taken up by others about the differences between U and non-U speech. Upper class people would never say 'cycle' but 'bike', never 'dentures' but 'false teeth'. Alan Ross, in the next issue of the magazine, tried to clarify the 'linguistic demarcation of the upper class' (1955:12). This led him to such insights as: 'To take a bath is non-U against U to have one's bath' (1955:17). If it was not so serious it would be laughable.

But it was serious, and it was part of a structure of feeling that the qualities which made the upper class worthy of everyone else's respect were under threat. The feeling that their position of leadership was being eroded by high taxation and that society was going to the dogs was one element of it (for example, Falls 1952). Possessed of a strong sense of the continuity of their status, they worried that their ranks would be diluted by those who were merely rich.

Nor was it merely people of upper class origin themselves who worried. Alisdair MacIntyre noted in an article in *The*

Twentieth Century in 1956 that many of the staff members of provincial universities remained nostalgic about their younger days in Oxford and Cambridge. He noted wryly: 'After one has heard from them a dozen times how grossly inferior Manchester or Sheffield or Leeds is to Oxford or Cambridge one begins to weary of a nostalgia which is as inordinate as that of Ovid's Black Sea exile, but lacks all his elegiac charm' (1956:123).

Yet Nancy Mitford was surely right to emphasize that the English aristocracy continued to have real political power through the House of Lords 'and a real social position through the Queen' (1955:5). But there is much more to it; business and social links among the senior directors of major British companies have always been strong and cemented by shared attitudes, values and relationships stretching into government and back to their public schools. In a brilliant little study of the 'ethnography of finance, politics and administration', Lupton and Wilson explored the social backgrounds of witnesses before the Parker tribunal which investigated the leaking of information about the Bank Rate in 1957 (1973). What the study showed was strong kinship links among leading banking families and among the directors of the Bank of England itself.

It was not until the end of the decade that some social scientists were able to describe in more detail that network of links which bound the elite groups of British society together. Until that point, the structure of elite domination of the major institutions of public life in the society was very imperfectly understood. Such understanding as there was was encoded in the term 'Establishment'. As used by Henry Fairlie in *The Spectator*, it referred not only to 'the centres of official power though they are certainly part of it – but rather the whole matrix of official and social relations within which power is exercised' (quoted Hennessy 1986:6). This particular journalist deployed the concept to explain the way in which the political damage to the stratum from which Burgess and Maclean came was contained, during the discussion in 1955 concerning their defection to the Soviet Union. The concept can be deployed as well to explain the composition of Royal Commissions, Civil and Diplomatic Service appointments, appointments to the judicial bench, elevations to the peerage and much else besides. But such discussion at this point was on the periphery of political debate and public awareness and based on very little carefully collected evidence.

What was not in doubt was the social visibility of elite groups and their essential self confidence. The popular press in the 1950s made much of the eccentric antics of some members of the aristocracy, like Lord and Lady Docker, who ostentatiously displayed their great wealth and at one point possessed a gold-plated Daimler, and it relished whiffs of scandal in high places. A prurient interest in royal affairs has always been a constant fallback for the press when other news was hard to find, and the early fifties royal story *par excellence* was the doomed relationship between Princess Margaret and Group Captain Townsend. What such reporting confirmed, however, was a sense of the separateness of Establishment figures and of the groups to which they belonged. That they were not damaged by it is clear, for the attitudes and values they represented remained intact for others to emulate and their occupation of key public roles, especially in local contexts, allowed them to continue to insinuate themselves into the public rituals of the society as a whole.

Contours of community

The local contexts in which it is vital to understand social attitudes, values and aspirations are defined sharply in Britain by the class differences of the society. The period of the early 1950s is marked in part by a growing awareness of those differences documented in a remarkably pedantic way by pioneer social scientists. What this record of research shows up is the clear differences in attitude and feeling between urban and rural areas and between older industrial areas and new estates and new towns. Overlying these differences, however, and something entrenched in the planning ideologies of the period, particularly the idea of the neighbourhood as the basic unit of all planning, was a pervasive sense that the ideal design for living was something resembling the closeness of the rural village (Dennis 1958).

Raymond Williams has shown that a nostalgia for a long-lost rural past has been a powerful structure of feeling in Britain, with its roots in the way people reacted to the industrial city throughout the nineteenth century (1985). The feeling that there was something essentially unnatural and inauthentic about the city carried on through into the twentieth century. Ronald Blythe, in his brilliant study *Akenfield*, even suggests that this attitude has become a sort of 'national village cult' (1969:17). The good life is, then, imagined as something lived beside a 'tall old church on the hillside, a pub selling the local brew, a pretty stream, a football pitch, a handsome square vicarage with a cedar of Lebanon shading it . . . a Tudor mansion, half a dozen farms and a lot of quaint cottages (Blythe 1969:17). The village pattern became the template for the design of new towns and housing estates.

The proportion of the population living in rural areas has remained steady at around 20 per cent for most of this century and the percentage of those involved in agriculture at about 5 per cent. Despite the towndweller's view of rural areas as timeless and changeless, the period of the 1950s was one of rapid mechanization of agricultural work and a dramatic reduction in the number of agricultural labourers, from 812,000 in 1951 to 617,000 by the end of the decade, resulting in the virtual destruction of the agricultural community (Newby 1977:81).

The social anthropology of rural Britain in the 1950s evokes a world as local in its concerns as the street-based communities of the towns, and highly differentiated on class lines. In his study of Gosforth in Cumberland, W.M. Williams detected seven social classes, and from the top to the bottom of the scale local people could recognize the educational, genealogical and linguistic markers which separated each from the other and controlled patterns of social interaction (1956). Older residents of the village fondly remembered the older way of life before the war when many were servants in the big houses. Williams claims that a typical comment in this context was 'They were proper ladies and gentlemen who were very grateful to you for what you did. They were people you could look up to, and it was a pleasure to work for them' (1956:119). This positive view of the past was coupled with a suspicion of strangers and some resentment of the newcomers who were increasingly arriving in the village.

Politically the countryside inclined to the Tories, especially in England, and a presence there has always been a hallmark of the traditional grandees of high Toryism. The cultural importance of their life-style, as something to which the merely rich could aspire, has been considerable. In the 1950s, however, the whole fiction had to be put on a sound commercial footing to exploit the widening opportunities for holidays and weekend travel that affluence was opening up for an increasingly mobile working class. Among other things, the opening up of the countryside and of its country mansions helped reinforce a sense of the history and heritage of Britain as something bound up primarily with the life-styles of an older aristocracy, which, though transformed through the twentieth century, had not been swept away and which retained strong local contacts in the countryside. That such an image of national heritage covers in a spurious unity the social and political divisions of the society is obvious (Bommes and Wright 1982).

Within towns and cities, social patterns and relationships were different, despite an obvious overlay of similarities in life-styles, leisure and attitudes. In what now appear as remarkably censorious, even prurient terms in what they realized afterwards had become a 'study of the cultural and spiritual life of the nation', Rowntree and Lavers were able to describe many aspects of everyday life from the interviews they conducted throughout Britain in the late 1940s (1952). It is a portrait of a society in which, in their view, there was a precarious balance between 'unsensational blessings', like respect for the law, 'good sense', 'freedom of speech', a 'tradition of voluntary work' and the best public libraries in the world, and many 'unsatisfactory tendencies' affecting the 'cultural and spiritual state of the people' (1952:XV–XVI). There follows an account of drinking, gambling, smoking and sexual promiscuity; they discussed, too, honesty, cinema attendance and newspaper reading habits.

What emerges is a strong sense of change and of the erosion of older values – particularly that of honesty – in the face of new material values. Cinema, they felt, often overemphasized 'false values'. 'We feel', they wrote,

> that the constant repetition of scenes of rather vulgar and ostentatious luxury, and the constant suggestion that 'having a good time' can only mean dining out and drinking champagne in expensive restaurants, dancing in night clubs, being waited on by several servants, and living in rooms of absurdly large dimensions, must have a deleterious effect upon a nation that has, above all, to realise that its future lies in plain living, hard work and in unsophisticated pleasures. (1952:239)

Offered as social investigation, the document reveals as much of the anxieties of some educated middle class people about popular culture as it does of the life-styles of ordinary people themselves. Nevertheless, what it describes of leisure habits is confirmed elsewhere in the social reporting of the period.

What the book did not do, however, was analyse and explain its observations. For that we have to turn to the sociologists of the period, to studies of urban redevelopment (Vereker et al. 1961), of new housing estates and how they contrast with older residential areas (Mogey 1956), of older towns (Kuper 1953), of mining communities (Dennis, Henriques and Slaughter 1956), and to studies which sought explicitly to relate the social phenomena they describe to aspects of change in social structure (such as Cauter and Downham 1954; Pear 1955). The new towns were described by White (1951) and Orlans (1952).

What these and other studies now represent is a rich source of observation and data revealing a society taking stock of change. The social surveys pointed to a strengthening of forms of home-centredness and of the values of material improvement and to the persistence of lines of social class differentiation, which, though changing in response to new opportunities in education, employment and housing, were still potent principles of social organization, attitude and feeling. What the record also reveals, however, was that the sociologists were not quick enough to identify other changes taking place around them, in the lives of young people, of women and, in some of the cities of Britain, of migrant workers.

The picture to emerge from this work has clear outlines and contrasts. The community experience of the older working class areas is shaped considerably by the often poor physical conditions of the housing. Three-quarters of the housing in the Liverpool district of Crown Street, according to studies by Vereker and his colleagues in the 1950s, was in need of repair (1961). Mogey's study of the Barton housing estate in Oxford describes a place 'almost bare of trees; the dominant colour is asbestos grey' (1956:12). To the extent that these are typical of both older inner city areas and pre-war housing estates, they reveal a social pattern of limited residential mobility, sharp demarcation in the roles of men and women, a very low level of participation in community organizations and in voluntary associations and a high degree of defensive privacy. Neighbours were kept at a safe distance and there was little social mixing across that great gulf between the roughs and the respectables.

Kuper's sensitively observed study of the Houghton area of Coventry, and in particular of Braydon Road, notes very similar circumstances (1953). He, too, detects low levels of aspiration among the ninety families he studied and no hint at all of any political interest among them. What this study shows is that the defensive privatism of the place is a response to very poor planning and physical conditions. Residents, for instance, were always aware of each other's noise:

Informants mention the wireless, the baby crying at night, coughing, shoes dropped at bedtime, children running up and down the stairs or on the bedroom floors, strumming at the piano and laughing and loud talk. In the connubial bedroom, the intimations from the neighbours may be shocking. 'You can even hear them use the pot: that's how bad it is. It's terrible.' (1953:15)

Outside lavatories contributed to an atmosphere of friction and embarrassment. A Mr Brown commented to Kuper: 'It's embarrassing for women when men are in the next garden.'

Little wonder that a prevailing norm was that neighbours

should be kept at a distance, although in times of trouble neighbours would help one another. Kuper notes that 'The polishing of a neighbour's front door step is a special demonstration of goodwill in times of difficulty. The man will lend a tubercular neighbour a hand with the garden work and their wives may assist in the house' (1953:44). The reference to TB is tellingly evocative. For the older people of the area that particular disease would have been something to dread and something which all would have had direct experience of.

The new towns, in contrast, were specifically conceived to contrast with such conditions. In Aycliffe, Basildon, Crawley, East Kilbride, Harlow, Hemel Hempstead, Peterlee, Stevenage and Welwyn, deliberate attempts had been made to build new kinds of community and to avoid the mistakes of outer estates and ribbon development. It was in the new towns that the neighbourhood concept in planning was strongest (White 1951). The notion of the 'balanced community' was important to the planners and community workers of the new towns, and through their community associations and village precincts they sought to recreate a sense of community and encourage the involved citizen in active rather than passive entertainments.

An early report on Letchworth and Welwyn noted, however, that 'whatever the town planners may desire, people have a marked tendency to segregate themselves by class and income. An area in which there are some noticeably large and poor families comes to be regarded as lacking in "social tone"' (quoted Orlans 1952:89). Stevenage sought explicitly to avoid one-class neighbourhoods and to retain a strong sense of the countryside, and many residents felt deeply ambivalent towards newcomers from urban areas.

In some of the older industrial areas, in south Wales, the north east, Yorkshire, Lancashire and central Scotland, workers in mines and docks and shipyards and heavy engineering factories continued to live their lives in densely populated areas of terraced housing, and often, as in the case of miners, in sharply segregated communities. Within such communities older working class values, attitudes and life-styles held firm.

Dennis, Henriques and Slaughter evoke in their study of 'Ashton' (actually the Yorkshire mining town of Featherstone) a world of tough, hard-drinking men, clearly demarcated conjugal roles and a class imagery which sharply divided the world into 'Them' and 'Us' (1956). The miners they studied lived for the present, giving little thought to the future; their attachment to the all-male peer group was stronger in many respects than that to their wives and families.

In many ways mistrustful of their union leaders, the men of Ashton nevertheless defended the need for a strong union, and in 1953 a lot of them were still of a generation able to remember the great industrial struggles of the 1920s and the depression years, which gave shape to a strong class consciousness (Slaughter 1958:245). The miners became the sociological model of the 'archetypal proletarian', but they had their counterparts in the shipyard and the dock. In their study of the Liverpool and Manchester docks in the early 1950s, Professor Simey and his colleagues charted the economic and social conditions of a tightly knit community, with strong patriarchal attitudes among the men and a high degree of industrial militancy nurtured by a historical memory of the miseries of casual labour (1956).

No summary can grasp fully the range of attitudes and values embedded in working class culture among different groups of industries, residential areas and regions of the country. In the patterns of that culture, there was a strong emphasis on the maintenance of boundaries – between men and women and between different statuses and occupations. Skilled workers in factories were jealous of their position as higher than that of general labourers. In leisure and life-style what stands out is order and predictability and a commitment to a particular place. Threaded through these attitudes was a well-tuned scepticism about the motives of those in authority, even among their own trades unions, and a general mistrust of employers. It amounts to a culture which is deeply conservative and defensive, and it is ironic that its basic tenets and perceptions left those who were part of it ill-fitted to make sense of the profound social and economic changes going on around them.

Change and crisis

The changes which were taking place in British society, and particularly those affecting working class people, were regarded by some people with deep ambivalence. The by now classic example of this is Richard Hoggart's book, *The Uses of Literacy* (1957). This was a pioneering attempt to assess the direction of change in working class culture from a man whose personal roots were part of it but who had, through education, escaped it. What he detected was a 'sense of social freedom' among working class people, 'the justified feeling of increased political and economic freedom' (1957:176). What he feared, of course, was that this new freedom could so easily atrophy into a sense that 'anything goes', into an acceptance of almost anything without objection, so that working class people could become either easy prey to the advertising copywriter or victims of what he called 'indifferentism' and a facile 'progressivism', which puts a premium on only that which is new and fashionable.

He was just as worried by the way many working class people lived their lives in a kind of timelock and showed no interest in the world around them. His comments on the popular radio programme hosted by Wilfred Pickles are both evocative of the period and illustrative of his fears. The programme, *Have a Go*, provided, claims Hoggart, 'a forum in which they [working class people] can express and applaud the values they still admire' (1957:169). These include 'straight dealing', 'good neighbourliness', 'looking on the bright side' and not being 'stuck up', and Wilfred Pickles himself played back to his audience their view of themselves as 'rough diamonds but hearts of gold' in a manner drenched in nostalgia and sentimentality.

Hoggart knew well, of course, that the world was changing faster than many working class people understood and in a direction which they and their leaders were powerless to control. Full employment and steadily rising living standards were part of a much more profound transformation in the structure of the economy and the composition of the labour force, which was to have great significance for the social structure of the working class of Britain. Three changes stand out: the steady increase of white collar workers, the growth in the employment of married women workers and, finally, the recruitment of immigrant labour to plug the gaps of Britain's labour shortage. Together these changes challenged in direct ways many of the assumptions of working class culture and political attitudes.

The growth of a white collar labour force was, of course, a long-term historical process bound up with changes in management and administration. Between the census years 1951 and 1961, the proportion of white collar workers in the labour force increased from 30.9 per cent to 35.9 per cent. During the same period the proportion of manual workers declined from 64.2 per cent to 59.3 per cent (Halsey 1972b:113). Substantial growth took place in the numbers employed in scientific and technical occupations. The significance of these changes began to dawn on social commentators and trades unionists themselves only later in the decade when the Labour Party anguished over its second and third election defeats at the hands of the Tories, who were appealing to an increasingly affluent working class's demands for yet higher standards of living.

The growth in women's employment was another subtle social change, challenging many aspects of both work and family life and eliciting reactionary responses from many quarters fearful about the break-up of the family, juvenile delinquency and wage inflation. Among many male trades unionists there were fears about the loss of wage differentials. The TUC had pressed for equal pay for women workers after the war, but did not really press hard for it. The dilemma for government was that pressures were building up for equal pay for women as a result of labour shortages in clerical work and in teaching. In 1955, the Burnham Committee dealing with teacher supply and employment conditions agreed to phase in equal pay for women teachers, a move resented by many male teachers. Among women themselves, however, work brought a sense of freedom and independence and their contribution to family finances was central to the servicing of increasing expectations for consumer durables. At this time, however, most women worked within a set of prevailing assumptions that their real purpose in life was to service their husbands and children (E. Wilson 1980).

The immigration of 'coloured' workers from abroad and particularly from the West Indies to help solve the labour shortage of the 1950s was something which both tested the institutions of British society and exposed the raw nerves of an underlying racism. During this period the numbers of immigrant workers were both small and not carefully recorded. In December 1958 the estimated black population was 210,000 (Halsey 1972b:456). When the ship *The Empire Windrush* docked at Tilbury in 1948 to disembark 492 Jamaicans, newspaper headlines announced the arrival of 'Five Hundred Pairs of Willing Hands' (Fryer 1984:374). By the late 1950s there were over 100,000 West Indians and 50,000 workers from India and Pakistan; but in that short space of time the climate of public opinion surrounding their presence in Britain had undergone a change.

'Disappointment and disillusionment of many kinds', writes Fryer, 'were the everyday experience of the 1950s settlers' (1984:374). What they encountered was prejudice and ignorance about themselves and their countries of origin. They met discrimination and misunderstanding. The response of some trades unions was to insist on quotas to prevent more than a predetermined number of immigrants being employed in one place. In West Bromwich, for instance, bus workers staged a one-day strike in 1955 against the employment of one Indian conductor (Fryer 1984:376).

Those who had settled here for many years in dockland communities in Cardiff, Liverpool and London already knew, of course, that they were not perceived as members of the host community and had been aware of discrimination against themselves since the period of World War I. Their experience was of being cordoned off, patronized and treated differently from their white compatriots in school and at work. A group who experienced the tensions of prejudice most acutely were the children of mixed marriages. One writer who researched this problem described them as 'anglo-coloured' (Collins 1955).

The popular description was 'half-caste', for people caught up in what the popular press of the time often referred to as 'the brown baby problem'. What these people were acutely aware of was the way their chances in school and work were severely circumscribed by the prevailing attitude that their status should be limited by their skin colour.

The period of the early 1950s is one in which an official awareness of the need for policy in this area was emerging. An interdepartmental Committee on Colonial People in the United Kingdom had been set up in 1947. During the early fifties both the Ministry of Labour and the Colonial Office co-operated to seek the dispersal of immigrants from areas in which they considered 'pressure' was building up against them. This was the case, for instance, in the Hull area, where in the early 1950s resentment was building up against black dockworkers and stowaways. Both government departments attempted to relocate Hull workers to Leeds to defuse the local problem (St Clair Drake 1955).

A particularly difficult area of inter-ethnic relations concerned contact between the opposite sexes. In her study of dockland canteens in London in the 1950s Enid Mumford observed an atmosphere of jovial bonhomie between white and black dockworkers. White women canteen workers interacted freely with the black men and this was tolerated. But only at work. Outside the canteen, sanctions against any such association were powerful (1959).

The overall state of inter-ethnic relations and attitudes is too complex to characterize and for the period in question there is little reliable research evidence upon which to draw. Two points must be made, however, if the character of those relationships is to be properly understood. The first is that they were changing and that alongside the racist responses of many white people there were, too, many others in churches, voluntary bodies and trades union who sought to help black workers; and black workers themselves were beginning to organize their own community associations. The second is that the response of this host community must be set against changing political circumstances in Britain's colonial policies.

This was a period during which British troops were engaged in Kenya against Mau Mau and in which the rise of black nationalism threatened colonial interests in the Gold Coast, Nigeria and Tanganyika. The popular press of the time was full of atrocity stories from Kenya, and Mau Mau itself was portrayed as a feature of African barbarism. The involvement of British troops in the Suez Canal zone helped sustain a whole series of other popular and derogatory stereotypes about Arabs. The Labour Party during the early 1950s had a clear commitment to anti-colonialism and supported Commonwealth development, and the government itself was acutely conscious of the need to play down the issue of the 'colour bar' in Britain in order not to alienate African and Caribbean opinion further, in a world where colonial loyalties could easily shift to what was seen as an aggressively expansionist Soviet Union (St Clair Drake 1955:212).

The outcome was that official policy towards immigration was tolerant and geared, however inadequately, to achieve the acceptance of black workers by their employers and workmates and neighbours. The government of Winston Churchill was committed to the policy of maintaining freedom of movement between Commonwealth countries, and resisted calls from some of its MPs, the most vociferous being Cyril Osborne, to impose controls (Layton-Henry 1980:53). This atmosphere was, of course, to change.

Affluence, Teds and angry young men

While their parents pursued their hopes of prosperity, a significant movement of attitude and feeling developed among young people; the early 1950s sees the emergence of a youth culture which distinguished itself sharply in fashion and music from the older generation. While age is an important principle of social differentiation and organization, it should not be forgotten that differences of age are overlain by those of class and gender. To speak of the younger generation is therefore misleading. By the mid 1950s, however, the contours of generational identities became more distinct than they had ever been before.

In addition, by the middle of the decade and after the general election of 1955 which gave the Tory Party a second victory at the polls, there was the emergence of a structure of feeling among some sections of the educated that British society was ripe for radical change. This sentiment was confirmed for them by the crisis which unfolded in 1956 over the Anglo-French-Israeli invasion of Egypt. There was also the Russian invasion of Hungary, which not only brought the Cold War to a dangerous level but caused a profound reassessment among the Marxist Left in British society of the meaning of socialism, stiffening simultaneously a political resolve which was across party lines to maintain a strong defence posture against the Soviet Union.

The emergence of young people as a group presenting distinctive problems and values was a consequence of three things – full employment, the Americanization of popular culture and the way in which adult society reacted to what was taken to be the broadened realm of freedom of the young. Musical styles symbolize the change dramatically. In the early 1950s the BBC Light Programme was dominated by the dance band music of Victor Sylvester. Popular programmes like *Two Way Family Favourites* played American crooners singing sentimental songs. *Friday Night is Music Night* thrived on an anodyne diet of popular classics, nostalgia and light orchestral music. Rock'n'roll burst onto this scene in 1954 with a sound the young found excitingly different; for them it became a vehicle of escape from the structured world of school and youth club or the strict order of work or military service. The fashions and forms of dancing associated with the new sound allowed its followers to develop an identity distinct from that of their parents. The starkest symbol was the Teddy boy, a working class youth with Edwardian style suits, duck's arse hair style, crepe-soled shoes and a reputation for ripping out cinema seats and for violence (Rock and Cohen 1970:303).

They were a minority, even among working class young people. Others pursued their apprenticeships or their education, quietly assumed adult responsibilities and found their pleasures in cinema, youth clubs and coffee bars, coping as best they could with parents, sexual relationships and those in authority over them. And on the edges of the conventional world, among some university students, among artists and musicians, there was a world of slightly seedy jazz clubs attracting a bohemian clientele with existentialist leanings, increasingly known as 'beatniks', who enjoyed 'rave-ups' like all-night jazz sessions. The book *Owning Up*, by the jazz musician George Melly, evokes this scene rather well (1965).

Teds were young men who, with their girlfriends, were enjoying the fruits, as they saw them, of an increasingly affluent society. For them the society was not a problem, even if they themselves were viewed as such. For the group of writers known later as the 'angry young men' – John Osborne, John Wain, John Braine, Kingsley Amis and Colin Wilson – society itself was seriously flawed. They railed at snobbery, materialism and conformity. John Osborne's play *Look Back in Anger* was something of a landmark. Thought of as shocking by many critics and outrageous by sections of the press, it represents a new and critical mood in British society. Osborne's main concern was with what he took to be the absence of feeling and commitment throughout the whole of British society (1958:65). He represents a broadside attack on those values, institutions and qualities which many, and certainly including many in the labour movement of the country, thought made Britain great.

It has been suggested that the angry young men were reacting just as much to a dearth of ideas in British cultural life as to the state of the society itself and in particular to its persisting inequalities and its materialism (D.E. Cooper 1970). Maybe: but this was also a time when more people, particularly the politically involved, were becoming more aware of how persistent the patterns of social inequality were in Britain, an awareness built up from official reports, sociological research and, in the case of politicians like Anthony Crosland, informed social and political analysis.

Affluent Britain may well have left behind the austerity of the 1940s, but the promise of the welfare state looked unfulfilled and by the mid 1950s it was also clear that the British economy was not growing or changing as fast as those of Britain's major competitors, particularly in Europe. From both the Right and the Left the point was underlined that the performance of the economy and the achievements of the welfare state were inseparable. What then opened up was a discussion about the meaning and purpose of the welfare state, which itself reflected the emergence of new ideological divisions in Britain and served to define for the main political parties what their priorities should be. The Tories put the emphasis on economic growth; the Labour Party did not disagree but linked that problem with another, that of social inequality and the growing awareness of its dimensions in Britain in relation to housing, health, education, pensions systems, wealth and income.

This awareness itself owes much to the social research carried out from the London School of Economics under the leadership of Richard Titmuss, David Glass and T.H. Marshall, all working within a framework of concern with its roots in the Fabian Society, the work of R.H. Tawney and a distinctive British tradition of empirical social policy research.

In 1954 the Early Leaving Report showed that working class young people were much more likely to leave the grammar school than middle class children. Social observers like Rowntree and Lavers reported confidently that, on the basis of official research, 2 per cent of the population aged about twenty-one was illiterate and between 15 and 20 per cent were semi-literate (1952:287). It was revealed in Parliament on 21 October 1952 that one in five national servicemen were semi-literate, suggesting that about one quarter of those passing through the secondary modern schools could barely read and write (Middleton and Weitzman 1976:334).

Social research into educational opportunity in the early 1950s clearly demonstrated sharp social class differences in the probability of children gaining access to grammar schools, as well as in scholastic attainment in secondary schools (Glass 1954). The research carried out as part of the social mobility survey at the London School of Economics demonstrated the strong link between educational opportunities and social mobility and pointed out that, although the chances in all classes of gaining access to grammar schools were increasing, differentials between classes still persisted (Halsey 1954).

Such evidence gave rise to heated debates about the quality of schools, the merits of comprehensive education and levels of public investment in education. It was the same with health; the story was one of general improvement and a lessening of mortality. But class differences in mortality still existed (Titmuss 1958a).

It is significant that it is during the mid 1950s that the welfare state was brought increasingly into question. From the political Right, particularly in the famous pamphlet by Ian Macleod and Enoch Powell, 'The Social Services – Needs and Means' (1949), the fear was that too much was being attempted and that, as a consequence, benefits for those who were really poor were inadequate (Rees 1985). Through the influential work (influential at least so far as the Labour Party was concerned) of Richard Titmuss, the argument was countered with claims that unacceptable inequalities were eroding the quality of welfare for everyone (1958a). And in his book, *The Future of Socialism*, Anthony Crosland sought to draw out the implications of an increasingly affluent but unequal society for the political strategy of the Labour Party, producing the first major post-war revisionist statement of the party's aims (1956). The thrust of the book was to urge the party to a serious commitment to promoting equality of opportunity over the old-fashioned idea of equality, and to embrace the mixed economy in preference to the dogma of nationalization, as the best guarantor of the economic growth upon which all other programmes depended.

These were discussions among the academics and political elites and the social commentators of the quality press. There is little evidence of heightened political awareness throughout the society. Improving living standards were what mattered to most people. Working people looked to their leaders in the unions and the political parties to secure their prosperity. Most people were much more interested in sport or crime, which was reported in lurid detail in the popular press. The 1950s were good years for murder stories – the Christy case and the Ruth Ellis case stand out, because they heightened a public interest in the ethics of capital punishment. This was a time, of course, when ordinary crime was reasonably well contained. Within the normal routines of family life, the world for most people looked fine. Science and technology seemed to be delivering great benefits in communications, such as television, in medicine, in transport – particularly in aviation – and in materials. Radio programmes like *Journey into Space*, matinee cinema serials like *Flash Gordon* and comics like *The Eagle* underlined for the very young the importance of science and scientific progress.

For those who were older, the image of the new was balanced by a reassuring celebration of the old and the familiar. British film makers in the 1950s found a healthy market in what Hewison calls a comic museum view of Britain, with such films as *Genevieve* (1953), about old cars, or *The Titfield Thunderbolt* (1953) about steam trains (1988:177). War offered endless opportunities to celebrate an image of British determination and pride and to recall memories of the social solidarity of wartime. Films like *The Wooden Horse* (1952), *The Cruel Sea* (1953), *The Dam Busters* (1954), *Cockleshell Heroes* (1955) and *The Bridge on the River Kwai* (1957) were of this genre; all underlined a nostalgic version of a distinctively muted British greatness, reinforcing simultaneously a view of the Japs as cruel and the Germans as authoritarian sadists. Americans, despite the fact (or even, perhaps, because of it) that Britain's security depended largely on American military might, remained brash and merely rich, wholly deficient of any admirable qualities.

The self congratulatory tone and complacency of all this was balanced, of course, by the atmosphere of threat sustained by the Cold War; by stories of spies and by such incidents as the disappearance of Commander Crabbe in Portsmouth harbour during the visit of Khrushchev and Bulganin in 1956, and by a general awareness of tension in eastern Europe and in the Middle East. It was all brought to crisis pitch in 1956 with the Russian invasion of Hungary and the Suez crisis.

Suez

This is not the place to recount the murky politics of the decision by the Eden government to invade Egypt jointly with France and Israel. Its significance for this account is that it brought to an end a phase in Britain's post-war history. It challenged Britain's pretence to world role status and brought into question both the competence and the legitimacy of many aspects of the conduct of British political life. Eden's premiership was ended by the Suez fiasco, but it did nothing either for the reputation of Labour leaders, who were widely thought to be sympathetic to Eden's view of Nasser as another Hitler and still committed to redundant strategic ideas about the need for Britain to control the Suez Canal.

Eden sent British troops into Egypt in 1956 knowing that, on the basis of the October Gallup poll of public opinion, 47 per cent of Conservative voters would approve of such an action and only 54 per cent of Labour voters would disapprove (Goldsworthy 1971:398). Richard Crossman noted in his diaries that, although there was a general feeling of bewilderment about the Suez invasion, 'There are many more Labour people than we sometimes think who feel they would like to have a go at Nasser and who, when faced with the prospect of Britain's ceasing to be a great power, are emotionally repelled' (J. Morgan 1981:517).

This same point was made by Lord Butler, who as Lord Privy Seal had been a senior minister of the Eden government, when he commented in his memoirs on the illiberal sentiments quite widely expressed against Nasser:

These were deep-seated emotions affecting liberal-minded people, but they coalesced only too easily with less generous sentiments: the residues of illiberal resentment at the loss of Empire, the rise of coloured nationalism, the transfer of world leadership to the United States. It was these sentiments that made the Suez venture so popular, not least among the supporters of the embarrassed Labour Party. (1971:189)

Leave on one side Butler's obvious delight at finding such a weakness in the stance of the Labour Party. He is clearly right to set the Suez episode in the context of Britain's transformed world role and prevailing anxieties and resentments about the loss of status it implied. It was to be Harold Macmillan's great achievement to rescue the Conservative Party from its post-Suez unpopularity and to focus public opinion on the domestic politics of economic growth. This left the Labour Party to wrestle with its splits on economic policy, particularly over the relevance of nationalization, and above all, over defence.

The Suez crisis occurred simultaneously with the Russian invasion of Hungary, confirming for many the view that Russia remained the danger it had always been, even after Stalin's death and denunciation. Both events fused into the same sense of crisis. The effects of Suez have been described by one writer as 'irritatory', particularly for the intelligentsia in Britain (Hewison 1988:197). Hungary shook the faith of many of them, however, in the Communist Party, and those who left it – more than 7,000 people did so – were to contribute significantly to and to define the terms of political debate in Britain. What later became known as the 'New Left', formed from the Communist Party historians' group – men like E.P. Thompson, John Saville and Christopher Hill – and from a group of Oxford under-graduates mistrustful of both Communism and the Labour Party, and including in its membership Stuart Hall, Raphael Samuel and others, was to play an important role in the internecine disputes of the Labour Party and to support actively the Campaign for Nuclear Disarmament.

Conclusion

The essence of the discussion of social change in this chapter is this: between 1951 and 1957 the social and economic reforms of the reconstruction period were consolidated. Within that framework of the NATO Alliance and the welfare state, the British economy grew steadily and most people experienced a growing prosperity. The predominant image of the 1950s is of a drab decade. What is clear, however, is that British society was undergoing profound changes of a kind which brought into question many of the values upon which post-war reconstruction had been achieved.

It is during this period that the economic weaknesses and social inequalities of British society became clearer. Growth, however, blunted the determination to do much about them and the priority for working people became the maintaining of that steady improvement in living standards and opportunities which they had come to see as their right. The pattern was therefore set of garbing affluence with its distinctive political cloak – complacency – and of trying to sustain both of these with political and economic institutions ill-adapted to meet the challenges of an increasingly unstable and competitive world.

5
Affluence Achieved

In his address to the Labour Party conference in 1959, following its third consecutive election defeat, Aneuran Bevan, then the party's treasurer, described the affluent society in the following terms:

> This so-called affluent society is an ugly society still. It is a vulgar society. It is a meretricious society. It is a society in which priorities have gone all wrong. (Foot 1982:642)

This speech, according to Michael Foot, was one of the best of Bevan's life; it represented a brave attempt to rescue the promise of a socialist Britain. His thesis was that people in Britain had so improved their material conditions that their discontents had been reduced, leaving them 'satisfied with the framework in which they live'; they were no longer conscious of 'frustration' or of 'limitation' and 'constriction' as they had previously been. The lesson for the party, he argued, was to educate people, to expand their personalities and not merely to adjust its policies to what he called the 'contemporary mood' and pander to the kind of greed that capitalist society thrives on.

For these reasons Bevan was opposed to Gaitskell's attempt to drop from the Labour Party's constitution the commitment to nationalization, a commitment which the right wing of the party felt was an electoral albatross in an affluent society. Whether the Labour Party could ever be re-elected was the underlying question, and one sharpened by a strong impression that the social basis of electoral support for the party had been significantly altered and that the problems of capitalism which the party had been formed to combat – unemployment, poverty, the loss of trades union rights – had all been overcome.

This was the key question for the Labour Party: was a

socialist analysis of Britain still a credible platform on which to launch a successful election strategy? Or, as the 'contemporary mood' seemed to indicate, was socialism an out-of-date solution to the problems of the past which, since they had been overcome by a reconstructed capitalism, were no longer relevant to the future? Even after the debacle of Suez and a leadership crisis, the Tory Party under Harold Macmillan achieved in 1959 a substantial electoral victory over Labour, raising the question whether, given that affluence and full employment had been achieved without inflation, Labour must inevitably lose. This question underlies much of the political and sociological discussion of the period from the late 1950s to the late 1960s.

In this and the following chapter I shall show that the period in question is one of considerable and rapid social change; it is a period of stocktaking in which, from many viewpoints, different assessments were made of what had become of British society since the ending of the war and the early years of reconstruction. The aim is to relate changes in social perceptions, attitudes and feelings to changes in social structures and life chances, in a way which reveals the altered balance of opportunities of a society still markedly stratified but in which class differences were taking new forms.

For most people, the period is one of steadily improving living standards, the foundation for a structure of feeling which was essentially complacent and self satisfied, in which the expectation of increased prosperity and the ambitions woven into it – for education, for holidays, private cars and, perhaps above all else, home ownership – are the clue to how people organized their lives.

Among some groups of what T.R. Fyvel, with some typically English hesitation, in 1968 called the 'intellectuals', and particularly among those on the Left, there emerged in this period a sense of moral outrage about British society and political life (Fyvel 1968). They scorned the apathy they associated with affluence and scoured their libraries for the sources of a new political morality. In political movements like the Campaign for Nuclear Disarmament, which gathered pace and strength in the late 1950s, many found the conviction politics absent in the rest of society. It is nicely ironic, however, that the critics of the affluent society were among its prime beneficiaries, finding a secure place for themselves in the expanding system of higher education, in the public services and in the arts.

Regret became a potent feeling; among many working class people it was articulated as a sense of loss of community. Such a feeling among those living in new housing estates had its analogue in the writings of men like Raymond Williams (1958), Richard Hoggart (1957) and Brian Jackson (1968), who regretted much about what they saw happening to working class people in the affluent society and struggled in their writings to redefine a notion of community and 'common culture', in a way which would rescue the best from the working class traditions they most admired, to fit the circumstances of the new society.

Regret was also a feeling among some sections of the political Right, who felt acutely the loss of Empire and of Britain's position as a world power. But it was not just Empire which was at stake; there was, too, Britain's relationship with Europe and the humiliation felt by many at de Gaulle's veto on Britain's application to join the Common Market. Among some working class communities, such regret became refocused as racism as one way of coping with the presence of colonial immigrants, who had come to Britain to meet the labour shortage which throughout the 1950s had threatened British economic growth. Colour bar turned, in 1958, to 'race riot' in Nottingham and Notting Hill.

Colour bar and loss of community are potent themes of this period; so, too, is welfare, and they are all connected through bad housing and poverty. It was during the period of the early 1960s that those who had been bypassed by the affluent society were rediscovered – the poor, the badly housed, the old and chronically sick and disabled, those on low incomes and the single parents, the poorly educated. It was one of the remarkable achievements of British social science that this nether world of affluence was carefully charted. The writings of Titmuss (1958a and b, 1962) and his younger collaborators Peter Townsend (1963) and Brian Abel-Smith, who produced in 1965 *The*

Poor and the Poorest, inspired a whole generation of social scientists and contributed substantially to the political emergence of a strong sense of moral indignation that the affluent society was unprepared to secure the conditions of a decent life for its most vulnerable members.

The years between 1956 and 1968 are marked by a heightened awareness of social change which ran ahead of the conventional ways of making sense of it all. The editorial of the first issue of the weekly *New Society*, a magazine which became during these years a very important vehicle of social comment among social scientists and public service professionals, commented:

We live in a climate of uncertainty. Our jobs and income may be relatively secure, but few of us are not assailed by doubts about our – and our country's – position in the world, about what moral or ethical standards we should follow, about the nature of human personality and about the whole structure of society. (1962:3)

Arthur Marwick has summarized the social and moral changes of this period as 'the end of victorianism' (1982:140). Homosexual law reform, abortion law reform, the *Lady Chatterley* trial, the hectic development of youth cultures and of fashionable London, liberalization and realism in the theatre and in film and the emergence into a general popularity of Cambridge satire, on stage and on television in programmes like *That was the Week that Was*, all fuelled a general feeling throughout British society that much had changed.

For writers interested in the mass media, there was a pervasive sense that much of the change was for the worse and that a popular culture was emerging which was bland and under the control of advertisers glamorizing a 'consumption-for-its-own-sake civilization', in which a tolerant and apolitical public acquiesced (D. Thompson 1964:21). Scandals like the Profumo affair revealed a moral ambiguity and double standard in British society that many found deeply disturbing.

The centre and the periphery

The avuncular yet patrician grouse-moor image of Harold Macmillan captures much of the complexity of British society in the late fifties and early sixties: a society which had 'never had it so good' with a political framework and class system still cast in a very old mould. Macmillan symbolized the political Establishment of Britain and the network of elites which made it up. His was a government dominated by men with public school and Oxbridge backgrounds, of whom over half had direct connections through the board of directors with leading industrial and financial institutions (Guttsman 1963). Yet it was this government which dismantled much of what remained of the British Empire, while giving the strong impression of being deeply wedded to the status quo at home.

Governments set political agendas within the constraints set by the performance of the economy and the articulated political demands of mass electorates. Macmillan certainly took the view that the economic challenge was to modernize and achieve sustained growth without inflation. He was pressed forward in this view by his own party, as well as by the opposition, because so many different groups in society saw growth and what it would bring as the best way to realize their highest hopes. It was not only, therefore, the older political elites of which Macmillan himself was representative which saw profit in maintaining the broad social and political framework of orderly growth. Trades unionists, managers, scientists and technologists, civil servants and public servants as well as millions of ordinary workers were united in that overarching commitment. Their experience of it lent credence, too, to the idea that their success was the product of individual achievement and effort. The corollary, of course, was that the failure of those who were not well off was seen as evidence of their own failings and not as a structural fault in the society itself.

The conservatism of British society had its deepest roots in real economic interests and not just in the broad social values stressing tradition and deference, where some political scientists

such as McKenzie and Silver (1968) and Nordlinger (1967)
located it. That coalescence of interest and sentiment, favouring
change only of a kind which prevailing notions of prosperity
and improvement could define, can be thought of as representing the political and economic centre of society. People who
occupied places in that centre experienced steadily rising living
standards during the Macmillan years and widened horizons of
opportunity for their children.

Those outside that charmed circle of full employment and
subsidized private housing – the old, the chronically sick, low
paid families with children, the unemployed, the badly housed –
were driven to the periphery of society as inexorably as those at
the centre got better off. The tragedy for both, of course,
though it was not well understood at the time, was that, relative
to the performance of Britain's industrial competitors, the
country's achievements were not as substantial or sustainable as
most people imagined.

A full account of the groups comprising the centre of society
cannot be given here. The centre does embrace, however, the
growing white collar, technical and professional labour force.
Between 1951 and 1971 the percentage of white collar workers
in the labour force increased from 30.9 per cent to 42.7 per cent.
There was a corresponding decline in the percentage of manual
workers from 64.2 per cent to 54.7 per cent (Brown 1978:75).
During this twenty-year period the number of professional
workers increased from 1.2 million to 2.7 million; that is, from 6
per cent of the labour force to 10.9 per cent. This growth was at
the heart of discussions among social analysts of such topics as
the managerial revolution and whether capitalism in its classical
form had been superseded by an entirely new kind of society for
which old political analyses were no longer relevant. This
debate was particularly acute on the Left, where it touched to
the core debate about the Labour Party's electoral strategy.

The debate among the political intelligentsia about the significance of the 'managerial revolution' was and remains inconclu-
sive. What it did achieve, however, was some prominence in
public debate for a rhetoric of economic policy according
special privilege to notions of efficiency and productivity and

the rights of management. What it gave prominence to was a managerial ideology which, while playing down the 'Them–Us' division of British industry, nevertheless reinforced it by forcing many groups of workers into an attitude of industrial defensiveness to protect staffing levels, skill differentials and traditional methods of working.

It is significant in this context that the period from 1955 onwards is one of growing unrest in industrial relations, as workers bargained hard for, and management conceded, the pay increases a still growing economy could meet. Power in trades unions increasingly moved from national executives to the shop floor, making more intractable the problem of wage drift, which pushed up pay packets without solving underlying weaknesses of productivity.

That a division existed in the minds of many trades unionists and business managers between 'Them' and 'Us' is clear. It was rooted, as will be seen, in real differences of income, status and power and therefore reflected and found expression in differences of life-style, education and ideological sentiment. But over and above these differences there was something those in employment had in common – a determination to secure for themselves the high material rewards that capitalism promised them. In an unequal society some groups of workers – those who, in general, are better educated and better organized – will secure higher rewards. Economic growth during the 1960s allowed most groups of workers in employment to achieve higher living standards. Those who have not yet found their place in the labour market or who are out of it all together are at greatest risk of being pushed to the periphery of the society and denied their full share of growing wealth and opportunities. The manager, the professional and the 'affluent worker', each in different ways, were prime beneficiaries of prosperity; in each case and in comparison with workers in declining industries or in older industrial areas, a growing confidence and optimism can be detected as the decade progresses.

That confidence and growing sense of their own importance, both in occupational and political terms, is clear in the case of managers and professional workers generally. In the early 1960s there were no business schools in British universities; by the end of the decade there was a 'spate of development of management education' (Nichols 1969:55). Senior management personnel may not have been trained in management but several commentators detected some common and essentially ideological themes in their outlook on their companies and their place in society. The idea of the separation of ownership from control of industry as the hallmark of modern industrial organization had, as Nichols argues, basing his conclusions on interviews with managers in the north of England, 'a high ideological potential for managers' (1969:55). They placed great stress on such values as efficiency and the necessity for profit and identified their own personal goals with those of the organizations which employed them. British managers placed a high value on their possession of social skills rather than technical ones and, as Alan Fox pointed out to the Donovan Commission on industrial relations, they tended to view the firm as a team in which there were no necessary conflicts of interest (1966:11). Such a 'unitary perspective' functioned, Fox argued, to reassure managers and confer legitimacy on their actions. But it is a perspective which also nurtures resentment against trades unions and their representatives.

Professional employees were not, however, averse to joining trades unions and did so in growing numbers throughout the 1960s (Blackburn and Prandy 1965). They did so because, as civil servants or bank employees or as technicians in large companies, their work was becoming increasingly subject to bureaucratic control. Particularly significant was the growth of public sector professional employment in teaching, medical care and social services. Between 1961 and 1971 the proportion of the labour force employed as professional and scientific staff and in public administration increased from 15.3 per cent to 20.3 per cent (Brown 1984). Not only did their numbers increase; so, too, did their contribution to what one sociologist called the 'moral climate of society as a whole' (Halmos 1967:14). Indeed, Halmos detected the emergence of a new kind of industrial society – the 'personal service society' – in which professional values drawn from the caring professions would gradually extend to other contexts such as industrial management.

The presupposition of such a shift is itself significant, quite apart from the accuracy of the assessment; for what lies behind it is a sense that some of the older solidarities of class and social differentiation were breaking up. This sense of change is particularly clear in the case of manual workers. The early 1960s is the period of the discovery of the 'affluent worker' and the argument that, through social mobility, manual workers were increasingly coming to resemble those from the middle class. This was referred to in a famous paper by Goldthorpe and Lockwood as the embourgeoisement thesis (1963).

Goldthorpe and Lockwood demonstrated convincingly that the claim that affluent workers were becoming middle class was overstated. Affluence was one thing; identifying with and being accepted by middle class people was quite another. What they did suggest, however, and this is borne out in part by a later study by Runciman (1964), was that affluent workers were much more likely to become 'privatized' in their life-style, and instrumental and opportunistic in their voting behaviour.

It was not just the sociologists who tried to take stock of what had happened to the working class. The British film industry explored the same question in a way which was inspired by an obligation to social realism. Films like *Saturday Night and Sunday Morning, Room at the Top, A Taste of Honey, The Loneliness of the Long Distance Runner, A Kind of Loving, Billy Liar* and others allowed producers such as Karel Reisz and Lindsay Anderson to make films, building on the novels of John Braine and Alan Sillitoe or Kingsley Amis, which explored many facets of change in working class experience – affluence, the relationship between men and women and between different generations. Such feelings are themselves reflections of change and helped define a structure of feeling in which those who commented on working class life could worry at how it was not deeply touched by socialism any longer, and those who lived it could enjoy the pleasures of affluence and a sense that working people had at last found their place in British society.

The critics of the embourgeoisement thesis could rightly

point to persistent inequalities in British society and to the fact that middle class life-styles were not at all widely diffused. They could point to trades unions and a growing industrial militancy to underline the point that the working class, after all, still worked and that industry was still run and organized on class lines. This line of argument was much more clearly codified by the end of the decade by writers on the New Left still insisting on the relevance of class as an explanatory principle of British politics (Miliband 1969; Westergaard 1972).

There were areas of agreement, however, which transcended the obvious differences of class and status; they were found in the values according to which people organized their lives and in the way different groups of people became committed to the continuation of the same social order because their interests and ambitions and hopes were realizable within it.

Life on the periphery was different. Its contours were drawn by poor housing, poverty and hopelessness. Poor housing conditions in British cities meant that many families were condemned, not only to inadequate accommodation or over-crowding, but also to the persecution of private landlords. The term which entered the language to describe this in the early 1960s was 'Rachmanism'. It referred back to the gangster-like activities of one London landlord, Peter Rachman, who terrorized tenants to extract higher rents than were allowed under the 1957 Rent Act.

Peter Townsend's work on the elderly, particularly those in old people's homes, revealed a shocking degree of poverty and neglect and loneliness among those old people who lived in institutions (1962, 1963). Although former public assistance institutions housing old people were relatively few in number, they housed a third of the elderly who lived in homes.

The problem of poverty was not confined to old people, although one third of the elderly were entitled to national assistance but did not actually take it. Pride and a detestation of charity were the underlying reasons for this. But there were other groups in poverty – those dependent on national assist-ance, those in employment with low wages. In her review of the evidence then available in her pamphlet *Poverty in Britain*

Today, Harriet Wilson, a sociologist and member of the Society of Friends, noted that welfare state legislation had had a 'peculiar lulling effect', leading people to believe that all the insecurities between the cradle and the grave had been relieved (1964:6). In fact, she notes, although the poor 'may not look as ragged today as they did a generation ago', compared to the 'general prosperity of the average family the lives lived by people who are dependent on National Assistance allowances are full of strain and anxiety' (1964:6). In 1962, 2.9 million people were in receipt of national assistance; 700,000 pensioners lived on incomes below national assistance levels; at least as many as 400,000 low paid workers were refused supplementary payments from the National Assistance Board. Following Peter Townsend's calculation, Wilson estimated that 9 per cent of the population or 5 million people were living on incomes below subsistence level (H. Wilson 1964).

Harriet Wilson claimed that the consequences of poverty in a world of high pressure advertising are that the poor come to feel unworthy, humiliated, rejected, dependent and anxious. Their children suffer the stigma of poverty and do less well at school. Parents, she claimed, could barely cope with their responsibilities as parents. In a sharply observed passage reflecting on how an unskilled labourer she knew organized his life, she wrote:

In times of trouble like this, people tend to become over-sensitive to the reactions of others, testing their own value all the time in terms of what the neighbours said, how the man from the National Assistance Board or the health visitor dealt with them, and how others behaved who tried to help them. If the officials are not aware of this they may by a hurried answer, or an inattentive response, upset a man like Mr. S. out of all proportion to their intention. He will feel once more rejected, and his suspicion that people cannot be trusted, that society is against him, and that he can never hope to get out of the mess, will grow. (1964:18)

Her solutions to these problems centred, as did the later work of the Child Poverty Action Group, which was formed in 1965 and in which she and Peter Townsend were among the founding members, on increased benefits, particularly family allowances, and legislation to increase the value of minimum wages.

In retrospect it is clear that the 'lulling effect' of welfare legislation that Harriet Wilson noted was not something which could have been easily challenged by the sort of research-based campaigning the Child Poverty Action Group was engaged in. It is not sufficient to make an appeal to the facts of poverty and hope that public opinion and political decision will be changed through that. It is important, too, to change attitudes and feelings and ways of thinking.

The political climate of the society in the early 1960s was against them, despite the research evidence and a growing awareness in Britain of President Johnson's 'Great Society programme' and its anti-poverty measures. Conservative policies towards the welfare state still rested on a concern with its costs and consequences for levels of public expenditure and insisted on increased selectivity and means testing of benefits. Arthur Seldon of the right-wing Institute of Economic Affairs commented in 1963, for instance, that 'Universality is out of date; humanity and efficiency requires discrimination' (1963:12).

Affluence was a much greater problem for the Conservatives than poverty. A report commissioned by Macmillan's government in 1962 from the Central Statistical Office underlined their worry that affluence was leading people into debt and a 'grasping after unearned wealth' (quoted *New Society* 1962). This report, based substantially, though not exclusively, on interpretations of 1961 census data, revealed a debt to the building societies of £2 billion and over £400 million of hire purchase debt. It noted an 'alarming development of crime amongst young men and boys' and declining sexual standards. It regretted the annual gambling bill of £762 million and noted this was an expenditure of £14 per head of the population.

The election of a Labour government did not alter the climate of opinion about the poor in any substantial way, despite the fact that writers like Titmuss and Townsend and Abel-Smith had done much to shape Labour's policies on social security. The problem was that the Wilson government attached a high priority to maintaining the value of sterling and to holding back public expenditure and home consumption to improve the country's export performance. This broad policy framework meant increased taxation and it was here that the government came up against some of the resentments of its own supporters, especially among the affluent working class and lower middle class. Both resented high taxation and too much generosity towards the poor (Deacon and Bradshaw 1983). It was the firm view of the Labour government that the problems of poverty and inequality could be overcome only in the context of sustained economic growth and that achieving this had to be the priority of any realistic government. It was a view of poverty which pitched the Labour government into a long and often bitter argument with the poverty lobby, which saw progressive taxation and policies for the redistribution of wealth as the central priorities.

Ruling ambitions: education

Though they benefited in different ways from affluence, and their positions and life chances in society were dissimilar, middle class people and many groups of affluent workers shared a common concern. It was that their children should have better educational opportunities than they themselves had had. This is hardly surprising. In post-war Britain, occupation and education were closely linked and the possession of educational qualifications was increasingly seen as what, above all else, made social differences legitimate. The idea of the meritocracy, with its associated value of equality of educational opportunity, was widely endorsed even though there were major disagreements about what form of educational system would realize such goals.

Education confers more than qualification; it nurtures self respect and confers status and opportunity on those who benefit most from it. The centrality of education to the ambitions of different groups in Britain is clearly indicated both in the level of official concern from the late 1950s onwards about the performance of the system and in the social research of the period. What that research showed was marked class inequalities of educational opportunity which reflected not only the cultural and social differences in society but the way in which the educational system itself was set up and functioned.

The tone of reasoned outrage which underlies much of the commentary on education in the late 1950s and 1960s can be deceptive. It reflected honestly enough both official concern and professional judgement that much was wrong with education in Britain and pointed to the need for yet further expansion and change. The rhetoric to justify this was liberal and concerned with the further development of individual potentialities; it was also egalitarian, according special privilege to the notion of equality of opportunity for children whatever their social background.

So far, so good; but it was not radical in demanding a fundamental restructuring of the educational system and the values which underlay it. Indeed, the inequality of the system was what made education attractive to many people. What it offered through its grammar schools and independent schools and universities was an opportunity for people, including working class people, many of whose children benefited handsomely from the grammar schools, to succeed and be legitimately different to those they thought to be less able and therefore less deserving.

The inequalities and inefficiencies of the 1944 settlement in education were charted in a remarkable series of educational reports. The Crowther report of 1959 dealt with fifteen to eighteen year olds and the inadequacy both of school education, particularly in the secondary modern schools, and of post-school provision for the further education of apprentices (Central Advisory Council for Education 1959). The Robbins report of 1963, set up by the Macmillan government in response to a growing sense of a crisis in the supply of trained people to a changing economy, dealt with higher education and the need to expand Britain's universities (Committee on Higher Education 1963). The Newsom report, *Half Our Future*, dealt with less able pupils and the system's poor provision for their needs (Central Advisory Council for Education 1963). The Plowden report of 1967 examined the primary schools and identified major problems of educational deprivation, particularly in older inner city areas of the conurbations (Central Advisory Council for Education 1967). Interwoven in the public, professional and political discussion of these reports was the work of sociologists exploring social class differences in educational opportunity and relating these to many features of the social and cultural organization, both of education and of family life.

This is not the place to recap in any detail what such work discovered. The thread running through it was a demonstration of structured inequalities of opportunity which had remained relatively stable over time, and of a system of education too inflexible to cope with the growing demands placed upon it or to promote the reserves of ability in the society at large (Westergaard and Little 1964; Committee on Higher Education 1963, Appendix One:54).

At the apex of the system were the older universities, Oxford and Cambridge, fed from a public school system supported by the well off precisely for that purpose. Rose and Ziman noted in 1964 in their study of 'the ancient universities in the modern world' that 'Camford' still attached great importance in its admissions procedures to the social backgrounds of applicants. Some of the colleges, they note, 'have thought as much in terms of shaping a continuous community as of backing individual merit. They care for the traditions of their college, and are mindful of family ties and immemorial school alliances' (1964:28).

The student world in higher education in the early 1960s was overwhelmingly male and middle class. Ferdinand Zweig explored the world of students in Oxford and Manchester in 1962 and described them as follows:

What emerges from these pages is a picture of honest and sincere young men taking their studies very seriously, with a sense of responsibility and a sense of duty ... On the whole they are self-disciplined (both in general and sexually), restrained, quiet, with an altruistic frame of mind, religiously inclined ... They are not angry young men. They want to find their own niche in a society as good and respectable citizens ... They are conscious of a debt they owe to society ... The rowdy and intemperate student, the jolly joker, the man of the song, 'Gaudeamus igitur', are on the way out. (1963:xiii)

The model student of the later chapters of the book is still male: he appears interested in politics but is not active. He resents the class system of society:

Disapproval of the class distinctions is very widespread at both universities. But the students are not radicals in this field. They do not demand the abolition of the class system, only the loosening and widening of it to allow for the full emergence of talent and merit. (Zweig 1963:208)

In the course of the next five years this image was to be radically altered and, as will be seen later, there was a growing radicalism among some students about nuclear weapons which Zweig did not pick up. The point for the moment is the predominantly male ambience of the system. Women fitted uneasily into university life. Elizabeth Wilson recalls that the principal of her Oxford college – St Anne's, a women's college – told the students they were being educated to become diplomats' wives (1982:44).

Students of working class origin continued to find higher education something of a threat and to sense a growing alienation from their class. Those who made it did so, in contrast to their contemporaries from the public schools who looked to careers in the professions or public administration, to find employment as teachers or as scientists and technologists in industry (Kelsall et al. 1972). Musgrove's telling little study of undergraduates entering the university of Bradford in 1966 found working class students more inclined towards technical courses and strongly oriented to the success goals of the affluent society: 'Their reference group', he writes, 'is top-level managers with large, comfortable houses and two cars' (Musgrove 1967:313). Their ambition, in short, was to achieve a status their parents could recognize but one which, nevertheless, lifted them out of their class.

The values woven into the practices of the secondary schools reflected strongly those of a divided society which had found ways of rendering those divisions legitimate by, in part, encouraging working class people to aspire to succeed by them. The public schools had set the model for the grammar schools, and in the early 1960s still performed an important function in elite recruitment. One fifth of seventeen year olds still at school in the early 1960s were in public schools; over one third of them went to university and of those who did more than half went to Oxford or Cambridge (Wakeford 1969). That experience, with its distinctive rituals, snobbery and social connections, was and remains an important one in securing the social solidarity of elite groups in British society.

The grammar schools were the avenue of mobility for bright working class children and much in them reflected the traditions of private schools. The expansion of grammar school places in the 1950s and 1960s was a major piece of social engineering which did indeed open up new opportunities for significant numbers of children from working class backgrounds (Halsey et al. 1980). It was an expansion supported by the Labour Party, and Labour local authorities were rightly proud of what they had provided. A Labour Party policy booklet in the early 1960s, *The Future Labour Offers You*, explained that the party's support for comprehensive schools was not an attack on the grammar schools: 'We nail the lie', it said, 'that our aim is to abolish grammar school education. On the contrary, we shall open it up to every child who can benefit by it, and extend the tradition and standards of the grammar school throughout secondary education' (quoted W. Taylor 1963:153).

Those children selected for grammar schools from a working class background were typically cast in the 'best pupil' role in their junior schools, and one of the consequences of being brought together with children from different junior schools and from other parts of town was a feeling of isolation from their peers compensated for by a strong new bond of identity with the grammar school itself (Lacey 1970). They were educated in an institution which was unequivocally middle class in its values. Their teachers valued honesty, truthfulness, tolerance, scepticism and having wide interests (King 1969). Such schools placed a high value on the school itself as a community and attached much importance to activities like debating, theatre visits, amateur dramatics and classical music, and disapproved of teenage 'pop' culture. By the mid 1960s they had largely overcome the problem identified ten years earlier of early leaving among working class pupils.

There was great competition for school places and ambitious parents were anxious about the results of the selection examination, the 11-plus. This anxiety and its associated ambition was carefully charted in 1962 in the book *Education and the Working Class* by Jackson and Marsden, in their study of their native Huddersfield (1986). What it also revealed was that the grammar school was in need of reform. For some parents it was the vehicle for the realization of their ambitions for their children. One of the parents interviewed, a Mr Chapman, explained how he drove his children on to get them through the grammar school and into university. Speaking of his son he said, 'When he was small I used to try and impress on Derek the need for work. I'd point to a man sweeping the road and say, "That's what happens to people who've got no ambition and don't work hard when it's necessary"' (1986:30).

Yet for other parents the grammar school was a humiliating experience. Mrs Teasdale, one of the working class parents they interviewed, felt she had no encouragement from the teachers. She left parent–teacher meetings feeling 'right depressed, right downhearted'. She also felt angry – 'We're good citizens, aren't we? We might be poor folk around this way, but we've as much bloody right as any other buggers in this bloody town' (1986:136). The point is this: in terms of both its social function and its internal arrangements, the grammar school divided children from one another, even those from the same social class background. In doing so, it gave its support to the social divisions of the society and simultaneously set the conditions to nurture in its pupils a sense of their social superiority, which was later confirmed in the way they secured better jobs than their peers who had failed the 11-plus and were educated in secondary modern schools.

It was during the 1960s that the deficiencies of the secondary modern schools to which the bulk of children were sent became evident. Novels such as Edward Blishen's *Roaring Boys* or E.R. Braithwaite's *To Sir With Love* described the negative features of the secondary moderns. The Newsom report charted the extent to which they failed the 'less able' children, particularly in older industrial areas where schools suffered from inadequate resources and high staff turnover (Central Advisory Council for Education 1963). Part of the problem, as William Taylor pointed out, was that in addition to being the poor neighbours of grammar schools in resource terms, their staff were themselves grammar school products, could conceive of few alternatives to the kind of education they themselves had had and too often regarded their pupils as educational failures from the start (1963). David Hargreaves's research into the social and academic organization of a secondary modern school in Manchester confirmed vividly that staff attitudes and practices, particularly that of streaming, added to the weight of social differentiation bearing heavily downwards on education to identify the less able and the troublesome and make certain that those who conformed to staff values got more from the school (1967).

Education both fuelled and blighted ambition. It lent credibility to the idea that educational achievement was the result of some children being innately gifted, and in that way endorsed publicly the private sense of pride parents could have in their successful offspring. Pride, ambition and a strong sense that social and economic differences between people were in many ways inevitable were the potent ingredients of a way of thinking and feeling which bound together those who had achieved success in this society, despite much that otherwise divided them. Those who failed in an educational system which many believed was open to talent could either regard themselves as intrinsically unable to do well at school or as deserving the just rewards of indolence.

Not widely acknowledged but clear nevertheless was the fact, too, that education in Britain was divided on lines of gender as well as social class, so that those who could claim a rightful place in the centre of society were overwhelmingly male. The

Crowther report, an otherwise progressive document which looked to ways to expand educational opportunities, saw a need to reflect in the education of girls their interest in courtship and marriage. 'At this time', the report noted (that is, in adolescence), 'the prospect of courtship and marriage should rightly influence the education of the adolescent girl ... her direct interest in dress, personal appearance and in problems of human relations should be given a central place in her education' (Central Advisory Council for Education 1959:34).

This view clearly had wide support in Britain. In an address to the National Association of Probation Officers the director of the Cambridge Institute of Education urged that secondary modern schools, which, sadly, had 'so few windows into their souls', should provide a challenge to girls. The primary interest of girls, he told the conference, was sex 'and schools should take advantage of this interest rather than avoid the issue. More should be made of their desire to dress attractively, and girls should be encouraged to look forward to looking after a home' (*The Times*, 29 September 1958). Such widespread attitudes entered into the way girls came to think of themselves and privileged domestic roles over occupational ones as those to which girls should aspire.

The expansion of education at all levels in Britain in the late 1950s and throughout the 1960s was a response to demographic pressure combining with social and political demands for widened opportunities. This was the context for the political debates of the period over the merits of comprehensive schools, the elitism of the public schools and the need to reform the tripartite system of secondary education. The economic imperative to increase the supply and quality of trained people to the British economy as a necessary precondition to its modernization is something which also influenced discussions of education. The setting up of the colleges of advanced technology and, later, of the polytechnics were measures aimed at reducing a shortage of highly trained personnel. For most of the period of the 1960s there was a happy coalescence between the needs of employers for well-trained staff and the aspirations of middle class people and affluent workers for expanded educational opportunities.

Those in the centre of British society experienced these years as years of growth and opportunity, despite the fact that social researchers had already by this time exposed education's organization on lines of class and spelled out its limitations. The message of that research found a receptive audience among politicians, particularly, though not exclusively, those in the Labour Party. When he became Minister of Education in Harold Wilson's Labour government, Anthony Crosland, the man who had done so much in the 1950s to move the Labour Party away from its older class war politics, worked closely with social researchers and commentators like A.H. Halsey, John Vaizey, Michael Young and David Donnison, all of them leaders in social research in Britain – and none given a drink at the minister's home until the serious business of the discussion was done with (Kogan 1971:185).

The outcome was this: a strong moral concern with equality and values like equality of opportunity became linked with a very different set of concerns about economic efficiency. The two came happily together to legitimate policies such as the expansion of education, the development of the comprehensive school, in which ability would not be wasted through inefficient systems of social selection disguised as sound educational practice, and the growth of higher education both in the universities and in the public sector in the form of the polytechnics. Such policies captured the imagination of white collar workers, the socially mobile, the professionals and, not least, a post-war generation of working people whose expectations were no longer impoverished but who looked confidently to improvements in their living standards and opportunities for their children. From the late 1950s onwards those expectations were realizable; steady economic growth, science and new technology and better management – all conditional on improved education – sustained an optimism and confidence that *all* hopes were realizable.

Politics and privatism

The political history of the period from 1959 to the late 1960s cannot be recapitulated here. The period covers the election of a Conservative government under Harold Macmillan, his resignation and replacement by Alec Douglas Home as Prime Minister and then, by a hair's breadth, the election of a Labour government under Hugh Gaitskell's successor as leader of the party, Harold Wilson, in 1964 and again in 1966. Three themes stand out, however, which exemplify changes in attitude and feeling in British society during this period.

The first is the emergence of a distinctive middle class radicalism which questioned both Britain's role as a nuclear power and its claims to be a modern industrial society. As will be seen, it was a radicalism with distinctive social roots and a strong moral tone, and one which demanded high levels of personal involvement in a way which translated political commitment into questions of personal authenticity and life-style.

The second is a loss of legitimacy on the part of the traditional social and political elites of the society. Harold Wilson played on this in the 1964 general election campaign when he ridiculed Alec Douglas Home as the 'thirteenth Earl', a symbol of an old elite no longer relevant to a technological Britain; but it was exemplified as well in the emergence of political satire and in particular in the unfolding of the Profumo scandal.

The third theme is the consolidation of privatism in social and family life which reinforced an indifference to and lack of involvement in politics, strengthening the boundaries between public and private life which were one of the major features of the affluent society. It meant that radical political thought and feeling could find expression only outside the formal frameworks of politics. It meant too, however, that under the weight of obligations to earn more and spend and improve living standards and cope with the demands of an ever more complex everyday life, indifference to politics, except in the most formal sense of voting at elections, deepened. Related to this is a growing concern from different political and ethical standpoints about what kind of society was emerging in Britain. The role of young people, the position of women in society and the pattern of family life were three key issues here. They focused discussions about morality, welfare and social relationships and in so doing charted the contours of regret, indifference and conflict woven into the social structures and institutions of modern Britain.

Harold Macmillan may well have symbolized an older Britain but he presided over a rapidly changing society, whose role in the world, despite what many people wished to believe, was no longer that of a great power with a colonial empire. Indeed, Macmillan himself and his Colonial Secretary Ian Macleod did much to facilitate decolonization and to reorient British foreign policy towards stronger links with both the United States and Europe. Yet it was still a country whose leaders, particularly though by no means exclusively in the Conservative Party, sought to maintain an independent British nuclear deterrent through possession of the hydrogen bomb and a wing of Vulcan bombers. This commitment became from the mid 1950s the focus of political involvement for a significant minority in Britain supporting the Campaign for Nuclear Disarmament (CND), which was launched in February 1958 by Bertrand Russell and Canon Collins.

The Campaign was a prominent feature of British politics for the five years between 1958 and 1963. It has been typified by one contemporary sociological observer as a campaign of middle class radicalism (Parkin 1968). His claim, based on interviews with those who joined the Easter Aldermaston marches, is that 'much of the movement's attraction derived from the fact that it also served as a rallying point for groups and individuals opposed to certain features of British society which were independent of the issue of the Bomb, but which the latter served dramatically to symbolize' (1968:5). Those involved in the campaign clung to the belief that politics was also about morality and that in ditching its nuclear weapons Britain could give a moral lead to the whole world. Not surprisingly Parkin found that CND supporters were also likely to be opposed to capital punishment, apartheid, racial discrimination and censorship; that they would support increased aid to poorer countries and support liberal positions on homosexual law reform or abortion. Many supported the Labour Party but resented what they saw as its electoral expediency.

None of this was integrated, however, among the movement's middle class supporters into a coherent ideological framework. CND, Parkin claimed, 'provided a cause without an ideology' (1968:56). His interpretation of this is that because protest of a class or economic kind typical of the 1930s had been routinized and stabilized, the springs of political radicalism had now to be essentially moral and non-ideological in character.

CND provided a framework of symbolic protest for a wide range of groups – the churches, far Left political parties, the Labour Left – but it was not, Parkin claims, until a body of nationally known intellectuals began actively to support it that the movement really developed. Among those who did were A.J.P. Taylor, the historian, Kingsley Martin, editor of *New Statesman*, Bertrand Russell and J.B. Priestley. The young writers and dramatists described in the 1950s as the 'angry young men' were also in support – John Osborne, Arnold Wesker, Robert Bolt – and so were writers like Doris Lessing, Shelagh Delaney, David Mercer and Marghanita Laski. Parkin suggests that a significant number of such people had experienced directly the strains of marginality associated with being upwardly mobile from a working class background and resented the class system of the society.

That can be debated; what is clearer is that CND had a strong base of support in its younger members and this was seen by many commentators as something new in British politics, the attitude of young people towards politics having been traditionally apathetic. A survey of the political attitudes of the young showed '90 per cent find politics a bore. They have no generalized empathy for public affairs' (Abrams and Little 1965:95). With CNDers it was different. They came from middle class and skilled working class backgrounds and were well educated. What Parkin found was that their parents and particularly their mothers were likely to support the aims of CND, and that they came from homes, even those not supportive of CND, in which an interest in politics was high. CND served for many as a political baptism into a wider political radicalism.

Parkin, in retrospect erroneously but for perfectly credible reasons at the time, attributed some of this radicalism to the effects of higher education encouraging students to question the world around them. He was not alone in believing this. Another sociologist, Philip Abrams, commented that, 'In so far as we do teach children about their society in ways that realize the educationalist's professed aims we are going to produce impassioned critics of society, "irresponsible beatniks", "marchers", "socialist fanatics" and so forth' (quoted Parkin 1968:174). This idea seemed to explain why attitudes among students varied, too. Engineering students, one survey revealed, supported the Conservatives by a ratio of 2:1 while social scientists supported Labour by a ratio of 3:1 (Parkin 1968:171). Of pro-CND students, 70 per cent were following humanities or social science courses. Scientists and technologists were not, in general, supportive of CND.

Among its adult supporters public service professionals were well represented. Parkin attributed this to the fact that professional occupations were more likely to attract those with a radical disposition because they allow a high self identification with work without entailing the compromises and conflicts which are generated in industrial employment. These professional occupations, of course, were occupational categories growing in importance in the changing labour market of modern Britain.

Only 12 per cent of CND's active support came from a manual working class background and CND was acutely aware of its inability to recruit working class members (Parkin 1968:17). But it is in the realm of the politics of the labour movement that the significance of CND lies, for debates within the trades unions and the Labour Party became divisive and bitter over the bomb. Aneuran Bevan, the champion of the Labour Left, had caused dismay among comrades in 1957 by declaring calls for the support of unilateral nuclear disarmament an 'emotional spasm', but by 1960 such had become the official policy of the Labour Party and the fulcrum of bitter internal strife. Debate about the bomb became a vehicle for different groups to try and define the soul of the Labour Party itself.

What happened, in essence, was that the Right and Left divided on this issue, with the major trades unions aligning themselves with the unilateralists. Gaitskell managed in the course of 1960 to have the unilateralist resolution of the Scarborough Conference reversed. This was achieved largely because the trades unions decided to attach higher priority to something of much greater importance to their rank and file members than nuclear disarmament, namely party unity. With Hugh Gaitskell's untimely death in 1963 the intra-party dispute about the bomb ended. His successor, Harold Wilson, widely thought of as the Left's candidate for leadership, was to define a different set of issues for the party's agenda, as Labour looked for the first time in over ten years to have some realistic chance of taking office.

The prospect of a Labour government after, as the party's propagandists had it, 'thirteen wasted years' of Tory rule was something made possible by Labour staging a credible claim to be the party of economic efficiency. It was in the economic domain that Macmillan's government had faltered. But failure there was compounded by the crisis surrounding the Profumo affair, in which a senior government minister was exposed as having had a dangerous liaison with a 'society' prostitute, who herself had intimate connections with Russian agents in Britain. Press discussion of that did much to undermine the authority of Macmillan in his government and create a general climate of 'outraged morality' in society at large (Irving, Hall and Wallington 1963). A heightened public awareness of strip clubs, call girls, homosexuality and spying were all part of it; so, too, was a sense that, through the humiliation of de Gaulle's veto on Britain's entry to the Common Market, Britain's irrelevance to the Cuban missile affair and the country's growing economic difficulties at a time when expectations had never been higher for yet better living standards, something was seriously wrong, both with the Tory government and with Britain itself. And woven through all of this was a strand of irreverence towards the traditional elites of British society and symbols of their authority. One small manifestation of this was the popularity of the television programme *That was the Week that Was*, which brought political satire into many front rooms.

British exports performed badly in the early 1960s and the balance of trade went into serious deficit. There was a sterling crisis in 1961 followed by economic measures which Labour, to its advantage, characterized as 'stop-go' policies. By the winter of 1963, unemployment had reached 800,000. The government's interest in indicative economic planning, regional policy – Lord Hailsham was sent to the north east of England with a cloth cap to regenerate the region's declining industries – and incomes policy was insufficient. Labour moved in to capitalize on a pervasive sense of economic malaise.

The national executive of the Labour Party produced in 1963 a document called *Labour and the Scientific Revolution*, which set out a 'new deal for the scientist and technologist in higher education, a new status for scientists in government, and a new role for government-sponsored science in industrial development' (quoted Sked and Cook 1979:215). Harold Wilson secured for Labour a positive identification with science and technology, and through that made a direct appeal to middle class technocrats and all those who in the post-war period had benefited from higher education. Judith Hart, a left-wing member of the party, announced that 'socialists and scientists together can make their dreams a reality' (Sked and Cook 1979:215). The 'white hot heat of the technological revolution', which Wilson proposed to harness as a way of modernizing Britain, became a symbol of unity for the Labour Party and simultaneously endeared it to whole sections of the middle class.

The election of a Labour government committed to planning and to the development of science and technology was a marked break in the political pattern of Britain. But it was a government with a small majority and commitments to maintain many of Britain's overseas military bases, the NATO alliance and the role and value of sterling. In this respect it turned out to be a very conservative Labour government in the context of a fast-changing society. Change, however, was uneven; its costs were borne unequally and it was experienced in very different ways by different sections of the community. The young, the old, men and women and working people as distinct from middle class people all experienced the affluent society in different ways, depending on their purchasing power and political clout.

The young and their sexual morality provided opportunity for much public comment and concern. The poet Philip Larkin (1979) captured well how some of the older generation felt about the apparent freedom of the young, when he wrote in his poem '*Annus Mirabilis*' that:

> Sexual intercourse began
> In nineteen sixty-three
> (Which was rather late for me) –
> Between the end of the *Chatterley* ban
> And the Beatles' first LP.

The BBC Reith lecturer in 1962 said at the beginning of his third broadcast: 'I am going to talk about teenagers and that means, almost inevitably, that I am going to talk about violence and sex' (Carstairs 1964:43).

The young people in question were fully employed and free of the obligations of national service. They were the post-war children, the inheritors, the ones for whom the war itself had been fought and won. But therein lay the source of many of their problems, for the reaction of adult society to their behaviour was punitive and critical. Targeted as a growing market for fashion and popular music, their purchasing power was nevertheless sufficient for them to determine what would be sold to them. Mark Abrams described the teenage consumer market (teenagers, some 13 per cent of the population, spent £900 million by 1958, £15 million of it on records) as:

almost entirely working class. Its middle class members are either still at school or college or else just beginning their careers. Not far short of all teenage spending is conditioned by working class tastes and values. The aesthetic of the teenage market is essentially a working class aesthetic. (Quoted Harker 1980:74)

This was the audience in which groups like the Beatles achieved such success, and popular music – supplied outside the BBC after 1964 by pirate radio stations – provided young people with a way of mapping out their identities in sharp contrast to those of their parents or their teachers or youth leaders. In an unequal society, young people from different social backgrounds both express themselves and experience the world in different ways. The distinct youth subcultures of Mods and Rockers were based on a rivalry rooted essentially in class differences of education and occupation. That rivalry erupted into over-reported ritualized aggression at seaside resorts (Cohen 1972).

This was the context in which youth workers, encouraged by the National Association of Youth Clubs, began to acknowledge the special needs of the 'Unattached' (Morse 1965). These were the unclubbable ones and frequently delinquent; as Mary Morse described them, basing her account on the field notes of youth workers in four urban settings in England, they were the young who sought excitement, who rejected adult authority and whose attitudes to the society around them were cynical and embittered. They were the bored and aimless ones who accepted 'with apathy and indifference the idea that there was nothing that could be done to improve things' (Morse 1965:121).

Her account of the position of unattached girls in 'Northtown' is particularly revealing of a set of attitudes in which resentment towards adults was mixed with a strong feeling of insecurity or inadequacy and a sense of social inferiority, compensated for by a forceful denunciation of anything 'posh' (1965:123). In relation to their work in the factory these girls were bored, apathetic and resentful and found release only in the commercial pleasures of popular entertainment. It is against this background that the figure has to be read that in 1961 just over 30 per cent of married teenage girls were pregnant at the time of their wedding (Carstairs 1964:48).

The reaction of older people to the behaviour of the young was described by one sociologist as a 'moral panic', something rooted in fear and incomprehension and a pervasive sense of the loss of discipline and order (Cohen 1972). This is almost certainly an overinterpretation coloured by an oversensitivity to the importance of headlines in the press. In the ordered worlds of older working class communities from which the young people came, youthful high spirits were easily contained; the factory and the street and the still important links of kinship stretching, as the Institute of Community Studies found, across three generations combined as a powerful instrument to bind the young and old together (Young and Willmott 1957; Townsend 1963). But that world was itself changing fast under the impact of urban renewal and economic change. Many of the implicit norms of family life and social relations, particularly those between men and women, were also being questioned.

Discussions about family life in the late 1950s and early 1960s were framed by a concern for its stability, given increasing divorce rates, and by the conflicts some detected in the roles women played as wives, mothers and workers. Family instability was widely seen as the root cause of delinquency and the decline of authority in society. Much of this criticism came from churchmen but not exclusively so. Ronald Fletcher, whose book, *The Family and Marriage*, set out to demonstrate that the critics were wrong, quoted a secondary school headmaster complaining that there is 'a complete and all-out worship of money and what it can buy', and the sad effect of this in his opinion was 'in the time taken from home and its life in pursuing this aim. Many parents are too engrossed to live with or for their children' (1962:13).

None of the available evidence suggested that family life was in any way threatened by women working. Indeed, the opposite was the case; the working mother often created opportunities for grandparents to play a stronger role in the family and in many cases women could work because the family unit was supportive and well integrated (Thompson and Finlayson 1963). The overall climate of opinion in the society was still dominated, however, by the assumption that the appropriate role for women was in the home, and within that climate it was difficult for women to articulate their own thoughts and feelings about the life they were expected to lead.

The nuclear family was widely seen as the setting in which most people would find their deepest satisfactions in life, and the growth of the post-war consumer goods industries served to construct the family rather than the individual as the unit of mass consumption. Nevertheless, some saw in this opportunities for moral improvement. Ronald Fletcher, for example, fending off the moralizers who feared the family's collapse, saw the development of 'companionate marriage' based on equality of status and mutuality of consideration between men and women as a vast improvement on anything that had gone before (1962:144). Sensitive to the fact that the nuclear family could become 'a narrow, self contained, little den in which people suffocate each other with their possessive, stagnant, and petty emotions' and aware that the lot of women could be improved, Fletcher's study remained overall sanguine in its assessment of the changing role of women (1962:136).

Other men detected problems, however. The Reith lecturer G.M. Carstairs reported conventional medical opinion that there was a high rate of neurotic ill health among young married women, which physicians called 'suburban neurosis' (1964:64). The doctors understood this as a reaction to a sense of uselessness, the result, Carstairs claimed, of society's failure to provide a constructive role for these mothers since it had not wholly abandoned the Victorian ideal of the fully domesticated wife. When women asserted themselves and sought a life outside the home they often felt both guilty and anxious about their actions.

Such feelings can be seen in retrospect as facets of the way changes in the economic roles of women outstripped the social and psychological adjustments of family life. Just as forcibly, however, they can be seen as a consequence of powerlessness and invisibility on the part of women who were unable to articulate in a publicly legitimate way their deeply felt frustrations about family life.

The problem, of course, is that there are few studies of women in the early 1960s which approached their lives in this way. An important exception to this is Gavron's book, *The Captive Wife*, first published 1966. What this young sociologist demonstrated was that young married women experienced a loss of confidence in themselves and often felt trapped (1983).

Among the working class mothers in her sample there was strong evidence of loneliness and isolation and, in contrast to the picture of the working class painted by the kinship studies in the East End of London, which had been carried out by the Institute of Community Studies, Gavron detected in her sample 'a rather isolated, extremely family centred existence, with the focus not on the extended family but on the nuclear family' (1983:94). For middle class women the picture was somewhat different; decent housing, money and extensive friendship links outweighed some of the constraints of living with small children, but the advantages did not wholly remove doubt and anxiety about the quality of life as married women.

Gavron's book was well publicized. Newspapers picked it out in 1966 with headlines like 'Alone with the gadgets' (*The Listener*) and 'Is your wife just a bird in a plastic cage?' (*Sunday Express*), and 5,000 copies of the book were sold. Ann Oakley, in her preface to a later edition of the book, argues that Gavron's 'early endeavours in charting the contours of women's captivity helped to fashion a new way of seeing the world' (1983:xvi). That way of seeing the world was one in which women's troubles were located very firmly in the social and political organization of the society. Gavron did not anticipate that change would come about very much through the action of women themselves. Her work, nevertheless, is indicative of a changed structure of feeling in British society, bound up with the way in which women experienced the contradictions of their roles in a male-dominated world in which the formal institutions of politics, geared primarily to sustaining the growth on which affluence depended, responded hardly at all to their needs.

The pattern of social relationships within families – those between men and women, parents and children, the generations – and the relationships between families as neighbours in a community and citizens in a state are inseparable from the prevailing arrangements and values of society as a whole. Britain in the early 1960s can be characterized in this respect as a society in which some of the older solidarities of class and community were breaking up and in which people sought within the privacy of their own families the goals which were central to their lives. Some writers on the Left saw great dangers here. Richard Titmuss viewed such developments as part of what he called the 'irresponsible society' (1960). It was defined by a concentration of economic power on the one hand and by political indifference on the other. For Titmuss, the problem was that the privileging of private affluence undermined the capacity of people to resist the centralization of power. The two together posed the threat that both the social conscience and democratic values of modern society could languish.

Titmuss believed solutions to these problems lay in an enhanced moral discourse and informed government action to modify the play of market forces in the society. For Raymond Williams, the problem was the moral decline of the labour movement itself, exemplified in the way too many people had come to see the Labour Party, or the trades union movement, merely as vehicles with which to achieve a greater share of what capitalism had promised them (1965:328). The result, he argued, was that the concepts of the consumer and the market determined the whole character of the country's economic life and there was no principled opposition to them. The doctrine of 'I'm all right, Jack' was not, he felt, an accurate description of the social feelings of the majority of the people of Britain, but it was something which should be challenged as a false representation of how people's lives were actually organized and how the 'social poverty' of the society could be transformed.

Such ideas were, however, far removed from the minds of the majority of ordinary people in Britain, for whom affluence had brought definite benefits. In 1948, 7.2 per cent of the population owned motor cars. By 1966 that figure had grown to 53.1 per cent. The number of foreign holidays increased from 2 million in 1955 to 5 million in 1967. In 1955, 39.8 per cent of the adult population had television in the home. The figure for 1964 was 90.8 per cent (Halsey 1972b). Cinema attendance collapsed during this period as television consolidated itself as the dominant cultural force of the society. The importance of these changes is still debated. The point to be stressed here is that affluence entrained increasingly privatized life-styles and focused both expectations and ambitions on high levels of individual consumption of consumer goods and commercialized leisure experiences.

Conclusion

The thrust of the argument of this chapter is this: Britain in the early 1960s was a fast changing society in which most groups of people experienced a substantial improvement in living standards. It was during this period that the values of individual success and home-centred privatism achieved a central place in the moral order of the society. The pace and complexity of social change meant, however, that this was not a stable situation and the divisions of the society ensured that the benefits of affluence were not distributed equally.

The social divisions of the society also nurtured a new awareness of its changing forms and possibilities which was not easily contained within its conventional political forms. The political consensus which had carried Britain through the 1950s began to break up in manifold ways during the early 1960s. The political forms of that consensus, particularly those of the labour movement, were not adequate to cope with new forms of political radicalism such as CND or to capture the interests of the young or to deal creatively with the changing needs and demands of a labour force in which women were a significant group.

Nevertheless, the achievement of affluence blunted the edge of discontent so far as the majority of ordinary workers were concerned. But not for long; the remainder of the decade, and right up to the first oil price rise in 1973, is a period in which the political and cultural contradictions of rapid change exposed and intensified structures of feeling which, while building on older forms, were nonetheless novel in their intensity. In the following chapter the period of the late 1960s is examined with special attention to the themes of conflict, corporatism and critique.

6
The 'Swinging Sixties'

The aim of this chapter is to examine the social changes which took place in Britain during the second half of the sixties decade and up to the oil price rise of 1973. The period under review is one in which governments struggled to modernize the British economy and halt its apparently inexorable decline. The strategies devised to achieve this were corporatist in character; governments sought to work closely with the representatives of both business and the trades unions to control levels of investment, incomes and prices and achieve, through planning, a steady growth in productivity and export performance. Conventional politics became increasingly a matter of economics but by the early 1970s the long post-war consensus that the economy could be managed in this way began to crumble. What then developed among political and economic commentators was a sense of crisis in the British economy.

This same period was for many groups in society, despite the economic gloom, one of optimism and liberation, a period when a new kind of politics – what R.D. Laing called 'the politics of experience' – became possible (1967). This was the period of anti-Vietnam War protest, the student movement, 'flower power', pop festivals, psychedelic drugs, the Beatles, Bob Dylan, Mary Quant, 'swinging London'; throughout these years a New Left set out its criticism of corporate capitalism and the first real signs of a revived feminist movement became clear. The social and cultural tone of the period, at least among some groups of the young and the well educated and particularly among the cultural avant-garde, was unconventional, anti-authority and experimental.

Much has since been written to demonstrate that the 'expressive revolution of the 1960s was no revolution at all but an adaptation of cultural styles to the social and economic forms of a mobile and privatized society (Martin 1981). One early commentator on the significance of the fashions, protests and styles of the period claimed they amounted to no more than a 'psychic epidemic' and that the world quickly settled down again to its ordered routines (Booker 1970; Martin 1981).

The view developed in this chapter is that there were profound cultural changes in Britain during the 1960s and that they followed from the way in which new opportunities for cultural expression opened up for a range of different groups in the society. In this sense, the critical and creative processes of what Raymond Williams called 'the long revolution' speeded up in the 1960s (1965). This process is one involving a search for new meanings and values, for new areas of 'feeling and expectation' to give shape to a world different to that of the past (R. Williams 1965:381). In a divided society it is to be expected that such a search will produce conflict and dissent, following closely the fracture lines of social divisions, power and experience. To concentrate too much on the 'expressive revolution' of the period, on changes in the arts or ideology, would therefore be too narrow an approach. The challenge in making sense of the 1960s is to trace out the ways in which different groups of people experienced their world and made sense of it, and to link such an understanding with the changing economic and political circumstances of a country which itself was part of, and open to, changes taking place on a wider international stage.

The approach of the chapter is to trace out the search for new values and meanings in relation to three main issues. The first of these is the meaning attached to nationality. The aim is to explore what being British conveyed to different groups in the society and what they felt it should mean in the contexts firstly of the broader international order of the world and, secondly, of the changing ethnic composition of the country.

The second theme concerns the changing contours and significance of class differences; the period under review is one in which the patterns – the constraints, opportunities, attitudes, values and stresses – of working class life were altered radically. Urban and industrial changes together with those in the field of social policy were part of this; so, too, were affluence and its accompanying hopes and expectations. Affluence for some was achieved at a cost to others. Optimism and hope that the future would be inexorably better than the past had their counter-balance in strong feelings of despair and rejection among those on the periphery of the affluent society, whose existence and problems were carefully charted, though not transformed, during this period.

Finally, the search for new meanings and expectations took active forms outside the conventions of formal politics. The student movement, the women's movement and the develop-ment of more militant forms of politics – on both the Right and Left of the political spectrum – together with the renewal of nationalist sympathies in Scotland, Wales and, of course, Northern Ireland, are each in different ways part of that search.

National identity and race relations

The Labour government which took office in 1964 came in with an agenda to modernize the economy and build a stronger Britain, a Britain no longer playing the role described by one of the younger ministers, Peter Shore, of 'the sick man of Europe' (quoted Warde 1982:97). The party's manifesto asserted that:

The Labour Party is offering Britain a new way of life that will stir our hearts, re-kindle an authentic patriotic faith in our future, and enable our country to re-establish itself as a stable force in the world today for progress, peace and justice. (Warde 1982:100)

The foreign policy stance of the Labour government insisted on a British military presence east of Suez, particularly in Malaysia and Singapore and in the Arabian Gulf, and a deter-mination to retain a strong naval presence in the Indian Ocean. The Prime Minister, Harold Wilson, commented in 1965 in a speech in New Delhi that 'Britain's frontiers are on the Hima-layas' (Darwin 1988:291). Resting on a belief that Britain could still play a role as a world power and lead the Commonwealth, this foreign policy was also framed to deflect Tory criticism that

Labour was not a patriotic party. The government, it has been claimed, was particularly concerned, especially because of its precariously small parliamentary majority, not to offend the patriotism of its traditional working class supporters (Darwin 1988:290).

Patriotism is a way of thinking and feeling which, though anchored in traditional institutions, symbols and rituals, is altered and redefined in response to changed national and international circumstances. Harold Wilson's Labour government drew on a patriotic rhetoric which linked pride in the nation with economic vitality and a world political role. That role was one tied to the NATO Alliance, the special relationship with the United States of America and the leadership of the Commonwealth. Each of these commitments created strains and tensions for a weak economy and political problems for a government which had to deal with complex and bitter conflicts arising from the international role it played. These concerned opposition to the worsening events of the Vietnam War, the unilateral declaration of independence by the racist government of Ian Smith in Northern Rhodesia and the East African Asian crisis, which put the whole issue of immigration high up on the agenda of British politics.

No one patriotic rhetoric was adequate to describe how different groups in British society felt about these changing political issues. Some on the Left felt saddened at the way the government appealed to older patriotic symbols to justify its actions. The political Right became increasingly racist in its response to immigration. Yet others felt regret at Britain's loss of world status and straitened circumstances and found their national identity in nostalgia for an idealized past. The inability of the Labour government to prevent UDI in Rhodesia despite protracted negotiations, or to hold on to its military presence in the Arabian Gulf, or to have any serious effect on America's disastrous involvement in Vietnam, are all testimony to the long-term decline of a world power. Compelled by cost to withdraw troops from east of the Suez Canal in 1968, the government prompted in Philip Larkin a typically mordant little poem, 'Homage to a Government', indicative of how many older people must have felt:

> Next year we are to bring the soldiers home
> For lack of money, and it is all right.
> Places they guarded, or kept orderly,
> Must guard themselves, and keep themselves orderly.
> We want the money for ourselves at home
> Instead of working. And this is all right.

He goes on to say that 'Our children will not know it's a different country. / All we can hope to leave them now is money' (Larkin 1974). What he articulated here was a sense of loss of greatness and fear that only material values now mattered. That sense of greatness was, however, preserved; people could find it together with their own sense of national identity and purpose in those ritual occasions when a divided and failing society could claim some kind of mystical unity.

Royal ceremonial, national sporting events and the death of statesmen are the grist to this particular mill. The death of Winston Churchill in the winter of 1965 was one of those occasions when the older, traditional and nostalgic version of patriotism was asserted to evoke a particular version of the country's greatness. It was widely interpreted at the time as being simultaneously a requiem for Britain as a great power (Cannadine 1983:157).

Churchill's dying days had been reported in great detail in the national press and his funeral was organized as a major state occasion with a lying in state at Westminster Hall, six gun salutes and a funeral procession through London. Ray Gosling described it all in *New Society* as 'Winston's Wake', seeing in the crowds and the reverence evidence of the fact that 'In peace we haven't been able to love one another: we've given life little magic' (Gosling 1972:31). What the funeral did was evoke a now mythical time when, during the war against Hitler, people did come together for a common purpose and lived their 'finest hour'. Gosling caught the mood of it:

At Victoria homegoing commuters were snapping up the Churchill souvenir editions like they were five pound notes. Bankers and brokers and jobbers were off to Bromley and Haywards Heath to hold hands with their wives and watching TV re-live their finest hours in civil defence, the home guard, or the RAF. (Quoted Gosling 1972:26)

Even Gosling, already an established anti-Establishment writer with politically radical credentials, found the occasion moving. He described his own thoughts, standing in the queue to the lying in state, as 'unutterable', and reflecting on the people around him he commented: 'Most of us, I'm sure, came not just to mourn or say thank you, but to live again those few short days in our lives when we had meaning and glory and fulfilment' (1972:29).

What Gosling described was an emotionally supercharged mood centred on one version of the country's greatness. Kingsley Amis may have been right just two years previously to note in an *Observer* series on patriotism that 'The would-be big stuff – It's Great Britain Again – demonstrably won't hold up any more' and that 'Poor man's imperialism' was a 'neurotic affliction', not even fashionable in ruling circles (1963). But he underestimated the potency of such ideas when they were evoked for ordinary people, when the need was pressing to take stock of themselves or their society in moments of political crisis, or on occasions like Churchill's death when the past pressed heavily on the present.

Churchill was and remains a complex symbol. His funeral in 1965 provided an opportunity for the imperial elements of national identity to be recalled. By 1965 those elements had taken on a distinctly racist character, and racist thought and sentiment became a key feature of British political life, as the numbers of immigrant workers in the country increased and the government responded to the crises of East Africa in which Asians, themselves part of Britain's imperial arrangements, were expelled from Kenya and came, as was their right to do, to Britain.

Immigration from the West Indies and from the Indian subcontinent increased steadily through the 1950s. Workers came to Britain because their skills were in demand in an economy suffering labour shortages. They came to a country with a serious legacy of poor housing and a legal system which tolerated blatant acts of racial discrimination. In the late 1950s and early 1960s immigrant workers looking for accommodation would see hundreds of adverts in shop windows saying 'Room to let: no coloureds'. Landlords justified their actions on the grounds that while they were prepared to let rooms their neighbours would object. At work there were other indignities – poorer rates of pay, discrimination on promotions, employment below their levels of skill and racist attitudes from fellow workers. On the streets there was always the possibility of verbal abuse and, increasingly after 1959, physical violence.

The history of the changing relationships between immigrant workers and their families and the host society in which they lived is one that is woven into the history of housing, employment and the law; it is found in the political responses of the major parties as well as among immigrants themselves. It must be traced, too, in the attitudes, values and feelings of both immigrants and people of the host society, for these framed the responses of both to the changing contexts of their contact. The structures of feeling and of perception involved are powerfully charged with resentment, fear, anger and suspicion, all aggravated by poor housing and economic change. Racism became for some people, a minority, a way of asserting a national pride in a way which offered a self respect denied to them in the normal course of their ordinary lives, at work or at home.

Anti-racist thought and feeling must be described as well. Organizations like the Campaign Against Racial Discrimination (CARD), which was formed in December 1964, drew together people, many of whom had been active in CND or the Movement for Colonial Freedom, who were deeply opposed to racism and racial discrimination (Heineman 1972). There was, as now, a further set of attitudes found throughout the major political parties, in which the predominant value was of liberal reasonableness, a view that immigration brought problems which could only be overcome through education and the careful assimilation of black people into the structures of British society. Such reasonableness was, however, vulnerable to a sinister right-wing interpretation. In 1959, for example, Oswald Mosley, former leader of the pre-war British Union of Fascists, campaigned in the 1959 general election in the North Kensington seat on a platform to repatriate immigrants. He insisted that 'we are going to treat these people fairly', and then added, 'but we are going to send them home' (quoted Deakin 1970:97).

In the early 1960s, a framework of thinking among the liberal intellectuals, who took race seriously as an issue, laid great stress on concepts like assimilation and integration (Patterson 1963). Divisions among those who thought themselves to be anti-racist in their thinking and opposed to all forms of racial discrimination were, however, sharp. They erupted to divide the Campaign Against Racial Discrimination between those who looked for radical political action of a kind which would empower black people to solve their own problems, and those who sought solutions to racial discrimination using the methods of non-party political pressure groups seeking to influence public opinion. These discussions were informed by a growing understanding of what was taking place in the United States civil rights movements and the problems of the ghettoes in American cities. The fear was that unless Britain acted quickly to improve the lot of immigrants, trouble would flare up just as it had in America.

Underlying the public debates on such issues as immigration control and housing there was, of course, the experience of black people themselves and their everyday contact with white people. Seeing Britain as 'the mother country' and encouraged by their education to believe they were part of it, what they found instead shocked and dismayed them. Two social researchers, Ruth Glass and Harold Pollins, noted the fears many white people had of black people:

coloured people are feared as competitive intruders; they are thought of as promoters of crime and carriers of disease; they are resented when they are poor; they are envied when they are resourceful and thrifty. They are looked down upon; they are patronised; occasionally they are treated like everyone else. (Quoted Fryer 1984:375)

Sheila Patterson in her study of 'dark strangers' in Brixton in the late 1950s suggested that the hostility of many British workers in Brixton to immigrants was rooted in a fear of unemployment and a belief that newcomers would dilute the services of the welfare state. A local government clerk told her: 'I don't think it's right all these foreigners and blacks should get all the benefits of the welfare state and health service straight away, without paying towards it' (1963:146). A factory foreman told her: 'A lot of them just come over here to live on National Assistance; and we have to pay for them to hang around the streets doing nothing' (1963:146). Only a handful of white people in Brixton had ever visited a coloured family's home and many told Sheila Patterson of their fears of mixed marriages.

The position and experience of migrants from India and Pakistan was different to that of the West Indians, for they came from a religious and cultural background very unlike that of the host society. Dr Bhikhu Parekh, commenting on their experience in 1978, said that: 'The first generation Asian immigrant in Britain ... was not used to the mores and practices of an industrial society. His presence was resented, and he suffered racialist insults and indignities' (quoted Fryer 1984:376). In Bradford, an observer in 1964 noted a 'subterranean resentment on both sides, that threatens racial harmony in a city where today nearly one in twenty inhabitants, one in every thirteen workers, one in every four busmen, eight in every ten nightshift workers are coloured' (Barr 1964:6). Racial coexistence, he felt, was a fact and one summed up accurately by one white worker with the comment: 'Ther a'reet sa long as they don't botha me.'

Both fear and resentment must be seen in context. In the early 1960s there was very little research exploring ethnic relations in Britain. But that began to change through the work of such bodies as the Institute of Race Relations and Political and Economic Planning. John Rex and Robert Moore were able to show, in their pioneering study of housing in the Sparkbrook area of Birmingham, that antipathy towards immigrants was rooted firmly in the context of the social and political relationships of housing and of housing shortage. There was a feeling among older residents that the former glory of the place was irretrievably lost (1967). In his study of race relations in the St Paul's area of Bristol, Anthony Richmond noted that a strong sense of loss of status among older residents was refocused as criticism of the younger West Indian families who moved into the area (quoted Deakin 1970:286).

The politics of race relations in Britain during the 1960s must be understood against the background of these powerful feelings. Three themes stand out. The first is the growing racist reaction of many groups in British society to immigration itself. The second is a shift in emphasis on the part of immigrant organizations, from policies which were accommodative and integrationist to ones which were defensive and critical of the host society. The third is the strengthening of anti-racist sentiment, especially among the educated and politically involved middle class, which took the form of moral outrage at the actions of the Labour government in making concessions to the anti-immigrant interests, in the ranks of the Tory Party as well as the traditional bastions of the labour movement.

A full history of these developments would trace them from concerns about race relations, following disturbances in Notting Hill and Nottingham in 1959. At the annual conference of the Tory Party in 1961, fears were expressed about 'uncontrolled immigration', a fear actively articulated by a lobbying organization, the Birmingham Immigration Control Association. The Macmillan government had responded with the 1962 Commonwealth Immigration Bill restricting entry to those with employment vouchers. In the 1964 general election Peter Griffiths stood successfully for Smethwick in the West Midlands on an overtly racist platform and defeated Labour's Patrick Gordon Walker, the man set to be Labour's Foreign Secretary.

With the election of the Labour government, the concern shifted to making racial discrimination illegal and the 1965 Race Relations Act was passed, making discrimination in public places an offence and setting up the Race Relations Board to investigate complaints. By the mid 1960s the race issue had become highly politicized. In 1967 the National Front was formed to fight further immigration; but the event which, above all others, brought immigration right to the forefront was a speech by Enoch Powell, the Conservative MP and right-wing iconoclast from Wolverhampton, when he foretold the streets of British cities flowing with the blood of racial violence.

The trigger for this episode was the expulsion of Kenyan Asians and their migration to Britain in 1967. This movement of people led the Labour government, fearful of electoral damage in areas with a high immigrant population, to further legislation to restrict immigration. This was done quickly, with the 1968 Commonwealth Immigration Act passing through Parliament in two days. In April of that year, Enoch Powell, by then on the margins of the Tory Party, made his famous speech to the Conservative Political Centre in the Midland Hotel, Birmingham. Claiming authority for what he said from the concerns ordinary people had expressed to him about the disgusting behaviour of immigrants, Powell said:

Those whom the gods wish to destroy, they first make mad. We must be mad, literally mad, as a nation to be permitting the annual inflow of some 50,000 dependants, who are for the most part the material of the future growth of the immigrant-descended population. It is like a nation busily engaged in heaping up its own funeral pyre. (Quoted Utley 1968:182)

Like the Roman, he said, 'I seem to see "the River Tiber foaming with much blood"', a reference to a future in which British cities would experience the same conflicts as had taken place in America when the ghettoes burned.

In his sympathetic account of the Powell speech in his political portrait of the man, T.E. Utley records that within a few days of the speech Powell received over 100,000 supportive letters of congratulation (1968:43). There were street demonstrations in his support by London dockers, Smithfield meat porters and Midland factory workers. 'Enoch for Prime Minister' was a commonly heard cry. 'In the aftermath of Powell', writes Peter Fryer, 'Asians and West Indians now went in daily fear of their lives' (1984:385). Racism had become respectable as an element of what it meant to be British. Against a background of economic difficulties and imperial decline, some people could find self respect in it.

Throughout these years there was a distinct shift in the political attitudes of black people in which their community organizations, formed initially to be self help, cultural and welfare organizations, took up more radical political agendas as a way of defending themselves against racism, and rejecting assimilationism as a policy relevant to their needs or interests (Deakin 1970). Among those writers who were concerned to combat discrimination and racism and who were active in campaigns like CARD, or who worked through the Institute of Race Relations or who researched this area of British society, this was a depressing period. For what the growing volume of research evidence pointed to was poor housing for black people, poor schools, prejudice and discrimination of a kind made worse by the legislation designed to prevent them.

What was showing up particularly clearly was that the children of immigrants, the second generation, faced special difficulties of poor educational opportunities and rejection. A West African sixth former described her position in a British school in a BBC discussion programme in the following way:

Well let me put it this way. They think we are sub-human. They don't think us equal to them. So we have no right to own a house, have chairs, eat with a knife and fork, or drink from a glass, or dance to music or us girls to wear mini-skirts. They don't think we are equal to that. (Quoted Deakin 1970:308)

The evidence was building up of black young people experiencing discrimination in finding jobs and taking work beneath their abilities for the sake of having a job. A working party of the Liverpool Youth Organisations Committee detected among black youth in that city a 'deep sense of unease' and insecurity when they left the coloured quarter of the town (Deakin 1970:312).

Surveying a sample of 2,500 people in several British cities, the Institute of Race Relations claimed to have detected only a hard core of about 10 per cent of the population hostile to black people, and claimed that this was linked more to the characteristics of their personalities than to any significant social or demographic feature of the society. At this stage, the Institute believed, effective policies to combat racial discrimination could be implemented, if their target was seen as the city and its problems and not race. Policies on housing, education and the relations of employment could all be improved.

What the Institute was clear about was that the 'liberal hour' had not yet passed, so that improvements could be achieved in race relations (Deakin 1970). In retrospect, it could be claimed that this was too sanguine an interpretation, reflecting too much faith on the part of social scientists and policy makers that social engineering could transform attitudes and values. But this was a distinctive feature of political and social thought in the 1960s. Such thinking, as will be seen, influenced directly the way in which British cities were transformed in the 1960s and, through that, shaped directly attitudes and feelings which for some people – the affluent – were confident and optimistic, but which for others – those on the periphery, those in the inner city – were despairing and aggressive.

Class, corporatism and urban change

For most of the 1960s politicians from different parties were at least agreed on this: that there was a fundamental structural weakness to the British economy which, limiting the amount of wealth produced, constrained what could be achieved through social policies of various kinds to improve living standards and the quality of life of people living in Britain. The differences between the major parties lay more in disagreements about the means to improve matters than in the ends they sought.

Two closely interlocked issues illustrate the political and economic constraints within which British society developed during the late 1960s. They are the issues of planning economic growth and bringing about urban renewal in British cities. Policies in both areas effected changes in the structures of class relationships and patterns of community life. During this period managerialism as an ideology struck firm roots in both the public and private sectors of the economy, encouraging the view, at least among the managers and planners, that old class divisions were disappearing.

The growth of private housing reinforced such a view. More and more people came to see their investment in their own home as the symbol *par excellence* of their success and their freedom, tangible proof that it is through hard work that both people and societies gain success. Such changes and beliefs strengthened the materialism and privatism of hopes and ambitions.

For those left behind on the council estates or in what was increasingly recognized as the inner city the predominant mood was one of apprehension, of loss and hopelessness, some of which translated, as has been shown, into hostility towards ethnic minorities. In the older industrial areas, heartlands of Labour support, marked features of political life became political apathy and a mistrust of the motives of politicians, despite a Labour government (Hindess 1971).

Among the securely employed, the upwardly mobile and middle class people in general there was a mood of confidence. Home ownership, expanded educational opportunities for their children, foreign travel and rising incomes combined to sustain it. For those with strong political interests the late sixties, as will be seen, was a time of opportunity to engage in radical political debate outside the constraints of older party politics and to enjoy the feeling that ideas mattered in changing the world.

The broad economic policies of the Labour government were clear. Economic planning and new technology were at the heart of them. They implied state intervention in the economy to control the growth of incomes and prices. The government set up a Prices and Incomes Board to manage that relationship. Technology and planned investment were two of the government's key economic concepts. The new Ministry of Technology, under the trades union leader Frank Cousins, was set up to modernize British industry, and the Department of Economic Affairs, under the volatile George Brown, was created to plan the economy and wrest economic control from the Treasury. The involvement of the trades unions in the planning machinery of government was an integral element of this approach, since it was hoped that such involvement would result in greater industrial discipline. One writer has summed up this whole approach as 'technocratic collectivism' (Warde 1982:106).

Because it was an approach which stressed the importance of economic values over political ones, it was widely criticized on the Left, particularly on the New Left, for its pragmatism and for masking the way in which the state was in fact acting in the interests of capital rather than labour. Even within the ranks of the party there was grave disquiet. Richard Clements, editor of the left-wing paper *Tribune*, commented as early as 1965 that 'The first year of the Labour Government has sadly disillusioned many active socialists. Indeed so deep is the frustration and despair that in some cases members of the Labour Party are unwilling any longer to take part in its activities' (quoted Hill 1977:155).

The Labour government faltered almost from the beginning in the area of its policies on industrial relations, and the industrial history of that period is one dominated by a growing number of strikes and by a widespread feeling, particularly among Tory supporters and some sections of the middle class, that trades unions were holding the country to ransom. The seamen's strike of 1966 was particularly bitter, prompting from the Prime Minister the comment that it was being driven along by 'politically motivated men'. The government's response to strikes, the white paper *In Place of Strife*, published in 1969, sparked off much acrimonious in-fighting both in the government itself and in the trades union movement.

John Goldthorpe identified the industrial relations 'problems' of Britain during this period as those of strikes, restrictive practices and wage drift (1977). But he then went on to point out that, defined in that way, they were problems for management. Workers, he noted, might well see the same issues as reflecting their interests in autonomy, earnings and control. On this analysis those who sought, as did the Donovan Commission on industrial relations, to reform industrial relations from within, through an appeal to moral codes which stress the importance of honouring agreements, were missing the point. The real issue, suggested Goldthorpe, centred on the kinds of expectation which ordinary workers brought to their work. These derived from a wider set of concerns about their lives in society, not only in the work place. Because of this, it was not possible to detach reform of industrial relations from a more general restructuring of British society and the aspirations it nurtured.

Those aspirations were at the centre of the discussion which took place among social scientists, managers and politicians about the affluent worker and the nature of industrial work itself. It was a discussion central to the work of radical social theorists seeking ways to transform the structure of industrial capitalism and searching for the revolutionary class to bring it about.

What were those aspirations? How were they nurtured and how had they changed? These questions were at the core of the work of John Goldthorpe and his colleagues on the affluent worker project, a major sociological study carried out in Luton, 1964–8, explicitly to examine the claim that affluent workers were becoming middle class (1971). What this study claimed to have shown from interviews with factory workers was that such men were not becoming middle class in the conventional sense. Their values focused on affluence and not on a felt need to improve themselves socially. They accepted tedious and monotonous work for the money. Hardly any of those interviewed expressed any hope or desire for improving the status of their jobs; 'the typical aim', the researchers write, 'was not a progressive series of jobs but the wherewithal to sustain a progressive advance in the material conditions of their out-of-work lives' (1971:77). The workers' hopes focused on material improvement and particularly on improvements in their housing.

These workers had high expectations for their children and preferred selective secondary education as a way of realizing these. The language of 'Us and Them' was noticeably absent from their accounts of their social position. Politics was something only marginally relevant to these men and their concerns of their private life. Goldthorpe and his colleagues argued that such men would support Labour in the polls to the extent that they saw personal advantage in doing so. With a prescience they must now be proud of they predicted a Labour general election defeat to be followed by a lengthy period of Conservative rule. That defeat did, in fact, happen in the general election of 1970 which returned a Tory government under Ted Heath.

The claims of this study have to be put in context. Elsewhere in the motor industry, particularly in Liverpool, at the Halewood plant of Ford, car workers maintained traditions of industrial militancy and a strong 'Them–Us' view of the world. Huw Beynon's study, *Working for Ford*, written at the end of the 1960s, is a telling indictment of the monotony and conflict inherent in assembly line technologies driven hard for corporate profits (1984). The world his book revealed, based as it was on extensive interviews with shop stewards from the Halewood plant, was one of conflict, mistrust of management, detestation of work itself. Most were pragmatists: they hated work but did not imagine there was much else open to them. One man told Benyon:

Your choice of job is governed too much by money. You've got to be a realist. You've got to be a realist.

You don't achieve anything here. A robot could do it. The line here is made for morons. It doesn't need any thought. They tell you that. 'We don't pay you for thinking' they say. Everyone comes to realise that they're not doing a worthwhile job. They're just on the line. For the money. Nobody likes to think they're a failure. It's bad when you know that you're just a little cog. You just look at your pay packet – you look at what it does for your wife and kids. That's the only answer. (1984:124)

The militancy of the Ford workers is clearly related in this study to the organizational capacities of their shop stewards, the traditional class consciousness of Liverpool working people, the policies of Ford management and the logic of the assembly line. Workers felt no moral involvement with the firm and none wanted to stay with the firm for any length of time. Against such a background, it is hardly surprising that this group of

workers found the appeals made to them by a Labour government, to restrain their demands for higher wages in the interests
of the national economy as a whole, ludicrous. Nor is it
surprising that the demands they made of their union and even
of their jobs were essentially material ones to increase their
freedom outside of work. Huw Beynon's thesis was that these
features of life at Halewood were facets of the organization of
capitalist production itself and would not be challenged by
anything other than a vigorous socialist movement (1984:299).

The affluent worker of Luton and the Halewood assembly
line worker appear in the social research of the 1960s as very
different kinds of people. The differences, in fact, lie in the way
they were studied. What they have in common, though, is a
strong sense of the need to protect themselves against the
indignities of industrial work and to find a firm basis for their
self respect in the kind of lives they could build at home for
their families. For many workers during this period, the legacy
of poor housing in Britain's industrial cities and the disastrous
effects of urban development were features which made that
home life stressful and insecure. Neither factory work nor poor
housing are themselves sufficient conditions for the development of the socialist sentiments those on the Left still hoped for
in the working class.

The view that new technology and planning together would
solve the problems of British industry had its counterpart in the
fields of planning and housing policy. Here the emphasis was on
regional planning, the containment of urban sprawl and industrialized building of houses to solve the housing crisis of the
inner city areas of the older conurbations. The Labour government of 1964 came in with a mandate and a determination to
solve what was seen as a housing crisis by investing more in
public housing.

Conservative policy on housing during the 1950s had been to
encourage new building by the private sector, use public
resources to clear slums, and stimulate private landlords to
increase the quantity and quality of accommodation available
for rent. The Labour Party made great play of the failure of
these policies in the 1964 general election, seeing them as the

cause of 'Rachmanism', the thuggish harassment of tenants by unscrupulous landlords. In 1965 the new Labour government passed a Rent Act which sought to control rent levels. The other aim of the government, to help local authorities build more houses, faltered on the rocks of the poor performance of the economy and on the need, as the government perceived it, to hold down public expenditure as part of the defence of the international value of sterling.

Housing therefore remained a serious problem, particularly in the big cities and older industrial areas. The housing stock in 1967 included 1.8 million dwellings considered unfit for human habitation, most of which were in the privately rented sector – a sector which by this time accounted for only about one quarter of the total stock of dwellings (Rollet 1972). Forty per cent of the housing stock in 1965 had been built before 1919. Homelessness was a serious and growing problem in the 1960s. In 1967 the Department of Health and Social Security reported 4,805 homeless families in England and Wales. This figure refers to those who, on application, had been admitted to temporary local authority accommodation. In 1970 over 25,000 families applied for such accommodation and 6,220 were admitted (Raynon and Horden 1973, quoting the Harrison report 1971).

The constraints on the provision of new housing in the cities were not only economic. These constraints were clear enough, a combination of restricted public finance and escalating land values driven hard by property speculation. But they were also political. The housing shortage was overwhelmingly an urban phenomenon of the big cities. Local authorities in rural areas or green belt areas were unwilling to release land for the housing of city dwellers, so the cities were compelled to solve their own problems. The solutions took the form of slum clearance and the high rise flat (Dunleavy 1981).

The high rise flat was, as Dunleavy has demonstrated, a technological solution to a social problem, a short cut to social change. It was a solution promoted by the big building companies, local authority planners and architects and, for a while, a solution enthusiastically embraced by politicians. Between 1955 and 1975 nearly 440,000 high rise flats were built, mainly in

inner urban areas and housing people cleared from slum accommodation. The boom in such building was short-lived but by
1966 the high rise flat accounted for 26 per cent of public
housing approvals.

The effects of such building on the urban landscape of Britain
were dramatic. What is not so clear are the longer-term
consequences on the lives and communities of those who were
compelled to live in them. Dunleavy's review of some of the
research into tenants' attitudes indicated in the late 1960s a low
level of dissatisfaction with their flats. On the other hand,
people expressed concern about the appearance of their estates,
rising levels of crime and worries about the safety of children.
'Loneliness', Dunleavy reported, 'and social isolation are
perhaps the most frequently cited adverse aspects of high-flat
life' (1981:98).

For those who remained in the slums, the compounded
difficulties of poverty and poor housing remained. The social
research of the late 1960s, inspired by a shift in government
policies towards urban renewal, focused increasingly on the
character of social relations in the inner city. What that research
revealed was a world of poverty and hopelessness and damaged
lives, a landscape of unrelieved deprivation in the midst of the
affluent society.

The classic study of that landscape was conducted in the St
Ann's district of Nottingham by Ken Coates and Richard
Silburn (1973). Working with a group of students in a Workers'
Educational Association study group, they charted the poverty
and poor housing of this district of the city. Their claim was that
37 per cent of households were living below the poverty line.
Retirement pensioners, low income families, single parent families and the unemployed were its main victims. What the
research showed was a sharp contrast between the attitudes
towards the poor of those who were reasonably well off and the
experience of the poor themselves. What they have to say on
this matter reveals the subtle contours of suspicion and resentment and tolerance which are also part of a class-divided
society.

The researchers noted, for instance, that:

Since our interest in family poverty first started to attract local attention, we have received dozens of letters, not all from callous people, telling us that we were mistaken. 'Go to the Bingo Halls' we have been told. 'Look at the pubs; they're always full!' someone recently wrote to the local newspaper. 'They spend their family allowances on drink and betting', said a caucus of staid ladies at a Townswomen's Guild meeting which invited one of us to give a talk. (1973:69)

The reality, of course, was different. The research revealed poverty and overcrowding and very poor housing standards. It meant for housewives domestic labour which was unremitting and stark in its drudgery. Overcrowding and poor sound insulation encouraged feelings of annoyance, 'jealous resentment' and 'a dumb but potent hostility' towards neighbours (1973:107). People who lived in St Ann's reported a strong feeling that their area had declined; they resented newcomers, some of whom were black immigrants, and the people they described as 'problem families' whom they felt the local authority was dumping on them. Residents expressed real fears about crime, teenage vandalism, noise and friction between neighbours.

In such circumstances children are damaged and handicapped in their education and suffer high levels of emotional disturbance. St Ann's was an educational priority area with very low levels of educational achievement. Parents and children had to bear the burden of stigma attached to people who lived in the district. In a society in which many felt their living standards had never been higher – the affluent society – people in poverty felt rejected, isolated and unacknowledged; theirs was a world of stress, indignity and lonely bitterness. In addition to being poorly housed and on low incomes people in St Ann's suffered higher levels of illness and of infant mortality.

Despite their problems, the people of St Ann's were politically apathetic. Only about one fifth of those employed were members of trades unions compared to a national figure of about 50 per cent. Interest in politics was low and most people looked to private solutions to their immediate problems. For Coates and Silburn, the main problems in St Ann's were those of, on the one hand, a relentless loss of dignity and pride, which is how deprivation affects people, and, on the other, the way the problems of the poor are simply not understood by the better off. 'Not only', commented Coates and Silburn, 'do people not know how the other half lives: they scarcely know that the other half exists' (1973:129). Only an effective policy to combat poverty, they argued, could change the lot of the people of St Ann's.

A key element of social policy at the time was the idea of area-based solutions to poverty. This emerged in the context of housing policies in the notion of the General Improvement Area and, later, the Housing Action Area. In educational policy the guiding idea, defined by the Plowden report of 1967, was that of the educational priority area in which special support would be provided for schools in socially deprived districts (Central Advisory Council for Education 1967).

Too often, however, the policy cures, especially in housing, created problems worse than those they were designed to solve. The wholesale redevelopment of inner urban communities was often carried out insensitively. 'Planner's blight' became a real problem in many communities, as did frustration at the overlapping ineffectiveness of diverse government departments, local authorities and voluntary bodies trying to focus their efforts in areas which lacked any coherent political focus (Dennis 1972; Midwinter 1972). What people who lived in inner urban areas experienced was accelerated change, often inflicted on them by planners, and always managed by an array of social workers, probation officers, community service volunteers, juvenile liaison officers, health visitors and other professionals strongly possessed of a professional ideology which placed a premium on ideas of community development and involvement. Eric Midwinter noted the effects of all this in the inner areas of Liverpool, where he directed the educational priority research project (1972). What he described there was a 'dislocated community', with a high incidence of social malaise and very low levels of educational attainment.

His comments on the life of Liverpool 7 and Liverpool 8 are worth recording, for they indicate that under conditions of turmoil and deprivation many people simply cannot cope. Midwinter noted that the anti-authority attitude of many in the area was probably motivated by a strong sense of loss of community. 'But', he wrote, 'infinitely sadder than any vandalism or small-scale crime, was the resignation of those who found themselves unable to cope':

Ground down by the ceaseless difficulties facing them, they had no longer even the boot-straps by which to haul themselves up. No glib half-truths about laziness or working harder sprang to mind; rather it was a case of there but for the grace of God. (1972:44)

The scene described by Midwinter in Liverpool had its parallels in other educational priority areas, and the attitudes and feelings which accompanied the poverty and deprivation described in Nottingham and Liverpool existed too in all other big cities (Halsey 1972a). The urban poor were, in very direct ways, bearing the costs of both the restructuring of the British economy and the rebuilding of the cities. It was part of their condition that they lacked the means to exert any effective influence on the political system which shaped their lives. The failures of both the Labour Party and the trades unions to build strong support among the communities of the inner city had their counterpart in widespread feelings in these areas that politicians were not to be trusted and in any case did not care what happened to the people who lived in places like Liverpool 8 or St Ann's. It is hardly surprising, therefore, that apathy and resignation, coupled with a sense of loss and fear for the future, especially among older residents, were prevalent attitudes among the urban poor.

In 1967, 27.1 per cent of households occupied dwellings owned by local authorities or new town corporations. Fifty per cent of those houses had been built after World War II, defining that distinctive feature of Britain's urban landscape: the council estate. Sid Chaplin, a writer and novelist from the north east of England, commented in 1964 that: 'Those millions in Coronation Streets and multi-storey flats and council estates constitute a great unexplored continent as far as fiction is concerned', and he wondered about how well old working class values would stand up to city life. 'What', he asked, 'will wither and die and what, on the other hand will flower? How will the individual stand up to it?' (1987:179–80).

What was true for fiction was less true for social science; the housing estate had been researched by the Institute of Community Studies and by social researchers (such as Willmott 1963; Jennings 1962; Elias and Scotson 1965). The attitudes and values to be found in working class housing areas were also the subject of comment by social observers and critics (such as Jackson 1968; Seabrook 1975). The picture to emerge from this work is a mixed one. Post-war affluence was something enjoyed by working class people and steady improvements in housing standards were part of it. But there is also evidence of a growing perception of loss among working people of a sense of community, of a pervasive feeling of isolation and loneliness and of an anxiety about personal safety and the quality of life on the estates.

The sociological answer to Sid Chaplin is that what flowered among working class communities were the values of private affluence and home-centredness. Willmott reported, in his study of Dagenham, the social contours of a maturing community in which patterns of friendship were intensely localized and in which social differences of a very subtle kind had stabilized. Political loyalties on the estate were still to the Labour Party but political interest and involvement were low. The prevailing social norms legitimated conformity to the life-styles of the estate and Willmott detected here one of the reasons why, in such a one-class area, children were not encouraged in the community to higher levels of achievement in school (1963:117).

Hilda Jennings noted in her study of the Barton Hill housing estate in Bristol that residents did not feel as strong a sense of belonging to the place as they had done in the older area from which they had been rehoused (1962). With few shops and pubs and, therefore, fewer opportunities for informal social contacts, there emerged in Barton Hill the 'isolated one generation family' and housewives reported a strong sense of loneliness (1962:221).

Sid Chaplin had asked: 'What will wither?'. Some of the contemporary critics would have answered unequivocally that it was the working class community which came under threat. Brian Jackson argued in 1968 that 'the habit of valuing people rather than concepts, and directness of emotional response are probably the main qualities that a civilized society should try to take over from working-class life' (1968:169). Reflecting, however, on his cultural journeys to his native Huddersfield, he found in the late 1960s a suspicion of the new, a scepticism about politicians and the police and a deep ambivalence about immigrants.

Jackson's case is that rehousing and planning and the rise of mass markets had all combined to transform working class life-styles and attitudes, and much of this had not sustained what was best in working class culture. Jeremy Seabrook put the same argument in a stronger form. Reflecting on the council estates of Blackburn – 'sweeping vistas of disfigured concrete', he called them, 'constructed with the greatest parsimony of compassion and amenity' – he claimed forcibly that, as human settlements, they 'invite violence and negation' (1975:236). The best that could be expected from people compelled to live there, he claimed, was 'a sullen and passive indifference' as the only manageable response to the economic decline and bleak materialism of their world.

Writers like Seabrook and Jackson were working within a framework of concern about the character of working class life which Richard Hoggart had pioneered in the 1950s. Their work can itself be seen as a reflection of a structure of feeling among a new generation of post-war writers, whose own personal and social roots were in the working class, but whose education and employment had taken them away from those roots. Deeply attached to what they felt were the best traditions of the working class, they despaired at the way in which affluence and materialism had blunted the vision of a better society among working class people and their leaders.

The concern they had with the changing values of working class life was part of a much more fundamental debate about the nature of modern industrial society which raged in the 1960s across the continents of a shrinking world. The themes of those debates are complex and varied but come together in a general mood of radical anger and optimism, which are lodged in historical memory as the expressive revolution of the 1960s, with the year 1968 as its great symbol. Those debates in Britain fashioned and legitimated areas and styles of political discourse and struggle of a distinctly radical kind which continue to influence the political agendas of British society. These debates are enmeshed with, and define changes in, underlying structures of feeling in the society. They ran well ahead of, and were opposed to, the corporatist politics of the period. The searching out and definition of different values to guide how people should live their lives reflected longer-term changes in the structure of the society and the distribution of power within it.

The personal and the political

The social and political forms of post-war Britain can be explained and understood as a series of compromises in the historic struggle between the forces of capital and labour. The agencies of that struggle – private companies, the state, the trades union movement, the political parties – each contributed something distinctive to the way it developed and to its outcomes. In the 1960s the political and ideological initiative, though not, in retrospect, the power, was seized outside the formal institutions of political and industrial life. Among the educated young, the supporters of the women's movement, the New Left, the 'underground' in the arts and the gay population, an interest grew – some might say, exploded – in alternative life-styles and radical political change. Those directly involved discovered new forms of political activity and experienced profound changes in their personal relationships and forms of self awareness. It was a period in which many people found new 'resources of hope' for themselves and their society (R. Williams 1983). But it was also a period in which, as Robert Hewison has so rightly pointed out, a right-wing counter-revolution took place which was to prove much more consequential for the future shape of Britain (1986).

The distinctive feature of late 1960s protest and radicalism was its internationalism. The civil rights movement in America had its supporters in Europe who linked it with the struggles of all oppressed people in the Third World. Vietnam, of course, pricked the liberal conscience everywhere and stirred among the young in particular a powerful feeling of disgust at the moral bankruptcy not just of America, but of capitalist society itself. The hippies of San Francisco had their supporters throughout the developed world exploring the outlines of a new kind of politics to realize new forms of freedom. Che Guevara, Angela Davis, Herbert Marcuse, R.D. Laing were among the political and intellectual icons of the radicals, symbols of Third World liberation, civil rights and sexual liberation. The contours of radical consciousness were further mapped out by the New Left's rediscovery of Antonio Gramsci and Rosa Luxemburg. The family and the media and the state were all subjects of radical 'critique'.

The various strands of radical theory and practice found new forms for their political work in the teach-in, the 'sit-in', the workshop, street theatre, surrealist art and humour, jazz-and-poetry readings, art 'happenings', the pop festival and the commune. The politics of commitment and opposition to authority, the celebration of the personal, were key elements in the whole radical *Weltanschauung*. Woven through the motifs of this cultural collage of new symbols and meanings were the smells and tastes of marijuana and the psychedelic imagery of LSD, the sounds of Bob Dylan, the Beatles and the Rolling Stones. It was the era of the 'dialectics of liberation', of the *Oz* trial, Mary Quant and 'swinging London'. It was the time of the student movement and the anti-Vietnam War demonstrations. The *'événements'* in Paris in 1968 provide some of the most potent historical images of that period.

Among the young, particularly among the educated in higher education, it was a period of considerable hope and optimism. Against the background of the Vietnam War, the shootings on the Kent State campus, a growing mistrust of bureaucratized

socialism of the kind that crushed the reform movement of the
'Prague Spring' in Czechoslovakia, students throughout Europe
fashioned for themselves a new image. It was that of the
intellectual worker destined for the bureaucracies of modern
capitalism. Seeing themselves in this way it was a short step to
believing that their interests and those of the industrial proleta-
riat were identical and that a joining of forces with the labour
movement could lead to the revolutionary overthrow of capitalism. This perspective led many to feel disillusioned with the
traditional parties of the Left, which were seen to be too deeply
incorporated into the apparatus of the repressive state (Crouch
1970).

The criticisms of the radical students were directed as well at
the institutions in which they were being taught. Miss Norris, a
Birmingham delegate to the 1972 conference of the National
Union of Students, can be cited as a good illustration of this. A
young woman, veteran of the Birmingham sit-in, she pointed
out that they were all assembled near the Chamberlain tower of
the university ('Chamberlain's last erection', as she described it)
and went on to say:

Here we are surrounded by the trappings of the system we are trying
to defeat . . . We have a palatial sports centre, an extensive library, well
equipped health centre, luxurious halls of residence and adequate
catering facilities at our disposal. We are also in Birmingham. No-
where else in the country is there such a collection of narrow-minded,
prudish, penny-pinching self-interested, reactionary Tory councillors
. . . Birmingham . . . owns slums that are described as the worst in
England . . . It has no plans for comprehensive education . . . Its policy
for union provision in F.E. colleges is absolutely appalling. (Quoted
B. Williamson 1984:260)

The tone is radical and committed, just as her student colleagues
at the London School of Economics had been four years
previously over the plight of the African working class at
Rhodesian independence.

The German sociologist, Jurgen Habermas, characterized the
student revolt in Germany as 'the first bourgeois revolt against
the principles of a bourgeois society' (1968:28). What he said

about German students fits the experience and feelings of many in Britain. Students, an essentially middle class group, had become

sensitive to the costs for individual development of a society dominated by competition for status and achievement and by the bureaucratisation of all regions of life. These costs seem to them disproportionately high in relation to the technological potential. The young have become very sensitive to the dangers of an order that does not avert aggression but increases risks on a planetary scale and creates the modern pauperism of the Third World. (1968:29)

The fate of the student movement ought properly to be the subject of another study; perhaps Trevor Fisk's judgement of it in 1970 has now to be accepted, although it was given then rather sulkily by someone who had been one of the moderate leaders of the National Union of Students and who had been overtaken by the radicals (1970). What he said was that student demands about welfare and discipline and for improvements in the quality of their courses would be far more significant in the long term than the minority advocacy of radical political views.

From within this same radical matrix came the women's movement, although even as late as 1970 the special problems faced by women in a male-dominated world were not widely recognized. The book by Crick and Robson which, in 1970, set out to chart the varieties of protest movements in modern Britain made no reference at all to women (1970). This was not surprising. Even those who were to become closely identified with the women's movement were not fully conscious of it till some time later. Ann Oakley, for instance, reflecting on her life in the late sixties as an educated but depressed young housewife, commented:

This was 1967 and 1968 and 1969 – the era before the women's movement. There was not even a murmur of feminism in English suburbia at that time; there may have been voices of dissent, but what they were dissenting about was a problem they couldn't name, '. . . a strange stirring, a sense of dissatisfaction, a yearning'; guilt, anger, loneliness, frustration, the dehumanization of women, their forfeited selves. (1984:70)

The quotation she used came from Betty Friedan's *The Feminine Mystique*, one of the classic texts of modern feminism published in America in the early 1960s. But it was not a well-known text in Britain until 1967 or 1968. Some writers, with Juliet Mitchell being, perhaps, the most important, were working out the terms of a radical feminism in the mid 1960s (1971). In so doing they brought into the political realm issues like the employment conditions of women, family life, sexuality, child rearing and patriarchy and demonstrated how these issues had been largely neglected by the labour movement and conventional modes of political discourse.

The women's movement developed in Britain through forms of political action and debate very different to those of conventional political parties. Women's groups came together briefly in a national conference in 1970, following on from a women's history workshop at Ruskin College, and for a while the National Co-ordinating Committee provided some national focus for the discussion of feminism. But the movement was too diverse in its aims and ideological commitments to hang together in a national organization. In any case, many women were attracted to women's groups precisely because they were non-authoritarian, structureless and built around immediate personal concerns faced by their members as women. These issues covered sexuality, child care, nursery schools and problems of housing and welfare benefits and women's health. They took seriously that radical stream of thought stressing that the personal was political. Through that, many women were led to a new understanding of themselves, and of the nature of the family in which many had been encouraged to believe their destiny lay.

The experience of involvement in the nascent women's movement was transformative. Elizabeth Wilson recounts in her autobiography, *Mirror Writing*, that she looks back to herself before the women's movement and cannot recognize the person she sees, that 'solemn girl of the 1950s and the enamelled butterfly of the 60s' (1982:2). Mary Ingham, reflecting on the weight of assumptions which in the early 1960s impelled girls into marriage, wrote about herself:

I suffered from the socially transmitted disease of conditioned helplessness to which my shyness made me particularly susceptible. I had been relieved that being a girl I would never get into fights and growing up as a woman I was deluded into the belief that staying inside a safe world would be a solution to my lack of self assertion. (1981:124)

The women's movement, however, as she notes later, helped her and many like her through this: 'it contradicted', she wrote, 'all the messages of failure flashing around us' (1981:170). It helped her, she now believes, to cultivate assertiveness and weed out her shyness and assured her that her achievements mattered.

Ann Oakley has argued that what involvement in the women's movement did for her was demonstrate the essential humanity of women, when she had previously seen them in an entirely sexist way herself. Through contact with other women she learned that her own uncomfortable experiences as a daughter, wife and mother were not hers alone. To have heard others, reflecting on their experience, reveal something of her own, was for her both a comforting and liberating experience (1984:77). The movement, she feels, quite literally changed her life.

There is a real sense in which it changed society, too. But that part of the story comes later. In the late 1960s and early 1970s the women's movement, despite connections many of its adherents had attempted to make with ordinary working class women (as, for example, during the struggles of the women workers at the Ford Motor Company for equal pay with men), remained a movement of the educated and largely of the young. Their commitment was not to the closed emotional world of the family. They sought to widen women's involvement in the public sphere and promote equal rights at work. They developed a vocabulary of protest and motive which allowed them to see their world, and themselves, in a new light.

The majority of women, however, particularly from the working class, gained little access to the new concepts. Denied through their education any real opportunity to understand their world outside the constraints and identities of their roles as wives, mothers, workers or schoolgirls, they coped with change within the resources of their experience and power. Both were changing; abortion law reform in 1967, the 1969 Divorce Act, the Equal Pay Act of 1970 were tentative steps on the legislative way to extending the rights of women in marriage and work. But the structured inequalities of the labour market, which kept women out of senior positions in employment and in part-time and low paid work, and patriarchal relations in the family, which constrained their domestic roles, still framed the experience of most women. The climate for discussing these issues, however, had unalterably changed, opening up a range of new identities for women.

Conclusion

The period of the late 1960s in Britain is, twenty years later, undergoing historical reassessment. 'Far from representing a transcending of capitalism (as some of Labour's fun-loving theorists were pleased to claim)', write Blackwell and Seabrook, 'the 1960s witnessed its extension into areas in which it had previously had no business' (1985:112). Their thesis is that 'it is now almost impossible to disentangle the energies of the counter-culture from its stupidities' (1985:127). The problem in doing so is that 'what was seen as rampant individualism and bizarre self-indulgence in the flower children had its counterpart in that vast merchandizing of goods and services which encouraged a whole society to dress up and play' (1985:127). Capitalism, then, cashed in on the search for individuality, authenticity and self expression.

The case is arguable and the fact that it is being argued at all is evidence of a continuing concern with the cultural forms and economic viability of advanced capitalism. In the late 1960s there was a prevalent mood that the economic growth of the post-war period was sustainable and that the aspirations it sustained would be endlessly realizable. Those closer to the economic realities of Britain knew different. Britain in the late 1960s was a society with an economy in serious trouble.

The story of the economy and, indeed, of the crises of the political system during this period is a tangled one to tell. A detailed account would trace out the way in which the long post-war boom in the international economy drew to a close. This exposed underlying weaknesses in the British economy which showed up in the indicators of a worsening balance of payments, over-valued currency, low productivity, falling profits, declining share of world trade, rising unemployment and inflation. None of these problems was remedied by the policies on prices and wages or sterling or towards industry.

The Conservative government under Edward Heath which succeeded Harold Wilson's Labour government in 1970 fared little better. Both governments struggled with the uncertainties of an increasingly unstable international situation in the Far East and in the Middle East following the Arab–Israeli war. Both governments were caught in the traps of a poor economic record, rising inflation, industrial conflict and political factionalism of a kind suggesting a loss of legitimacy of the British state itself. Both the main political parties lost electoral ground during this period to the Scottish and Welsh Nationalists. Both struggled fruitlessly with the escalating crisis of Northern Ireland and both had failed to solve the problems of conflict in British industrial relations. Both Wilson and Heath found themselves in a setting of rising expectations for increased incomes and the freedoms they would buy, which was coupled with a growing disillusionment about the capacity of politicians to deliver such hopes (Leys 1989; Sked and Cook 1979). The percentage of the electorate voting in general elections fell from 67.4 per cent in 1964 to 54.9 per cent in 1974, with each of the major parties losing votes.

The underlying problem was perhaps this: the political system of the country had become corporatist in character and incapable of solving creatively the problems of the economy. Those problems were entrenched in a class structure, and a history, which sustained attitudes and values of a kind which inhibited significant economic change and which focused conflicts in those areas of the economy most vulnerable to economic competition – the mines, the docks and manufacturing industry – and held back the longer-term improvements in education, research and development upon which any modern economy ultimately depends.

The outcome in terms of attitudes and values throughout the society was to privilege materialism and individualism and to attach inordinate importance to short-term measures of economic success. Changes in the class system, through education and alterations in the structure of employment, including the growth of public sector employment, had opened up opportunities for the socially mobile, middle class professionals and the well off, of a sort which confirmed for most of them a powerful sense of well-being. It left space for the radicalism of thought and feeling which has become something of a hallmark of the 1960s. For working class people in the factories and the pits the period has a bleaker aspect. For the urban poor, those who lived in the inner city – especially those from the ethnic minorities – the story was one of neglect, marginality and despair.

Seen in this light the radicalism of the period has to be interpreted as evidence of the failure of the consensus policies of the post-war years to cope adequately with the circumstances of a changing society in a rapidly shrinking world. The 1960s came to an end in 1973 with the rise in the price of OPEC oil. The naive optimism of the post-war boom gave way to a gloomier outlook. The story after that, as we shall see, is one of increasing ideological polarization in British society and a deepening sense of crisis.

7
Decline and Division

The period discussed in this chapter covers the time from the downfall of the Conservative government of Edward Heath in 1974 to the early months of 1982, before the outbreak of war with Argentina over the Falkland Islands. The thrust of the argument developed here is this: during this period the post-war consensus finally broke down. Corporatist solutions to Britain's economic problems were tried and failed and British political debate became overtly and thoroughly ideological. What became known as 'the New Right' made the ideological running and defined a political agenda for the radical change not only of economic policies but of social institutions and attitudes as well.

Such an interpretation is hardly novel. The central claim in this chapter, however, is that the political success of what has since come to be known as 'Thatcherism' is not the consequence of the political effectiveness of one faction of modern Toryism. That is part of it; but that success is symptomatic of something else – of change in the social structure of the society and in prevailing attitudes, values and feelings. British society produced Thatcherism just as much as Thatcherism changed British society. These changes are part of the way in which different groups of people, each responding to altered circumstances in the economy and the political system, acted to promote their interests, achieve their goals, and legitimate their claims for the recognition of others.

The social and political conflicts involved in all this occurred throughout the society. They can be seen in the arenas of industrial relations, taxation policy, social policy and the inner cities. They were reported and mulled over by a thoroughly biased mass media. They were fuelled by middle class resentment about trades unions, about workers' fears of inflation and hostility to the state's regulation of the economy. They centred on incomes policy, education – particularly the questions of discipline and standards in school – the inner cities and economic decline: they were focused sharply on the rights of women and the problems of unemployed youth, particularly from ethnic minorities. During the 1970s these issues were bound up with the general question of Britain's changing role in the world as a nuclear power and member of the European Economic Community.

The underlying structural problem, addressed in very different ways by writers and politicians from different points on an increasingly polarized ideological spectrum, was economic decline, and how it could be halted and reversed. The fracture lines of those debates followed closely the contours of social differentiation in the society. It is in the experience of blighted hopes, high expectations and the mutual resentments of an increasingly unequal society that the political struggles over the management of decline have to be located.

The political psychology of economic decline

The economic decline of Britain was clear enough despite the fact that during the period when public awareness of it was at its height living standards had never been higher. The problem of decline was, and remains, relative. Compared to Britain's major industrial competitors during this period, British economic growth was slow (Gamble 1981). Britain's share of world manufacturing output dropped from 9.0 per cent in 1960 to 5.8 per cent in 1975, and British productivity and levels of investment in manufacturing industry were among the lowest in the industrialized nations. Had it not been for the exploitation of the North Sea oil fields, the British economy in the 1970s would have been in a state of serious collapse.

The effects were clear: unemployment increased steadily during the 1970s. So, too, did inflation – reaching double figures between 1974 and 1977 (Gamble 1981:22). Between 1966 and 1981 employment in manufacturing industry fell by 34.1 per

cent, prompting a serious debate among politicians and eco-
nomists about the deindustrialization of the British economy
(K. Smith 1984). What emerged in the context of these discussions, from both ends of the political spectrum, was a heightened sense of crisis in the economic and political structure of the
society for which only radical solutions, it was widely believed,
were a serious option (Kumar 1988:292).

The implications of the economic crisis and the political
responses to it varied considerably for different groups in the
society. For working class people generally, but particularly
those who worked in the traditional heavy and manufacturing
industries, like steel and shipbuilding, this was a period of job
losses and terrible uncertainty. For those who became unemployed, it was a time of considerable hardship. Among women,
among the ethnic minorities and particularly among the young,
the crisis was experienced directly in the market for labour. In a
society which places such a high premium on employment, to
be unemployed, as will be seen, is to suffer a special kind of
pain.

The experience of workers in the older industries is inseparable from the way in which British capitalists, as well as the
nationalized industries, sought to rationalize their holdings and
their businesses. Modern capitalist economies are organized
internationally to secure maximum returns on invested capital.
The economic history of capital during the late 1960s and 1970s
is dominated by centralization and concentration and by a
widening field of international operation.

Between 1950 and 1970, in a process catalysed by the merger
and the takeover bid, the proportion of manufacturing industry
output accounted for by the top 100 companies increased from
21 per cent to 40 per cent (L. Harris 1985:24). A further thread
in that history is of attempts to achieve industrial change – in
technology, investment and efficiency, through state involvement in big industry by way of nationalization and bodies like
the National Economic Development Council and the National
Enterprise Board. The Labour government of 1974–9 believed
in the importance of working co-operatively with capital
through planning agreements, and with trades unions through

incomes policy, as a way of managing the economy in a counter-cyclical way to achieve steady growth.

The relevance of this to the experience of working class people is this: they had to bear directly the costs of restructuring British industry. It was they who had to cope directly with unemployment, redundancy, the rationalization of their work and increased productivity. The history of how that happened is one in which the values and experiences and self perceptions of working people were threatened and transformed. It was a process involving much conflict, much change, and much bitterness and anxiety. And many groups of workers interpreted what was happening to them in a way which echoed strongly the rhetorics of class conflict, which were still part of the political memory and traditions of Labour in this country. This, as will be seen, was particularly true of traditionally proletarian groups like miners. But the same sentiments were found in the docks, in heavy engineering, in vehicle manufacture and among unskilled manual workers.

Modern capitalism is a form of society most unlikely to fall apart in a paroxysm of revolutionary class conflict. It is much more likely to contain its contradictions by localizing its deprivations and by exporting its poverty overseas. One of the great tragedies of the 1970s is that resentment about economic decline on the part of employed or redundant working people was refocused, not on the inequities of the capitalist system itself, but on the poor or the ethnic minorities of British society. It was a response upon which the radical Right could capitalize, in the way it was able to attack the social foundations of that great post-war achievement, the welfare state.

The historical social psychology of this has been clearly set out by Zygmunt Bauman (1982). Building on Max Scheler's classical sociological account of *'ressentiment'* – an attitude built up of repressed feelings of hatred, envy and revenge which are refocused as *Schadenfreude* or malice – Bauman has explained why the failure of the economy to grow results in disappointment and anger of a kind which breeds, not a desire to change the world, but a sense of impotence and passivity. At its simplest the argument is this: growth feeds optimism, and in the consumer society of modern capitalism, self respect is equated with ever higher levels of material possession. Loss of growth breeds resentment. Workers in these conditions seek to protect differentials and puny privileges. Protecting the value of individual wage packets comes to be seen as more desirable than ensuring that social wages or goods of collective consumption – health, education, etc. – will be safeguarded. The result is that the poor and dependent are both neglected and resented as inflationary pressures increase.

Bauman put it this way: 'When global output is falling, unemployment rising and prospects of general improvement fading, group advantages seem a more rational strategy than solidarity with the underdog . . . Guarding one's position in the pecking order may become the supreme rationality, complete with its reverse side: devil take the hindmost' (1982:184). It was precisely this feeling that fed the politics of the radical Right in Britain in the 1970s.

If the underlying structures of feeling – differently expressed by different classes in the society – were characterized as resentments about decline, the overt political problems to which they gave expression and focus were set out as the constitutional question: 'Who runs the country?' This was the question the Conservatives put to the electorate in 1974 following Ted Heath's failure to bring inflation under control, achieve growth and bring order to industrial relations.

The Conservative government of Edward Heath came to power in 1970 with an agenda to reform industrial relations, cut public expenditure and improve the machinery of government. Dogged from the beginning by recession, low growth and rising unemployment, declining external balance and inflation, the government found itself by 1972 in the midst of a sterling crisis. It was a crisis made worse by accumulating difficulties with industrial policy and particularly industrial relations. The Upper Clyde Ship Builders workers led by Jimmy Reid had staged their successful 'sit-in' to save the yard. Rolls-Royce, contrary to the government's policy of not bailing out 'lame ducks', was bailed out. Political struggles over the Conservatives' Industrial Relations Act of 1971 became very bitter. The 1972 strike of miners, with the new weapons of mass picketing and 'flying pickets' and sympathy action by other workers, all contributed to a general public climate of disillusion about the British economy and considerable hostility towards trades unionism.

The political crunch for Edward Heath came in the context of his government's unsuccessful bid to hold a firm line on incomes policy. The decisive battle came once again with the miners. They were determined to cash in on their strengthened bargaining position following the Yom Kippur war – which threatened an oil shortage – to recover, as they saw it, ground they had lost in relation to other groups of workers. Heath imposed a state of emergency and, in the new year of 1974, a three-day working week to conserve energy. The mood among miners was militant. For many miners the struggle with the government was resonant with memories, handed down to them by their parents, of the great struggles of the inter-war years. Their post-war memories were of a steady rundown of the industry from 700,000 men in 1957 to 390,000 by 1972, with great social cost to the mining communities (R. Taylor 1978:359). Class conflict provided the template with which many ordered their experience of this, and their determination to breach the rigid constraints of Heath's pay policies brought the government down.

The Conservative government was replaced in 1974 by a minority Labour government, which strengthened its position at a second general election in October of that year. Heath's leadership of the Tory Party was conceded to Margaret Thatcher, who represented a different and radically right-wing strand of British Toryism. This was the moment when the post-war consensus finally came to an end; the *coup de grâce* was delivered in 1979 when a new Tory government came to power following the 'Winter of Discontent'.

The experience of workers during this period of Labour government up to the general election of 1979 is framed by a growing militancy among those organized into unions. For others, particularly the young, it was of unemployment; for those from ethnic minority backgrounds, it was of a growing awareness and experience of racial discrimination. For women workers, despite the Equal Pay Act of 1975, the experience of work was still one of discrimination and of blocked opportunities. And for a growing number of people outside the labour market altogether – pensioners, the long-term sick, the unemployed, single parent families with children – these were years of deepening poverty.

The militancy of organized labour, as might be expected, did not breed solidarity among different groups of workers. It bred a determination among some groups – the well organized – to press their claims at all costs. The full history of the wage bargaining, and of the incomes policies of the government to contain settlements within limits they believed the economy could afford, cannot be recounted here. It is interesting to note, however, that both from the Right and the Left of the Labour political spectrum, this period was seen, despite the militancy, as an essentially divisive one.

An early assessment came in 1978 at the Labour Party Annual Conference when Sid Weighell, leader of the railwaymen and acknowledged as a right-wing union leader, spoke out against inflationary wage claims and what he regarded as irresponsible collective bargaining. 'My union', he said,

helped create this party ... I am not going to stand here and destroy it. But if you want the call to go out at this conference that the new philosophy of the Labour Party is that you believe in the policy of the pig trough – those with the biggest snout get the biggest share – I reject it. (Quoted Whitehead 1986:279)

In his Marx Memorial lecture of the same year, Professor Hobsbawm, Marxist historian of the labour movement, wondered whether the 'forward march' of labour had been halted. His point was that the labour movement had not been able to unite different groups of workers into a common consciousness and that militant trades unionism of a sectional kind had actually 'set workers against each other rather than establish wider patterns of solidarity' (1989b:21).

For Hobsbawm the problem was essentially one of leadership. He was perfectly right in this: workers organized to achieve high wages, to enable them to buy the goods capitalists want to sell them, will almost certainly elect leaders who will agree with them. It is an entirely different matter, however, whether those workers will achieve the good life to which they aspire. Britain in the 1970s was a country in acute economic difficulties in which different industries, through job loss and rationalization, sought to modernize and compete more effectively. The embattled class consciousness of some groups of workers did not lead them to a stronger sense of solidarity with fellow workers, but to resentment, especially towards those unemployed.

The logic of resentment is well explained in a sympathetic study of workers in the modern process plants of the chemical industry in the 1970s (Nichols and Beynon 1977). Central to their interpretation of what the chemical workers told them about their work and their attitudes to the unemployed is the notion of sacrifice. The only way the workers, all men, could make sense of their hard, monotonous work was to see it as a personal sacrifice to ensure that something else should be gained for their wives and their children. 'It is only through sacrifice', they write, 'that a wasted life has value' (1977:194). So far so good: the problem comes when the chemical workers have to make sense of the unemployed. Here Nichols and Beynon encountered resentment; the workers frequently referred to the laziness of men on the dole. One worker told them:

There was a bloke who used to live in our street back home and he never worked. Well he worked down the pit once but all the time I knew him he never worked. But you know, he always had a roll of fivers in his pocket. I couldn't do that. In fact it drives me wild. Those buggers with a lazy bone lying around when they are fit to work. (1977:196)

The archetypal 'doley' was perceived by a large proportion of the men in the ChemCo plant being studied as a malingerer being well kept by the state. Another man told the researchers:

A chap who doesn't work! I would sort him out. I would literally see him starve. I would step over him starving in the gutter . . . Whereas perhaps a year ago I would have said: 'Oh well, give it to them.' But now it's got to the point where there are so many of them and they go around openly boasting that they do not work. (1977:198)

The researchers' interpretation of the 'doley myth' is that unemployment, insofar as it entails some men not working for their livelihood, makes an open mockery of the prevailing ideology of sacrifice, making it appear worthless, as if the working men's working life actually was a farce. Their work was meaningless to them, merely a means to end; but it was the very meaninglessness of it which justified the ends they sought. The worker relieved of the immediate necessity of work represented, so the researchers claim, a real threat to the self respect of those employed.

This same underlying attitude explains much of the behaviour of industrial workers in the modern world. They seek by all means to defend their jobs and keep their employment. During the 1970s this took the form of sit-ins and attempts to form co-operatives and well-orchestrated efforts to resist plant closures through, for example, workers' combines, such as the one which developed in Vickers Ltd as the National Shop Stewards Combine Committee (Beynon and Wainright 1979). The paradox, of course, is that workers organized themselves in a period of crisis to defend jobs which they, by and large, detested. The rationale, also of course, was to save something for the children. One Tyneside worker active in the combine committee told Beynon and Wainright:

That's what I'm doing all this for. Not necessarily for me but for my children and my grandchildren. It's important that we provide some sort of future for them: a future that is better than what we've had. As far as I can see at the moment there's going to be no bloody jobs. That's how I look at it. (1979:179)

The tragedy was that workers' organizations were outflanked by the far superior international organization of business and capital and that trades unionism had failed substantially to embrace groups in the society who were not in employment. Indeed, trades unions were themselves widely resented as being part of the problem their actions were designed to solve. They were too easily criticized for their resistance to change, their restrictive practices and their unwillingness to co-operate effectively with managements to achieve change and higher productivity. Conservatives were emphatic on this point. Sir Keith Joseph, one of the intellectual architects of the New Right's political and economic strategies, declared forcibly in 1979: 'We see the power of trades unions and the way it is used as one of the major obstacles barring the road to national recovery' (1986:98).

Looked at differently, the failure of trades unions to secure real gains for their members stems not so much from the fact that unions were strong and militant and therefore disrupted industry's capacity to deliver the good life: on the contrary, the unions were too weak to combat the ways in which industry was being rationalized and failed abysmally to do much for those on the periphery of the labour market – the unemployed, the young, ethnic minorities and growing numbers of poorly paid women workers.

They had failed, too, to offset a widespread view that they themselves were the cause of the country's troubles. One public opinion survey, reported in *The Times* in 1978, showed that 82 per cent of adults believed that unions had too much power (Seaton 1986). Television typically portrayed issues of industrial relations as being largely about strikes and portrayed strikes in an entirely negative way. In the 1970s a particularly prominent principle of interpretation of industrial stories on television was to treat inflation as the key issue and to imply that it was invariably caused by illegitimately high wage claims (Glasgow Media Group 1980). The industrial reporting of popular newspapers was dominated by strikes and a potent story line was to link strikes with *agents provocateurs* or Communist conspiracies.

It is difficult to know what importance to attach to such media images. Reviewing the small amount of evidence concerning public images of unions and media coverage of them, Jean Seaton concluded that middle class people were more likely to accept media interpretations of strikes than were working class people (Seaton 1986:284). Middle class women, those most distant from the world of industrial work, were particularly likely to blame strikes on 'greed'.

The social and economic changes of the 1960s and 1970s touched middle class sensibilities in fundamental ways. Many professionals employed in large organizations had lost their traditional autonomy and a growing number of white collar workers had turned to trades unionism. Bechhofer and his colleagues also noted, in their research into the changing social composition of the middle class, that social mobility had undermined something of the social distinctiveness of middle class life-styles (1983). These trends they associated with a growing phenomenon: middle class discontent.

They argued that it was this discontent, rooted in a belief that important social values had been eroded, which explains the growth in the 1970s of significant middle class support for right-wing movements or groups, such as the National Association for Freedom or the National Federation of the Self Employed. Strong middle class support for Thatcherite Toryism was based on support for such values as freedom for the individual, the responsibility of family life, the sovereignty of the market and the inevitability of social inequality.

Bechhofer and his colleagues suggested that many groups of middle class people had come to feel strongly a loss of their social separateness, which was compounded by a sense of growing powerlessness on account of their loss of autonomy and importance in the conduct of public affairs. It amounted, they claim, to a 'feeling of relative deprivation, to the feeling of being overhauled by those who were once unequivocally status inferiors and thereby to a loss of identity' (1983:111). Margaret Thatcher's appeal to prudence, hard work and individualism and her defence of inequality struck many responsive chords among the provincial middle classes.

Those same values were part of a distinctive structure of feeling. It had at its core the idea that all forms of collective provision for need were likely to undermine the responsibility of individuals. Thatcherite theoreticians had identified the welfare state as a socialist invention which privileged those who worked in it rather than those who were meant to benefit from its services (Mishra 1984; Gough 1983). Linked to this was the criticism that it undermined the responsibility of people to look after their own welfare and provide for their own needs. And for Margaret Thatcher, the idea of the welfare state was too closely linked to the idea of equality. 'What', she asked in 1975, 'is it that impels the powerful and the vocal lobby to press for greater equality?' 'Often', she answered, 'the reasons boil down to an undistinguished combination of envy and what might be termed "bourgeois guilt"' (quoted Walker and Walker 1987:10). That greater equality might be a precondition of effective citizenship, in a society which does not let the costs of social change be borne by those least able to bear them, is something lost on those who supported, and continue to support, this particular brand of Toryism.

It is not surprising that, as the sense of economic crisis deepened, the attitude of those on the political Right to the welfare state was critical to the point of hostility. This was the end of the post-war consensus. With economic decline and inflation the enormous diswelfare of growing unemployment became the most obvious symbol of how far the Beveridge welfare state had, indeed, collapsed.

Unemployment

The social scourge of the 1970s was unemployment. In 1971 unemployment stood at less than 3.0 per cent. It climbed to 5.0 per cent in 1979 and to 12.3 per cent in 1983 (*Social Trends* 1988:77). The numbers claiming unemployment benefit went up from 751,000 to 2,917,000. This took place at a time of rising inflation and falling employment in the productive sectors of the economy. Neither Conservative nor Labour governments could find solutions to it. Its roots penetrated deeply the economic and social fabric of the society as a whole.

Unemployment involves distinctive kinds of social relationships. Those who lose their jobs are victims of the decisions of others and find themselves in a state of dependency. Loss of income is only one of its major consequences; it entails, too, loss of status and respect and its effects on individuals ramify through their families and communities. An unemployed man from Sunderland captured something of this when he told Jeremy Seabrook:

I do know of people's lives that's been smashed apart by having nowt to do. Time. It can be a funny thing. There's times of the day that definitely go slower than others, did you know that? There is definitely times when the hands move slower on the clock. I hate the middle of the day. And the long summer evenings. I go for walks sometimes, to Hebburn, along the beach, in the wind. It helps block things out. You walk twelve to fifteen miles on an afternoon, come back tired out. That reminds me of coming home from work, when I felt tired out but knowing you'd given a good day's work. That was satisfying; something I haven't known since. You feel now you've got nothing to give, nothing to offer. You feel ashamed of yourself. (1982:111)

Unemployment need not necessarily have these consequences. Adequate income support and opportunities for retraining could mitigate its worst effects. In Britain in the 1970s, however, the unemployed were too often perceived as agents of their own fate, eliciting among the employed and the better off a strong feeling that the plight of unemployed people was in some way deserved.

This was picked out as a main theme in the interviews undertaken by Dennis Marsden in his work on unemployment (1982). What his work underlined was the persistence among the unemployed of a strong emotional investment in and commitment to the ideal of work. This makes the pains of unemployment difficult to bear. At the same time, Marsden detected both from his respondents and from the social commentary on unemployment a strong note of 'scroungerphobia' – the fear that the unemployed are abusing the benefit system, fiddling and not looking for work (1982:213). 'By European standards', commented Marsden, 'the British are remarkably more inclined to believe that the poor are "lazy"' (1982:215).

'Scroungerphobia' is not a simple distortion by the right-wing popular press or the inflation-induced resentments of the lower middle class, although it can be traced to both sources; it is a feeling, too, among ordinary working people and perhaps particularly among those who themselves were and are forced to supplement their low incomes by state benefits. Two researchers in Liverpool 8 picked up strong resentful attitudes from the low waged towards those unemployed and linked them directly to the poor level of wages in the district (Dennehy and Sullivan 1977). 'Throughout the period of our survey', they wrote, 'we were made increasingly aware of the bitterness of some of those currently working for such low wages towards their unemployed neighbours who they thought (often wrongly) enjoyed a higher standard of living' (1977:62).

The problem of youth unemployment became serious during the 1970s. The percentage of under-25 year olds unemployed increased from 27.3 per cent in 1970 to 44.1 per cent in 1979, and those at greatest risk were the least qualified school leavers (B. Williamson 1983:143). The problem was a Europe-wide one, a feature of the recession, and it exacerbated many of the ordinary difficulties faced by young people finding their way into the adult world.

The transition from school to work was a well-explored theme in the 1970s, approached from several different angles by social researchers. One line of approach was to explore the experience of young people in the light of the subcultural youth styles which gave that experience meaning and significance (for example, Willis 1977). Another was to explore how young people coped with school and to understand how they searched out job opportunities for themselves (for example, Ashton and Field 1976). The results of these enquiries cannot be adequately summarized here. What does stand out, however, is that young people's experience of education and of the labour market continued to be shaped powerfully by the class structure of the society. For many young people, particularly those from a working class background, the implicit contract between school and work – that work follows achievement at school – had broken down completely, breeding a sense of resentment towards authority and towards adult society in general.

Young people who, for reasons connected with both their

family background and the quality of education they received, did badly at school, invariably found themselves in unskilled employment. In the 1970s, though, that changed: such young people became unemployed or found themselves, from 1976 onwards, on special schemes organized by the Manpower Services Commission to provide them with temporary jobs and job related training.

For working class young people, the recession exposed the weaknesses of their education and the limitations on their life chances in a way which encouraged some, a minority, to come to an explanation of their plight which was distinctly racist and sexist. The pathological forms of this response found some sustenance in the youth styles of the skinhead. It was a response upon which extreme right-wing political organizations could capitalize by offering these young people opportunities, through racism and violence, to rescue something of the self respect society would otherwise have denied them. One such young man was described by David Robins, a London youth worker, in his study of a growing problem in the 1970s, that of football hooliganism:

Decent, law-abiding citizens, who still believe that England is basically a tolerant country, are definitely in for a shock if they ever meet Barry Watts. Bull-necked and shaven-headed, decked out in leather belt, boots and braces, a bewildering array of tattoos cover his muscular arms (he's a body-building fanatic): MOTHER, JULIET, WEST HAM UNITED, ENGLAND, WHITE POWER. On his skull is scrawled SKINHEAD, and on his cheek, immediately below the eye, is etched a small swastika. (Robins 1984:116)

Barry Watts was a school failure, unskilled and unemployed. 'Evenings', explained Robins, 'he and his mates patrol the forbidding streets around Mile End, looking to set on Asian workers coming home from nearby factories, or daubing walls with racist slogans' (1984:116).

As a member of the British Movement, a neo-Nazi fringe group, Barry Watts is not typical of his generation but he is a product of inner city decay, unemployment and powerlessness; people like him and his parents were and are untouched by the

institutions of organized labour. Threatened by an unemployment which denies them the means to fulfil their high expectations for material possession, and denied the ordinary social
recognition available to those who work, they vent their
frustrations through boisterous macho behaviour and racism.
The contrast with the experience of those young people in
employment or those who continued with their education was,
and remains, stark.

Structures of opportunity

As horizons of opportunity for many groups of workers and
many working class young people receded, new vistas of
achievement and potential opened up for others. Throughout
the 1960s and 1970s the occupational structure of the society
continued to change, with the number of white collar, technical
and professional jobs continuing to grow. In 1971 white collar
workers (including managers and professionals) constituted
42.7 per cent of the total labour force; manual workers
accounted for 54.7 per cent (Brown 1984:141). By 1981, the
percentage of non-manual workers had increased to 46.5 and
that of manual workers had decreased to 48.7 (Abercrombie and
Warde 1988:118).

Such occupational change allows higher levels of social
mobility. The work of John Goldthorpe and his colleagues on
the Oxford Social Mobility survey, which examined the mobility experience of different age cohorts of men in Britain in the
twentieth century, demonstrated a higher level of social mobility in the society than many commentators had expected (1980).
One part of that project, written up by A.H. Halsey and his
colleagues, demonstrated clearly enough that in the post-war
period, significant gains in educational life chances were secured
through the expansion of secondary education, particularly in
grammar school places, so that real improvements in the
educational life chances of many working class children were
realized (1980).

The personal experience of most people, excepting, of course, the marginalized and the poor, but particularly those in white collar employment, was typically one of social mobility and rising living standards and of increasing expectations for the education of their own children. This generation of young parents were the prime beneficiaries of the 1944 Education Act, whose entry into the world of work came at a time of full employment. Their occupational success, in the main, was a consequence of their education; tested ability and not inherited wealth or status guaranteed for most of them their self respect. It is understandable, therefore, that many would come to a view of their occupational success as being a consequence of their own abilities and achievements and to demand at least the same opportunities for their children as they had had themselves.

A fuller history of the cultural and political consequences of the post-war expansion of secondary education, especially grammar school education, would pick out a special theme – that of the social ambivalence of its working class products or, at least, of some of them. Their experience of being wrenched from their class did not lead inevitably to a strong identification with the ostensibly middle class life-style most subsequently acquired. Their education made them critical of its cant and hypocrisy. But their ties with their working class roots were well severed. George Charlton, a poet from Gateshead, reflected on this in 'Gateshead Grammar':

> There must be hundreds like us now
> Born since the war, brought up
> In terraced streets near factory yards
> And on expansive council estates.

In what he calls 'academic quarantine' they were 'taught to live like Spartans, than like monks' and to

> Suppress the local accent in our voice,
> Not to give ourselves away.
> And little by little we go home less
> To parents who seem to have fostered us. (1988:228)

An even more forceful evocation of the same feeling is in

Tony Harrison's poems, 'From the School of Eloquence' (1984). His angry reflection on the class-ridden patterns of the English language is an indictment of a society which denies opportunity to people. The poems speak tellingly of how he as a grammar school boy was wrenched from his Leeds working class background. But he does not see that as gain. Quite the opposite. He reflects with a great sense of loss, which was part of the price of his success, on his own education in the classical languages and in the modern ones he picked up later. 'I've studied', he writes, 'got the OED and other tongues I've slaved to speak or read':

> but not the tongue that once I used to know
> but can't bone up on now, and that's mi mam's.

Social mobility, then, was bought at a price, that of a cultural fracture in the working class, and despite the costs of it having been met in full by working class parents who sacrificed much to achieve their children's success, Britain was still not becoming a more meritocratic society.

What the Oxford mobility research also showed – and in this respect merely added further confirmation to ten years' worth of other social research demonstrating the same thing – was that the relative chances of children from different social class backgrounds doing well through education had remained stable over the post-war period. The main beneficiaries of educational improvement had, therefore, been children from middle class backgrounds.

Such findings help explain many aspects of change in attitudes towards education and in education policies in Britain during the 1970s. To begin with, they explain the prominence of debates about education in the context of British politics. Throughout the 1960s, both Labour governments and local authorities, driven by a commitment to the ideas of equality of educational opportunity while simultaneously seeking the votes of the skilled working class, had pressed forward with the development of comprehensive education. In 1971 just over one third of all children were being educated in comprehensive schools. By 1983, the figure was over 80 per cent (*Social Trends* 1985). During this same period the proportion of children being educated in grammar schools declined from about 18 per cent to 3 per cent.

This shift took place during a time in which the structure and operation of secondary schooling had become something of an ideological battleground. It was an arena in which many writers and groups on the Left, still working within the political problematics of the 1960s and concerned, therefore, with ideas of liberation and authenticity, found compelling evidence that schools were authoritarian, destructive of working class life chances and performed well, through the structures of their 'hidden curricula', their key role in capitalism as ideological apparatuses of the state. In that role they functioned to legitimate inequalities by making it appear that structured inequalities of educational achievement were the consequence of the inevitable inequalities in the distribution of abilities. One French sociologist, Pierre Bourdieu, who was much read in Britain at the time, referred to this as the 'ideology of giftedness' (Bourdieu 1974).

It was in this context that some radicals, such as the staff at the William Tyndale junior school in London, or at the Liverpool 'Free School', began actively to explore alternative forms of schooling and pedagogy. Writers like Ivan Illich and Paulo Friere, including a small host of American radical writers like John Holt and Paul Goodman, were avidly read by the pedagogues of the Left, and their ideas gave considerable shape in universities to courses on the sociology of education and through that influenced the education and training of school teachers, although how far that influence extended must remain a matter of considerable debate (Flude and Ahier 1974; Ahier and Flude 1983; Demaine 1981).

It was against this background that, in reply, the political Right brought to the educational agenda the issue, as they saw it, of declining standards of education – both in what children learned and in the discipline which guided that learning – and the dangers of pursuing the political goal of equality through educational policies. The danger they saw was the loss of excellence as bright children were taught in the same way as the ordinary ones. They saw, too, what they understood as the great danger of allowing schools and colleges to be hijacked by the radicals who would then be unaccountable to parents in the way they spent public money. This particular debate was well aired in what must be seen, in retrospect, as a series of the most important educational documents of the 1970s, the so-called 'Black Papers' edited by Professors Cox and Dyson and the populist Tory, Rhodes Boyson (1971, 1975, 1977). Certainly, the various strands of the right wing's criticisms of education were woven together to stiffen Margaret Thatcher's later successful attack on the social foundations and failures – as she saw it – of the social democratic welfare state (Dale 1983).

Political conflict over the form of education thus came to be central to an ever-widening political debate about what form society itself should take and what should guide it. That debate remains unresolved. What remained true, so far as education itself was concerned, was that the opportunities it offered people were still tightly constrained by class differences in the society and in the way those differences defined the educational experiences of students. Despite more than ten years of expansion at the pinnacle of the system, higher education institutions, particularly the universities, still continued to recruit the majority of their students from middle class families (Edwards 1982:73). Why this is so is a complex issue to explain. Without doubt, however, part of the explanation relates to the ethos of universities themselves and the way in which academics clung to an Oxbridge model of what a university is, insisting on admissions policies which were rigorously selective on a range of narrowly drawn criteria which almost inevitably favoured young people with a traditional public or grammar school educational background (Halsey and Trow 1971; B. Williamson 1981).

The relevance of this claim is that the structure of educational inequality in British society lent and continues to lend legitimacy to the idea that scholastic achievement – and all that it brings later on – reflects the qualities of the individual student. The rituals of school speech days and prize-giving reinforced it.

Headmasters of comprehensive schools invariably reported with great pleasure the successful sixth formers granted places at Oxbridge.

This same way of thinking explains the pattern of parental ambitions for and worries about education. Ambitious parents, particularly those who themselves had 'got on' in the world through education, worried about the achievements of their children and expected schools to push them on. Many working class parents, on the other hand, accepted the myth that their children did less well because they were inherently less able.

Those working class families caught in the traps of poverty and deprivation were particularly ill equipped to help their children do well at school. Wilson and Herbert, for instance, reported in their study of child rearing among deprived families in Birmingham that most of the parents interviewed had themselves painful memories of school failure (H. Wilson and Herbert 1978:186). 'Parental attitudes', they write, 'are rooted in deep-seated feelings of powerlessness. Their view of the world is dominated by mistrust and there is no curiosity about it' (1978:186). Parental feelings of failure, they argue, influence attitudes to education and the performance of children in school.

From several different angles, therefore, the performance of the educational system in meeting a range of different social needs was questioned. In 1976 the Prime Minister, James Callaghan, entered the fray in a speech at Ruskin College, Oxford, to question how effective schools were in preparing young people for the world of work. From then onwards the Labour government saw educational policy as an integral part of its whole strategy of industrial regeneration. It was a thrust in their policy with wide support in industry. On the other hand, its devaluation of the professional achievements of teachers and apparent retreat from a broad-based view of equality of educational opportunity was seen by many as a further erosion of democratic and socialist goals, and as an endorsement of the Conservative view that education had to service the needs of the economy and of authority in the society (Beck 1983). The debates about education were symptomatic of a much more pervasive mood that much was wrong with British society, and that radical solutions were needed to the country's malaise.

The position of women

Discussions of employment – and unemployment – as well as of opportunities in education were focused increasingly in the 1970s on the special problems faced by women in an unequal and male-dominated society. The growth in the women's movement and in support for it represents a major change in the social fabric of British society. It raised women's issues higher up on all the agendas of political life. It exposed the special difficulties women faced in work and in the family and pointed the way to how they could be overcome. And the movement achieved this through novel forms of political activity, which made available to women ways of thinking through their problems which were radically at odds with the prevailing interpretations of their plight in the main political parties. For women involved in these debates, it was an experience which altered their lives. It changed how they thought and felt about themselves as women and transformed the pattern of all their social relationships.

Working, as three of Britain's leading feminists put it, 'beyond the fragments' of their immediate and everyday experiences to explore the position of women in the society as a whole, the idea that came to be central to the thinking of active feminists was that women, unconsciously, had become accomplices in their own subordination (Rowbotham, Segal and Wainwright 1979). Reflecting on the nature of the political processes of the women's movement, Hilary Wainwright put it this way:

Much of the oppression of women takes place 'in private', in areas of life considered 'personal'. The causes of that oppression are social and economic, but these causes could only be revealed and confronted when women challenged the assumptions of their personal life, of who does the housework, of the way children are brought up, the quality of our friendships, even the way we make love and with whom. (1979:13)

The development of political demands around such issues as social security, nursery provision, child benefits, the attitudes of the medical profession, the issues of abortion and of rape, of women's refuges, changed the perceptions and feelings of all the women involved. It helped them to see that their private troubles were connected with their public roles and could be altered only in the context of broader changes in the society itself. The radicals among them drew heavily on the traditions of critical social theory, which were actively debated in the late 1960s and throughout the 1970s. Those traditions provided them with the conceptual tools they needed to dig behind the ideological facades of a society which, while pretending to value women, actually devalued them as human beings.

The idea of 'the women's movement' is, however, something of a misnomer. There were, and are, many different ideological threads running through it and a variety of specific political allegiances. Hilary Wainwright, for example, was active in the International Marxist Group. Sheila Rowbotham was a member for a while of the Trotskyist Socialist Workers' Party. Lynne Segal found her political home in what she describes as the libertarian Left. What helped provide coherence to this diversity was a growing debate about women's issues, pushed along by an increasing amount of feminist writing and social comment. That comment covered the experience of women as housewives and mothers, the education of girls and their sexuality. It explored the shifting meanings of femininity; it exposed pornography for what it was – an act of violence towards women. It questioned whether or not the promotion of women's rights was something which the major political parties could be trusted to carry out.

Perhaps the most significant comment was historical. The history of the subjection of women began to be charted in a way which directly influenced how women came to interpret their present-day experience and to comprehend the pattern of their own lives. It is hardly surprising, therefore, that the emerging women's movement attached such importance to women's writing and particularly to biographical writing. Women's history provided those who read it with credible accounts of why their lives were shaped to the convenience of men and of the women – particularly mothers – who dominated them. Nor is it surprising that the well-educated women who identified with the women's movement in the 1970s found, through that history, that deep down inside themselves there were strong feelings of not really belonging to the world that their parents had offered them (Heron 1985).

Valerie Walkerdine, in her contribution to Liz Heron's collection of essays on 1950s childhoods, evokes this vividly, writing about how, through her education, she lost any sense of belonging to the world in which her mother had lived (Heron 1985:74). But she felt no regret about that; indeed, what she felt was the opposite, a sense of renewed possibility. 'You should never have educated us', she writes, 'the ordinary girls of the fifties',

for we are dangerous. We are set on becoming, and you will not stop us now. But it is not the individuals you sought to make of us who believe we have made it, leaving all the pain and uncertainty behind in that other place. No, not that. We are beginning to speak of our histories, and as we do it will be to reveal the burden of pain and desire that formed us, and, in so doing, expose the terrifying fraudulence of our subjugation. (1985:76)

The commitment to women's liberation was for many of its activists part of a wider political struggle against all forms of discrimination, particularly racism. Without doubt, women writers developed a critical awareness of the discriminatory structures of British society which was fresh and radical and which challenged fundamentally the capacity of the main political parties, particularly of the labour movement, to do much about it.

There is perhaps only one sense in which what they were saying squared with the experience of ordinary working women. The claim that women were systematically disadvantaged in the labour market gained in credibility throughout the

1970s. During that decade the percentage of female workers in the labour force increased from 35 per cent to 42 per cent. Over two-thirds of women workers were married (Wainwright 1984). Whereas just over 2 per cent of male workers worked part-time in 1981, almost 35 per cent of women workers did so. Women accounted for just over 10 per cent of those employed in professional occupations and 68 per cent of skilled, non-manual workers. Despite the Equal Pay Act of 1970 and the Sex Discrimination Act of 1975 women's average gross weekly earnings remained throughout the latter half of the 1970s at about 57 per cent of those of men. These data reflect, of course, the structured inequalities of the society – in family life, education and employment – which disadvantage women and the failure of social policies to counteract them. It is the prevailing cultural values of the society which reinforce and legitimate those disadvantages, and they still remain intractable.

The importance of the employment of women both to their families and to the economy as a whole cannot be overestimated. The semblance of affluence enjoyed by the employed, including the growth in home ownership, has been achieved largely because of the employment of married women. The persistence of a gender-based division of labour within families, even among those dual career, middle class families which should have been different but were not, created enormous pressures for women.

What Raymond Williams once referred to as the short-range, short-term but 'decisive pressures of a capitalist social order' operate particularly strongly on women (1983:254). Such pressures leave little room for what Williams also described as 'affordable dissent', at least for ordinary women, whose access to new ideas is in any case constricted on account of their limited education. One of the consequences of this is the increased risk to women of experiencing breakdowns in their mental health. In the 1970s there was growing evidence of this. Ann Oakley summarized some of this work as indicating that: 'Women's energies in our kind of society appear to be devoted to "doing good and feeling bad"' (1981:81). In her view, all the evidence underlined the fact that depression among women and oppression were closely linked, both facets of a sex-divided society.

The women's movement developed ways of naming the problem of women's oppression. This was achieved, however, in an ideological climate in which, with divorce statistics climbing inexorably upwards, traditional family values and women's roles within the family were being reasserted by the radical right wing in British politics. In his *The Subversive Family*, Ferdinand Mount, one of Margaret Thatcher's advisers and speech writers, defended the family as the last bastion of freedom in a society in which the state encroached too far into the liberties and responsibilities of the individual (1982). Built, in his view, on a timeless biological imperative in which women find their deepest personal satisfactions as carers, the family had to be defended against those who wished to transfer its caring responsibilities to the state.

An important point about this argument is that it came at a time of rising unemployment and increasing concern among churchmen and some politicians about the stability of family life in Britain. The debate about the family was certainly seen by the feminists as part of an orchestrated attempt to confine women to traditional domestic roles (Segal 1983). If this was indeed the case, it was a powerful argument to reinforce what was already a strong propensity among women to identify with those roles anyway.

The evidence piled up in the 1970s that young women, unenamoured with either the prospect or the fact of routine work in shops or factories, expressed their highest hopes in the possibility of love and of happiness within the frameworks of traditional marriage. Influenced by their comics and women's fiction, limited by the gender assumptions woven into their education, and shaped by the assumptions of their parents, that is what they wanted (Sharpe 1976; Sarsby 1983).

Married women, particularly working class married women, continued to see their roles within the family in traditional terms. Pauline Hunt's study of family and work relationships in the Staffordshire mining village of Silverdale revealed relationships between men and women of a kind which seemed not to have changed much from those described by Dennis, Henriques and Slaughter nearly thirty years previously (Hunt 1980; Dennis, Henriques and Slaughter 1956). The worlds of men and women were sharply demarcated and women fell back on a diet of romanticism to get them through what would otherwise have been the tedious drudge of ordinary domestic life.

Jacqueline Sarsby has suggested an explanation of this (1983). Women who perceive their career and status as being in marriage and who are dependent on men, even when that dependency is sometimes on men who are unloving and perhaps even violent, cope with the anxiety and stress of their role by converting it to the idiom of romantic love (1983:108). It is one way to deal with the fact that they are powerless, exploited and lacking both reward and recognition for what they do. Through fantasy, reality becomes bearable.

What finally stands out in much of this work describing how women's roles were constructed is a paradox. It is that as women worked to be in a better position to build up their homes and enjoy the increasing privacy of a family life, which many of them described as constricting and tedious, their involvement in work, which was itself often boring and low paid, was nonetheless something they experienced as liberating. One of Susan Sharpe's respondents in her study of working women put it vividly:

And even those who work in places like Schooner Inns being a waitress, I know two or three of them who do that. They're Mum all day long, and a couple of nights a week they go down there to be a waitress and they turn round and say – 'Ooh, I love it down there, I'm not somebody's mum', it's you, and that's why they like it really . . . you're not sort of part of the wallpaper or the furniture, you're somebody in your own right, you're you, yourself. (1984:77)

Work provided women with a new basis for their self respect even when it was of a menial kind, suggesting to Susan Sharpe that the demand for work among women will not fall away. There remains, however, a challenge to find means of improving the conditions of women's work in a way which will improve their lives as a whole.

It is perhaps too soon to reach an adequate assessment of the significance of the patterns of women's employment for the society as a whole. What is clearly, for many, a vehicle of individual liberation, is simultaneously something essential to the changing labour markets of modern capitalist society. Work brings women out of the family into society, but in a way which reinforces the privatism of family life. It may, too, contribute to the development of yet more complex patterns of social differentiation in an already divided society. Ray Pahl observed, in his studies of work and family life on the island of Sheppey in Kent, the emergence of great differences in the life-styles and well-being of families in which women worked and those in which they did not, or in which both adults were unemployed (1984).

Self confidence and well-being, anxiety and despair are common feelings among both men and women. What stands out, however, is that private feelings are inextricably bound up with public facts. So far as women are concerned, the period of the 1970s was one, depending, of course, on their position in the class structure, either of an expanded awareness of radical possibilities for change in their lives, or of a tightening of the grips of domesticity and poor jobs and the growing risks of unemployment. Between those extremes most women continued to live out quite ordinary lives in the growing comforts of their private homes wholly unaware of the volatile debates among the educated activists of the women's movement.

Race, poverty and the inner city

The divisions in British society of class and gender are paralleled and compounded by those of ethnicity and of space. The period of the 1970s is one in which the special social and economic dynamics of the inner city were accorded particular attention by governments and by social researchers. For it was in the declining urban areas of the older industrial conurbations that the tensions and social divisions of British society were amplified. It is in the way in which different groups experienced and interpreted their lives in the inner city that a new twist was given to the despair, resentments and hopelessness that were the structures of feeling through which the poor made sense of their fast-changing world.

There is a long history to the inner city, stretching back to Engels's account of Manchester and Salford in the 1840s and through to the work of Booth and Mayhew at the end of the nineteenth century. Urban squalor has remained a feature of British urban life until the present day. But it was in the 1960s that the inner city was rediscovered. That rediscovery took place against the background of growing economic problems in the economy, which affected the older industrial cities badly. They lost population and jobs, and the local authorities which managed them were left with a legacy of older housing and with people and communities to care for who suffered from high levels of unemployment and poverty.

Government policies from 1968 onwards, when the Urban Aid programme was announced following Enoch Powell's 'river of blood' speech, all the way through to the white paper *Policy for the Inner Cities* in 1977 and the inner areas programmes which followed it, have to be seen as resting on the premise that the poverties to which the inner cities were subject were localized. Because of this, area-specific programmes of intervention, which sought to mobilize local support and initiative, were thought of as the best solution to the problems residents in the older areas faced.

The loss of employment was a major problem. So, too, was poverty. To the governments of the 1970s, particularly Conservative ones, poverty was also a localized phenomenon, a reflection of a particular subculture which transmitted deprivation from one generation to the next. The critics of this way of thinking pointed out that it treated deprivation as a residual problem linked to the behaviour of particular families, rather than to the arrangements of social policy and the job market (Townsend 1979).

The work of Townsend, indeed, tells another story. Using a

measure of poverty which acknowledged it to be a relative, not an absolute, phenomenon, and basing his conclusions on a major survey carried out in the late 1960s, supplemented by national data from the Royal Commission on the Distribution of Income and Wealth, he claimed that in Britain in the 1970s some 7 per cent of households were in poverty and 24 per cent of households existed at the margins of it (1979:301). The corresponding numbers of people involved were 3.3 million and 11.8 million respectively. The incidence of poverty was highest in single person households. It was high in households dependent on state benefits for their income, especially in families with three or more children, and among the elderly. His conclusion was that poverty was a feature of the organization of British society.

Townsend also claimed to have demonstrated that the idea that poverty is concentrated in the inner cities is a misleading one. The poorer districts of cities showed up on a number of indices of deprivation, but those areas account for only about 20 per cent of the poor population (1979:548). An area-based policy to combat poverty would not solve the problem or deal with the larger question of underprivilege. This is not to suggest, of course, that the poorer districts or the outlying and depressed council estates could be ignored. The real question concerned the kinds of changes needed in social policy and employment policy and taxation to bring about a redistribution of wealth and income, for it was only in this way, argued Townsend, that poverty could be overcome.

Whether such change could be brought about depends not just on the sensibility of governments but on the attitudes of those who elect them, and on the actions and attitudes of poor people themselves. The evidence about those who were well off was that they were very likely to blame poverty on the poor themselves or to deny its existence. The last thing they would do was correlate their own success and the privileges which the tax system gave them, through their pension funds, mortgage subsidies and the perks they got with jobs, with the poverty of other people in the society (Townsend 1979:337–68).

The effects of poverty on the poor are to reinforce a sense of separateness and isolation. Privacy is a defence mechanism; it protects the poor from gossip and the humiliation of knowing that they cannot share in the life-styles of the society as well as other people can (Townsend 1979:306). But there is much more to it than this. Brian Elliot, reviewing British studies of unemployment and poverty in the inner city, has set out the plight of the urban poor in the following way:

It consists of a constant struggle to make ends meet. It is rich only in fear: fear of the next unpayable fuel bill; fear of another humiliating and probably frustrating encounter with the officials in the DHSS offices; fear, especially for the isolated elderly, of robbery or physical violence; fear among the young and the black that once again they will be stopped and questioned by the police if they gather on the streets. There is little that offers hope. The prospects of better housing, of some substantial improvement in the decaying environment of the inner city, appear remote. (1984:40)

Elliot's comments refer to the book *Inside the Inner City* by Paul Harrison, with its telling subtitle, 'life under the cutting edge' (1983). A study of economic collapse in the London borough of Hackney, it presents a bleak picture of poverty and decay in dump housing estates and of people who, to all intents and purposes, had been abandoned by the welfare state. It describes an area with a high rate of street crime and aggressive behaviour between neighbours. It is an area in which the streets, as Harrison puts it, are 'schools for scoundrels' and in which parents, collectively, have lost control (1983:315). The police regard it as a tough patch to control. It is an area in which racial attacks are frequent and in which the police are not trusted. It was in areas such as these that some sociologists detected the emergence of a distinct 'underclass' in British society, especially among young black people (Dahrendorf 1982). The point is this: the capacity of poor people to group together to fight for their rights is seriously eroded by the conditions in which they have to live their lives.

The position of black people in Hackney leads to the issue of ethnic relations in British cities in the 1970s and to the question of how immigrant communities had come to perceive them-

selves and their position in the society. Two structures of feeling
stand out. Among black people the period is one of growing
alienation from many aspects of the host society, a feeling that,
in response to discrimination, intolerance and increasing racial
violence against them, they had to look to their own defences
and find strength in their own communities. Among white
people, there was a growing awareness of what they regarded as
a problem, but after that opinion divided. The 1970s is a period
of some resurgence of the fanatical and racist political Right as
well as of a determination from those who opposed all forms of
racial discrimination that action had to be taken against the
racists. That action included movements like Rock Against
Racism, formed in 1976, and the Anti-Nazi League in 1977.

An increasingly strong element of the reaction of the immigrant community to the society around them in the 1970s was
resentment (Rex and Tomlinson 1979). It is resentment born of
a discrimination felt at work, in school and on the streets and in
a political climate which they perceived as increasingly racist
throughout the 1970s. The expulsion of Ugandan Asians by Idi
Amin in 1972 had prompted calls for, and action to effect,
tighter immigration controls. In the years that followed the
National Front increased its political activity. Stories of racial
violence and police harassment, of racist demonstrations and
anti-racist counter-demonstrations, were regular features of the
daily news. Rex and Tomlinson, basing their observations of
race relations on research carried out in the Handsworth district
of Birmingham, noted that, particularly among black youth,
resentment was focused into attitudes hostile to the police and
to white society generally (1979:68).

A strong awareness among Asian and West Indian youth in
Handsworth that race relations were getting worse was
nonetheless coupled with a predominant view that there should
be more racial mixing and tolerance (1979:231). Rex and
Tomlinson were not in the least sanguine, however, that racial
tolerance would prevail. They detected a growing racism in the
white community and an increasing mistrust on the part of
immigrants which encouraged a growing militancy among
them. 'We do not see that this line of development will be

arrested', write Rex and Tomlinson, 'unless or until decisive action is taken with the support of all the major political parties to stop racial incitement, to attack racial discrimination, and to give West Indian and Asian-descended men and women a secure sense of citizenship' (1979:274).

Resentment and anger among immigrant communities came to be focused particularly in the one area where they felt their citizenship rights were most unjustly denied, namely the law, and in particular in their relations with the police. In the big cities where the majority of the coloured population of Britain lived – London, Birmingham, Liverpool, Manchester, Bristol – the evidence accumulated in the 1970s of deteriorating relationships with the police. Peter Fryer, in his movingly partisan account of this work, summed it up as follows:

The police, it was claimed, no longer merely reflected or reinforced popular morality; 'they re-create it – through stereotyping the black section of society as muggers and criminals and illegal immigrants.' Criminal procedure was being used to harass a whole community. The police refused to protect a community under constant attack from sections of the white population; and black people's efforts to defend themselves gave rise to police reprisals. (Fryer 1984:393)

The full history of how black people sought to defend themselves will have to wait for black historians to write it. The project, is, however, well under way. It will include an account of groups like the Anti-Racist Committee of Asians, formed in East London in 1976, which organized a march from Brick Lane to Leman Street police station to demonstrate against racist attacks and police harassment (K. Thompson 1988:107). For a while in the late 1970s Stoke Newington police station in Hackney was the focus of frequent demonstrations. The Bangladeshi Youth Movement and the Newham Defence campaigns, like the march of the Black Students' Action Committee and the strike of black school children in Brixton in 1973 to protest against police harassment, are further examples of the same phenomenon. A full account of the growing feeling that black people had to resist racism actively would discuss battles such as the three-month strike by Asian women workers at Imperial

Typewriters in 1974, to secure better pay and conditions and
better representation from trades unions (Moore 1975:77). The
strike of predominantly Asian workers at the Grunwick film
processing plant will figure prominently as a story of workers
fighting back.

Particularly important to the history of black people's resistance in Britain to the systematic racism to which they have been
subjected is the response of black women. That response is
something which is being actively researched by black women
themselves, and that research is in turn giving shape to the way
black people in Britain see themselves and their history, and
through that come to a view of how they can determine their
own future (Bryan, Dadzie and Scafe 1985).

Black women's organizations began to form in the early
1970s, and many of those active in them found more in the
experience of Third World liberation movements to illuminate
their experience in Britain than they did in the women's
movement of this country, which many saw as being a middle
class feminist movement (Bryan, Dadzie and Scafe 1985:149).
Organizations like OWAAD (Organization of Women of
Asian and African Descent), formed in 1978 and active until
1983, provided a framework for black women's groups to
organize and make sense of their own, as well as that of their
children's, experience of the discrimination and the racism of
British society. The cultural importance of this activity is well
attested by the authors of *The Heart of the Race*. 'As a
consequence of the Black cultural revolution of the past two
decades', they write,

an increasingly positive sense of self and blackness has come to
dominate the consciousness of Black women not only in Britain but
throughout the diaspora. As more and more Black women are able to
sing, write and speak out about the realities of being Black and female,
rejecting the myths and stereotypes and reasserting those aspects of
our lives which we have determined to be valid, the knowledge that
Black womanhood is a positive, vibrant force is re-entering the
consciousness of our community. (Bryan, Dadzie and Scafe
(1985:226)

Their experience of poor housing, low pay, racial violence and, especially among women of West Indian extraction, the failure of their children at school or to find work, was directly indicative of discrimination. By the end of the 1970s that discrimination was carefully described in official reports and in much social research (Ward 1983). What the women's organizations were able to do was help people to an understanding of that experience and to commit many women to an active defence of their children, who experienced such hostility in British society.

In the spring of 1981, disturbances involving black youth and the police broke out in London, Liverpool, Bristol and Manchester. Described in the press as 'riots', these disturbances, which lasted for over eight days, were to constitute a major symbol both of resistance and of the depths of anger and despair among black communities in Britain. The character of the policing of inner city areas, as Lord Scarman pointed out in his report of the disturbances in Brixton, may well have been the trigger for them (Home Office 1981). But the riots had a history in racism and in discrimination, in immigration legislation widely regarded as racist in intention, and in the economic problems of Britain's declining inner cities.

Conclusion

The emphasis in this chapter has been on the ways in which economic decline accentuated social division. The divisions between the old and the young, the employed and the unemployed, rich and poor, black and white, and men and women, took on new forms with many serious consequences for the social and political stability of the society. Everyone has a need for and a right to decent housing, but between those needs there was a wedge driven, setting apart the interests and identities of owner occupiers and council tenants, those with homes and the homeless, those in the inner cities and those in the suburbs. Residential segregation with all its cultural stigmata became a far more potent divide than those of income or class. The period of the 1970s is one in which the retreat from a commitment to the welfare of all reached its zenith and British society took on a new political hue. Profit and prosperity, choice and freedom became the buzz words of a rekindled Conservatism which overtook an obviously exhausted corporatism in the period from 1976 onwards and which led to Margaret Thatcher's general election victory in 1979.

The Labour government of James Callaghan left office in 1979 defeated by its own failure to solve the country's economic problems, and by a more subtle shift in the tide of public opinion in which radical solutions to the country's problems were being demanded. The economic failure was exemplified above all else in the government's inability to hold the line of its incomes policy. A series of strikes in the winter of 1979 broke the back of the government and the period has become lodged in political memory as the 'Winter of Discontent', when decent people could not bury their dead and rubbish piled high in the streets. It was a period in which the political divisions within the Labour Party itself between Left and Right deepened and in which public opinion was turned against the trades unions and the public sector of the economy.

When James Callaghan, as Prime Minister, returned from a Western leaders' summit on the Caribbean island of Guadeloupe on 10 January 1979 he commented, in reply to a question about the mounting chaos in Britain, that an interpretation of the country's problems in these terms was 'parochial'. The *Sun* newspaper headlined the interview the following day with words Callaghan himself had not used. 'Crisis – what crisis?' is what he is said to have said, and the phrase caught on as a symbol of the government's ineptitude. Certainly, a sense of crisis had come to pervade all commentary on the state of the British economy and society.

'Crisis' is a term of judgement and if it is used too liberally it conceals another important fact about British society at that time, a sense of well-being among different groups, especially those in employment in families with two incomes. A balanced assessment of what took place in the 1970s would have to identify, as Philip Whitehead commented, the 'winners and losers' (1986). Farmers in the eastern counties did well; manufacturers in the West Midlands did not. Northern Ireland was a loser whichever way success is judged. The rich continued to do well; the poor suffered. The 90 per cent of the labour force still in employment experienced real gains in living standards. By the end of the decade most households had a fridge, three-quarters had a telephone, more than half had a car and could drive freely on a network of motorways built in the 1960s, and do-it-yourself became a major leisure industry. The numbers going abroad for their holidays increased from 7 million in 1971 to 13 million in 1981.

These are the conditions which sustain a strong home-centred sense of privatism. Raymond Williams described it as 'mobile privatisation' which means, as he puts it, 'that at most active social levels people are increasingly living as private small-family units, or, disrupting even that, as private and deliberately self-enclosed individuals' (1983:188). Valued above all else as consumers, people find their deepest satisfactions in acquiring more and more of what retailers want to sell them. Their priorities come to be focused above all else on improving the living standards of themselves and their families.

Blackwell and Seabrook interpreted such developments as involving a 'violent restructuring of the psyche and emotions' of ordinary people so that their needs have become subordinated to the requirements of the economy (1985:184). Perhaps this explains why, in the general election of 1979, the Conservatives were so successful in capturing the votes of working class people. The swing to them from Labour was 11 per cent among skilled workers and 9 per cent among the unskilled. But underlying it all was a sense of unease, especially in the older industrial areas. Jeremy Seabrook had picked this up from his journeys around those communities in the late seventies:

If you talk to old working class people, however oppressive the poverty and insecurity under which they lived, they will always recall that the greatest consolation was the quality of human relationships; how comforting it was to share, with kin and neighbours, work companions. But now, in the face of vast improvements in material conditions, it is the people who are all wrong. Things are better; but all that has been gained has been at the expense of human relationships. (1978:72)

In Nottingham he found old Labour activists who felt bitter that their early ideals had not been translated into politics. 'People aren't satisfied, only they don't seem to know why they're not', one old man told him (1978:132). In Coventry factory workers told him of their fear of change and sense of isolation from one another.

Sennet and Cobb, two American writers, have made similar comments about workers in the USA (1972). They interpret the American worker's search for material prosperity as a way of healing doubts about the self in a culture which reinforces inequalities by creating a 'morality of anxiety' and 'discontent' (1972:171). Under these circumstances it is difficult for the Left to organize the working class; people are encouraged to turn against one another rather than against the 'system'.

In 1979, however, the 'system' was not in any sense safe. At the point when Margaret Thatcher's first government took office, and for the first three years of that government, Britain remained a society with serious economic problems to overcome and with political divisions of a kind which some people thought threatened the political unity of the country as a whole. That was the case right up until the war with Argentina in 1982.

8
Britain in the Eighties

Margaret Thatcher came to power in 1979 as Britain's first woman Prime Minister, with a well-prepared, radical agenda to rescue the country from what was widely perceived as a serious state of crisis. There were many layers to that crisis. The economy had faltered badly in the 1970s and high inflation posed a serious threat to the country's economic institutions. The Tories believed deeply that industrial relations in Britain, and particularly the trades unions, had become anarchic and were a serious obstacle to economic recovery. Of no less importance was the need, as the Tories saw it, to rein in public expenditure as a way of restoring financial discipline in the fight against inflation.

The political problems the new government faced included, in the Tories' view, the need to strengthen the authority of Parliament in the face of strong devolutionary inclinations in Wales and Scotland. They included the problem of maintaing law and order in Northern Ireland. On the international front, the Tories were determined to restore Britain's status as a nuclear power in a strengthened NATO Alliance and defuse the energies and confidence of a Europe-wide, resurgent peace movement.

Then there were the 'popular' issues to be dealt with – of law and order, welfare scrounging, permissiveness, the erosion of family values, ill-discipline and underachievement in education – and the strengthening of values like those of individual responsibility, prudence and national pride. The most coherently ideological and well-prepared of all post-war administrations, the Thatcher government saw itself as having an underlying yet central agenda, that of rolling back the powers of the state and defeating socialism. In the short run, that particular goal involved cleaning out the Augean stables of the Conservative

Party itself to purge it of Heathite corporatism and soft-headed attitudes to public expenditure. The theoretical justification for its programme was well worked out and drew heavily on the monetarist economic theories of Hayek and Friedman. What this meant in practice was that the government was determined to reduce public expenditure and control the money supply.

The government was elected with a 43.9 per cent share of the popular vote. Labour polled fewer votes than at any time since 1931 and, as Professor Hobsbawm shortly afterwards underlined, only barely beat the Tories in the votes it collected from the skilled working class (1989c:24). The election resulted in a Tory majority in the House of Commons of 43. Given the nature of the British political system this meant that the government had a clear parliamentary mandate, if not popular support, to implement its policies. It was a mandate made all the more feasible by disarray in the parliamentary opposition and by the emergence of the Council for Social Democracy (later the Social Democratic Party) as a breakaway group from Labour.

The aim of this chapter is to consider the ways in which the values of the Thatcher governments have both reflected and given shape to aspects of change in sentiments and attitudes throughout British society. The central claim is that, in the course of ten years of Tory government, the moral order of British society has altered. The structures of feeling which are dominant in the society, and which provide the main justifications for how people should organize their lives, commitments and hopes, lay stress on individual success as a priority greater than that of collective obligations. The privileged values of individual success lend further credence to the idea that social inequality is not only inevitable, but that it is also desirable in a society which seeks prosperity. For those who have become successful in these terms, the dominant way of thinking supports the view that their success is the result of their own efforts and is therefore deserved.

The view of the nature of society embedded in this outlook, namely that society does not exist and that only individuals matter, is one closely associated with the Prime Minister herself. It is a view wholly blind to the complex ways in which people are interdependent on one another. The 'success' of some people and the 'failure' of others depends not just on individual effort or ability, but also on how a society distributes its life chances and its subsidies. This view is deeply held by those who, over the years since World War II, have defended the welfare state and the state's role in managing the economy and who cling to the possibility of building a fair and 'fraternal society'. Central to this way of thinking is that all social change brings with it benefits and disadvantages, so that the success of one group is often bought at the expense of another. It follows that the good society is one which seeks, through its institutions, to recognize these 'diswelfares' and compensate for them (for example, Titmuss 1968; Halsey 1981).

Over the past ten years, however, such a way of thinking has been in political retreat. This is not something which can be blamed on Thatcherism. The ideological success of Thatcherism cannot be gainsaid; but it was possible because the moral foundations of the welfare state were insecure and because of political chaos among the opposition parties, particularly in the labour movement. The failure of the labour opposition lay in not being able to articulate a different vision of what a just and economically successful modern society might look like.

The logic of the situation in which most people in Britain now find themselves is one which encourages them to seek private solutions to the ordinary problems of their lives – in health, education, housing, transport, pensions – and to value the provision of public services against some assessment of their cost rather than the degree to which they are needed. Policies on the economy have come to have precedence over social policies. It is not that people have become more selfish; rather it is that selfish behaviour has become necessary. Private hopes and aspirations of a particularly narrow, materialist kind have come to have precedence in how people arrange their lives, construe the future and allocate their political support.

For many groups of people, particularly among those diverse groups pushed to the periphery of the society through poverty and the complex discriminations of gender and race, the situation in which they find themselves is one of hopelessness and, often, despair. They are the victims of a society in which the circuits of sentiment and fellow feeling have become disconnected; their plight is unrelieved because it is unrecognized and unfelt by the majority, who have achieved success in the narrow terms in which that has come to be measured. The glorious dawn of 1945 could not be further away.

Yet that is not the whole story. There are other structures of feeling which, in Raymond Williams's terms, are 'emergent' and which provide new resources for a 'journey of hope' (1983). These include, in Williams's view, the women's movement, the peace movement and the green movement. In Thatcher's Britain, however, the grounds for hope for many rest firmly on strong government, economic growth, tax cuts and steady improvements in living standards. For others they lie in nationalism of various kinds – Scottish, Welsh or Irish – and for a minority, hope rests only with God.

For the main political parties, hope rests in their ability to reflect the interests and temper of a changing mass electorate and win the votes on offer. What the politicians understand better than most, however, is that they are not in full control of what might happen. The best laid plans can be upset by events well beyond their influence. It is for this reason that any account of change in Britain in the past ten years must avoid interpretations of what has happened which rest on the dogma of historical necessity, as if it could all be explained as part of how British capitalism was reconstructing itself. That is part of it. But it cannot be the whole story.

If the Falklands War had been lost; if the miners had won their strike in 1984–5; if unemployment had increased more than it did; if the Labour Party had not split after the Wembley Conference; if the Chernobyl disaster had been more serious than it was; if Margaret Thatcher and most of her Cabinet had been assassinated in the Grand Hotel in Brighton; the pattern of politics in Britain would have been radically different. What would not have altered so radically are those underlying sentiments fused into the fabric of the society itself and into its recent past which, at least between 1979 and 1982, were strongly marked by a sense of decline, regret and anxiety about the future.

Margaret Thatcher's governments responded to these issues in ways consistent with their ideological predilections. What the government achieved in relation to rebuilding a sense of national identity and purpose, economic reform and alterations in the moral climate of the society, cannot be examined, however, apart from the changing international contexts of those achievements and the residual structures of feeling of British society itself, which recalled still a greatness and identity set in an older mould. It is to these three issues – Britain's role in the world, the economy and the moral climate of the society – that we must now turn.

Defining Britain

The government of James Callaghan held precariously to power with the support of the Liberals and Scottish Nationalists. Throughout the 1970s the electoral support for the two main political parties had declined. They collected 64.3 per cent of all votes in 1970 but by 1974 that figure had dropped to 54.9 per cent. By the 1979 general election the main parties had recovered considerably to gather 80.8 per cent of all the votes cast (Leys 1989:242). The success of the Liberal Party in the 1970s, as well as of the nationalist parties – Plaid Cymru in Wales and the Scottish Nationalists – was a marked feature of Britain's electoral politics. But that success was rooted in something else – in economic decline, and in the failure of the two main Westminster parties to acknowledge the growing strength of local loyalties and the ways in which people in Wales and Scotland (though decidedly not in Northern Ireland) saw a better future for themselves free from the domination of Westminster. And perhaps of greater importance is the failure of the British state to find the symbols which would sustain a credible national identity, and promote them to a former colonial power, now playing a poor neighbour role to the

European Economic Community in which it had been, for
nearly ten years, a reluctant member. Some writers on the Left
saw evidence here of what one of them, Tom Nairn, called 'the
break up of Britain' (1981). Others have since written of 'the
divided Kingdom' (Osmond 1988).

There are two parts to this; one concerns the way in which a
positive, forward-looking, British national identity began to
evaporate in the 1970s. The other is how an emergent structure
of nationalist sympathy emerged and acquired its distinctive
characteristics in a compound of myth, resentment and pride all
worked into a revived interest in historical and cultural traditions.

The loss of a distinctive national identity which anyone could
be proud of was one of the features of Britain in the 1970s.
Britain's joining the Common Market in 1972 was accompanied
by much opposition from both the Left and the Right. Sections
of the Labour Party saw dangers to the British economy and
sovereignty. Enoch Powell, a leading spokesman of the Right,
even counselled Tory voters to vote against the Heath government in the 1974 election because of the way it had given over
sovereignty to Brussels.

E.P. Thompson satirized support for the Common Market,
during the period of the referendum to decide whether to stay in
or not, when he pointed out that it was all about consumption,
about the belly (1975). 'The Eurostomach', he wrote, 'is the
logical extension of the existing eating out habits of Oxford and
North London.' He went on: 'Particular arrangements convenient to West European capitalism blur into a haze of remembered vacations, beaches, bougainvillea, business jaunts and
vintage wines.' More seriously, he catalogued what he called
'the offence of going into Europe' as fourfold:

First, we are there already. Second, Europe is not that set of nations
but includes also Warsaw, Belgrade, Prague. Third, the Market defines
the diversity of European cultures at its crassest level as a group of fat,
rich nations feeding each other goodies. Fourth, it defines this
introversial white bourgeois nationalism as 'internationalism'.

What Thompson called for was that, instead of the Market, the British people should maintain for a while longer 'their own sense of identity' so that the prospect of a 'cautious federation of socialist states' might emerge, each with jealous regard for individual identities. The problem, of course, at least for socialists, was that there was no agreement about what that identity was or should be.

For those like Edward Heath in the Tory Party, or right-wing Labour politicians like Roy Jenkins or David Owen, who supported the Common Market, two arguments were compelling. Firstly, a strong Europe could counterbalance the great powers and reduce the risks of a European war in the future. Secondly, both the opportunities and competition which would come from involvement in a large European market would revivify the sluggish economy and transform industrial and commercial attitudes in Britain.

For those who wish to turn the EEC into a cultural and political reality, the building of a European dimension into prevailing notions of a British identity remains a problem. The assertion of a traditional view of British national identity, at least among the white population of this country, poses no difficulties whatsoever. There is a rich store of chauvinism and imperial imagery for people to draw on, which is lodged in memories of a former greatness. Memories of Britain's role and achievements in World War II provide the most poignant stock of images to be called upon when there is doubt about the country's present status. Such images can be easily invoked, for they lie just below the surface of most people's self respect and are assiduously cultivated by the mass media.

Royal occasions sustain such images continuously. The changing of the guards at Buckingham Palace attracts tens of thousands of tourists; state occasions like the opening of Parliament ritually endorse all the symbols of authority of the state. The daily work of the royal family brings them into well-reported contact with thousands of people each year. The Silver Jubilee of the Queen in 1977 was an occasion for street parties all over the country and hours of documentary television retracing the great moments of her reign.

The marriage of Prince Charles to Lady Diana Spencer in 1981 capped the lot as an opportunity for millions of people to celebrate royalty and its symbols. All the ingredients of a great occasion were there – the heir to the throne, a beautiful bride, the royal families of Europe, a national holiday and all the pomp and circumstance of a carefully managed royal event, which stood out among all the others because this one was about the continuity of the royal line itself.

Two reporters from the magazine *New Society* evoked the day well in their street-level account of what was going on in London. They walked among the crowds in the Strand and in Hyde Park in an atmosphere which was relaxed, good humoured and happy. 'In Trafalgar Square', they wrote, 'a battalion of bare-chested skinheads swing arm-in-arm. Two of them are draped in union jacks. One has a face decorated with red, white and blue greasepaint' (Chappell and King 1981:176). 'We need cheering up', said one elderly gent, 'with the year we've had in this country.' Everywhere there was bunting and good-humoured banter about the wedding and what 'Lady Di' would be wearing as her wedding dress. The same scenes were repeated throughout every town and village in the country and neighbours assembled for street parties.

But their trip to Brixton was different. In Brixton there were no street parties, no bunting, no balloons. 'Gaggles of young blacks', they reported,

hang around a wire enclosure, their fingers looped through the holes like prisoners. The air inside the fence – a kids' playground – is thick with marijuana smoke. A monotonous reggae beat pulses from a couple of giant speakers near the entrance. There is an air of repressed hostility. I feel my presence is barely tolerated ... On a wall, a message reads: 'The world is dead and everyone in it a corpse. Blessed is the man who stand and shout it out – Haile Selassie'. (Chappel and King 1981:176–7)

The contrast is telling; by the early 1980s, the high rate of unemployment among young black people, and their experience of racism, had effectively destroyed any commitment they might have had to the conventional political identity of the British citizen.

The reaction of many white people to the presence of black people in Britain had by this time become routinely racist. David Selbourne visited Wolverhampton early in the new year of 1982 to talk to unemployed men and uncovered an angry sense of national decline, which some blamed on black people (1982). 'This bloody country's wrecked', an unemployed moulder told him:

Why? 'Too many Indians' he says without expression. 'Those riots at Brixton. I'd send all them darkies back home' . . . 'Ninety per cent of these looters are darkies.' 'He's got some funny ideas he has' say his wife, calmly (she herself wants to 'stand murderers up against the wall and shoot them'). 'I don't want to see them starved and beaten like Hitler done' he says 'but what I think, is what the majority think.' (1982:96)

This couple thought that Enoch Powell was great, 'the man to rule the country'. It was not Selbourne's purpose to explore what the unemployed felt about their nationality. It is not hard to imagine, however, that people denied a basis for their self respect in employment will search for it elsewhere in something no government can take from them and which they share with others – their national identity and the respect which goes with it.

The furore which erupted in and through the popular press over how the Labour leader, Michael Foot, was dressed at the Remembrance Day ceremony at the Cenotaph in 1981 is indicative of how the dominant version of the national identity can still be portrayed. Foot wore a green donkey jacket when the rest of the assembled dignitaries wore black suits or overcoats. The *Daily Telegraph* said the next day that he looked like 'a bored tourist at a bus stop' (quoted Wright 1985:136). The *Sun* and the *Daily Star* subsequently caricatured Foot as Worzel Gummidge the scarecrow, and presented him as an offence to the memory of Britain's wartime dead.

Patrick Wright has suggested that the real significance of this episode is that it represented a clash between 'opposed modes of public remembrance' (1985:136). One, what Wright calls the Establishment mode, is nationalist and militarist, concerned with glory rather than gore. 'Its essence', he writes, 'lies instead in the transfiguration which its ceremonies bring to bear on past war, introducing order, solemnity and meaning where there was chaos, disorder and loss' (1985:136). The other, which Foot himself sought to represent, seeks to remember the dead in an act of peaceful solidarity with them. 'Foot stood there', Wright claims, 'as bearer and manifestation of the history of the common people, of the aspirations, consciousness and courage which have produced and sustained the labour movement' (1985:137) Michael Foot's own defence afterwards was that 'respect for the dead isn't a matter of the clothes you wear.'

The significance of the whole episode has to be assessed against two other features of British society in the early 1980s. The first was its divisiveness. Wright argues that in response to this the British Establishment worked hard to revive a sense of common nationhood in a society badly divided by class differences. A similar claim has been made by Hewison, who interprets the development of the 'heritage industry' in Britain at this time as a way of clinging on to something which people could value, to offset the misery of the country's long-term economic decline (1987). 'In the face of apparent decline and disintegration', he writes, 'it is not surprising that the past seems a better place' (1987:43). Under such conditions nostalgia is something in which people can luxuriate, though it is a feeling inseparable from regret.

The second feature to consider is the growth of the peace movement. Michael Foot's long association with the Campaign for Nuclear Disarmament was also something which the popular press commented on, finding through that an opportunity to ridicule pacifism of any kind and to discredit CND for its weakness in the face of the Soviet threat. The peace movement had grown rapidly from 1979 onwards, when NATO took its 'twin track' decision to install American Cruise missiles in Europe, and the new Conservative government decided to buy the Trident submarine missile system. Divisions within the

Labour Party over nuclear weapons and unilateralism were a prime cause of the development of the Social Democratic Party, led by former senior members of the Labour Party. For many groups on the Left in Britain, the campaign against nuclear weapons became the vehicle for the development of a range of critical attacks on the whole structure of modern industrial society and the post-war settlement in Europe. From the point of view of the government, it was essential that CND should be discredited, but convenient that the Labour Party had adopted a unilateralist defence policy. Because of that, the Labour Party could be ridiculed for the way it was prepared to run risks with the defence of Britain.

The peace movement itself grew rapidly, representing a distinct structure of feeling, among some sections of the labour movement and the educated middle classes, that the world was becoming an increasingly dangerous place and that conventional politics offered no solution to its problems. In January 1980 CND had 3,000 members. By the autumn of 1981 it had over 30,000. By the mid 1980s that figure had risen to over 100,000. The general secretary, Mgr Bruce Kent, used to boast that 'Thatcher and Reagan are our main recruiting agents' (R. Taylor 1981). It attracted many to its membership who had been active politically in the 1960s and who were unenamoured of conventional modes of political activity within the main political parties. These were thought to be too compromised and constrained by the political orders in which they worked and too attached to the destructive forms of modern production and the modern state.

An important element in the support for the peace movement came from people concerned with the environment – with nuclear energy and waste and the effects on plant and animal life of industrial pollution. Cotgrove noted in the late 1970s that environmentalism was a movement of the radical middle class worried about the economism of modern society, the impersonality of bureaucracy and the loss of spontaneity and community in political life (1976). His survey of a sample of the membership of Friends of the Earth, an environmental group, showed them to be drawn overwhelmingly from the service sector of the middle class – from doctors, social workers and teachers; that is, people on the periphery of the major decision-making structures of both industry and the state. They express-ed deep concerns about depoliticization in modern society and a suspicion of modern science and technology, and saw values like involvement and participation as guides to what the good society should look like (Cotgrove and Duff 1980).

The peace movement of the 1980s was different from the earlier movement in the late 1950s and early 1960s in a number of respects. Dick Taylor and Nigel Young have suggested that there are four factors of particular importance to the movement in the 1980s – the European dimension, the 'Greens', the women's movement and changes in the Labour Party (1987a:291). The European dimension was very important to the active peace campaigners, for it underlined their view that responsibility for the Cold War and nuclear weaponry rested with the leaders of both the West and the East, in what E.P. Thompson characterized as a 'doomsday consensus' (1980). The conclusion which followed such an interpretation was that nuclear weapons had to be cleared from both eastern and western Europe, and that this could only be achieved by political activity of a kind which linked together the people of Europe outside the political forms which normally divided them.

The ecology movement was important because of the vision of a different kind of politics it promoted, which placed such emphasis on community involvement and on a radical re-orientation of personal values and relationships (Taylor and Young 1987:293). The slogan 'Think globally, act locally' encouraged supporters to relate the problems of British society to the whole structure of world underdevelopment, environ-mental chaos, and the arms race.

The women's movement was able to build on its own political forms to help women who had not been previously involved in political activity to develop their confidence, in groups which excluded men and all forms of competitiveness (Eglin 1987:243). Groups like Oxford Mothers for Nuclear Disarma-ment, Families Against the Bomb, Babies Against the Bomb, came together as women's groups because many of their members sought to make direct links between expenditure cuts in the welfare field and increased arms spending. They were people from the educated middle classes with space in their lives for dissent, and their activity contributed substantially to the political success of the movement as a whole. The women's camp at Greenham Common, set up as a women-only camp in March 1982, will stand as the most potent symbol of the distinctive contribution of women to the cause of peace.

The underlying issue in all of this was the kind of nation state the people of Britain should seek to develop and what kind of role Britain should play in the world. Active peace campaigners, who sought nuclear disarmament, imagined Britain could give moral leadership to the nuclear powers by putting its own defence on a very different footing. The Conservative government and its supporters, including many ordinary Labour voters, could not accept the CND line on unilateralism and what it would mean for Britain's status as a world power. The counter-argument to CND was that the Soviet Union still represented a serious threat to British and Western interests and that peace protesters were a sort of fifth column of unpatriotic hippies who should be strictly policed. Without doubt, the peace movement had forced into the open a discussion on Britain's nuclear policies and pressed the government to defend its actions. In so doing it stirred powerful political feelings and, without anyone intending this as the outcome, clarified how wide the ideological spectrum of British politics had now become.

The early years of the Thatcher government were dogged by economic failures and by a deepening world recession. Unemployment increased sharply along with political conflict between different factions of the Tory Party itself. The popularity of Margaret Thatcher was low and the Alliance parties – Liberals and Social Democrats – were credibly seen as being able to offer the British people a government which was not based on what they claimed were the class-confrontational policies of the two major parties. Social Democratic Party supporters were drawn overwhelmingly from the professional middle classes and regarded the class-conscious attitudes of many on the Labour Left as both outdated and divisive. Indeed, their solution to the problem of decline was to alter industrial attitudes and place more emphasis on the ways in which capital and labour could co-operate to their mutual interest. This was Margaret Thatcher's project, too, but even the pro-Tory *Sunday Times* carried a headline on 8 February 1981 which read: 'Wrong, Mrs Thatcher, wrong, wrong, wrong'. Some sociologists detected major alterations in party political alignments which predicted the possible demise of the two major parties, as they were unable to solve the country's economic problems or heal its political divisions (for example, A. Stewart 1983a).

The point to be underlined is this: despite its radical agenda and its determination to achieve its reforms, the first Thatcher government faltered at the hurdles of rising unemployment, slow growth, widespread popular dissatisfaction with politicians of the two main parties and growing ideological diversity within society. Britain had not been rebuilt. The 'enemies within' had not been defeated and the country was widely perceived on international fronts as the 'sick man of Europe'. Events in the South Atlantic changed all of that, and it is to these that the account must now turn.

The spirit of the South Atlantic

The invasion of the Falkland Islands by the military junta of General Galtieri in the early days of April 1982 provoked a strong reponse in the Thatcher government and in the British Parliament. By 5 April the first ships of the task force, led by HMS *Invincible*, had left Portsmouth to regain the islands, if necessary, by military force. In response to a pessimistic question from an ITN reporter about the likelihood of success, Margaret Thatcher said, echoing Queen Victoria, 'Failure? The possibilities do not exist.'

The military aspects of the campaign need no recapitulation. A naval task force of over 100 ships carrying 28,000 men from the Royal Navy, regiments of the British Army, Harrier Jets and helicopters and all the guns and ammunition they needed, recovered the islands in a few weeks of bitter fighting. To the catalogue of great battles won, from Waterloo to the Normandy landings, the Falklands added Goose Green, Tumbledown Hill and Port Stanley. The marines and the paratroop regiment wrote a new chapter for themselves in a tale of courage and glory. Among the tragedies to be recalled are those of Bluff Cove in which fifty-one servicemen died and the *Sir Galahad* was hit. All told, 256 British servicemen died and over 700 were wounded or seriously injured. Argentina lost 746 soldiers; 1,336 were wounded and 11,400 taken prisoner. In one of the most controversial events of the war, over 1,000 Argentine sailors went down with the battleship *Belgrano*, sunk by the British nuclear submarine HMS *Conqueror*. At the end of the war Margaret Thatcher told a Conservative rally in Cheltenham that victory meant that Britain had 'ceased to be a nation in defeat' (quoted Osmond 1988:250).

At the outset, however, there was no guarantee that the task force would succeed, and it must remain an important matter for speculation and future military planning to consider what might have happened if the seven Argentine Exocet missiles which did reach their targets, but did not explode, had done so. What was certainly there from the outset was a political determination to succeed. That determination had complex roots. Margaret Thatcher's political reputation rested on her management of the crisis and she knew it. But she was helped considerably by the Labour Party and by Parliament and by a groundswell of popular feeling which was itself fuelled by the jingoism of the popular press. It was in Parliament that the support held firm. Michael Foot, no longer Worzel Gummidge, expressed concern on 3 April that the government might have done more to prevent the invasion of the Falklands. On 14 April, in another Falklands debate, he spoke fulsomely in support of the task force and against Argentine oppression. David Owen, former Foreign Secretary, said after Michael Foot sat down that 'he had spoken for the whole house' (Hansard, 14 April: 1154).

The underlying feelings and attitudes, widely shared throughout the society, were of a kind many had thought long dead. One writer noted afterwards:

we cannot dismiss the war as something which was simply foisted on the British people by the militarism of the Tories, or the dithering of Labour, or the self-interest of the military establishment, important though all these undoubtedly were. The fact is that the war struck a ready chord among millions of British people: the myths, sentiments, and memories of the colonial empire are still alive, and still able to influence political events. (Spence 1983:25–6)

An editorial in the magazine *New Society* commented on 8 April that 'As the MPs try to out-jingo each other, it all sounds remarkably like Suez' (1982). The report went on:

There is Labour's defence spokesman, John Silkin, calling the Argentine president, General Galtieri, a 'bargain basement Mussolini'. Just as, 26 years ago, Anthony Eden called President Nasser a 'Moslem Mussolini'. The hysteria is understandable. The surrender of the Falkland Islands seems as shameful as the wartime loss of Singapore.

Two writers in the same journal, later in the month, commented on the images used in the national press to construct their accounts of the war (Cherry and Potts 1982). All the press images played on historical memories. Headlines like 'The Armada is underway' and 'Goodbye and God bless' were typical. The imagery polarized the roles of men and women. The *Express* of 13 April had a picture captioned 'The mother who waits', and there were many pictures of tearful girlfriends waving the ships away from Portsmouth. Another theme these authors detected was that of dignifying militarism. 'This is the British going to war', thundered the *Telegraph* on 18 April, 'and the Paras are looking forward to it' (Cherry and Potts 1982). Hugh Cunningham commented on the moralism of the politicians and the way in which they evoked World War II. 'The stifling power which the memory of the Second World War exerts over British public life', he noted, 'has rarely been more plainly apparent' (1982:132). The tone in the popular tabloid press was rampantly jingoistic. The *Sun* ran headlines like 'Up yours Galtieri', and when the *Belgrano* was torpedoed it celebrated the event in the now famous one-word headline, 'GOTTCHA'.

Enoch Powell wrote in *The Times* about a new unity that our leaders must not betray (14 May 1982). 'All of a sudden', he wrote, 'thoughts and emotions which for years have been scouted or ridiculed are alive and unashamed.' A 'matter-of-fact unanimity of purposes', he claimed, 'has painted out, in a way reminiscent of 1939 and 1940, differences of class, education, prejudice and party.' 'The British', he said, 'are never so formidable as when they are in this mood', and for him failure was unthinkable, not only in fact, but in its consequences if the nation 'should now be forced to recoil upon itself, in defeat, humiliation and betrayal.' It was a remarkable piece of writing, conjuring up the necessary abstractions of the nation and the people and fusing them both into a mystical unity of purpose.

Powell was right to assume the task force had strong public backing. Public opinion polls detected only 20 per cent of the population opposed to the war. Writers on the Left saw in the war the means by which the Thatcher government sought to pull itself out of the electoral doldrums and bemoaned the fact that military violence was still part of international politics. Anthony Barnett, an early critic, commented on the way in which the war invoked 'Churchillism' in Britain:

All the essential symbols were there: an island people, the cruel seas, a British defeat, Anglo-Saxon democracy challenged by a dictator, and finally the quintessentially Churchillian posture – we were down but we were not out. (1982:48)

What Margaret Thatcher was later to refer to as the 'spirit of the South Atlantic' became the historical heir to the 'Dunkirk Spirit', both symbolizing the essential grit and greatness of the British people. E.P. Thompson ridiculed it all as 'imperial atavism drenched with the nostalgia of those now in their later middle age' (quoted A. Barnett 1982:137). John Fowles, the novelist, commented in *The Guardian* of 14 August that the public could not oppose the war 'because they are hog-tied by false assumptions, by apathy, by tradition, by social myth and convention, by inability to think before words like "honour", "duty", "pride" and the rest' (quoted A. Barnett 1982:88).

For many of the people, however, the Falklands War released a strong patriotic feeling. The war did for them what Margaret Thatcher said it had done; it put the 'Great' back into Great Britain. And it demonstrated, as Hobsbawm pointed out in 1983, how potent patriotism could still be as a sort of compensation for feelings of decline, inferiority and demoralization for a population largely apathetic about politics and who felt entirely fatalistic about what changes they could bring about to their world (Hobsbawm 1989a).

The achievement of the task force cannot be belittled. It was a major military achievement. The performance of British troops in battle was far superior to that of the Argentines. Their training and fitness and the experience of many of service in Northern Ireland all contributed, as an American study has shown, to the success of battlefield tactics and quick response in combat (N.K. Stewart 1988:xi). Regimental loyalty in a professional army, a doctrine of leadership that officers should be with their men and lead by example, together with very effective training, all contributed to the success of military operations. It is certain, too, that the Falklands victory has conferred further legitimacy on the style, structure and position of the armed forces in British society as institutions close to many images of the nation itself.

The Falklands War has left a complex legacy. The policy of maintaining a garrison in the islands is a costly one (over £400 million annually) but its costs are not part of the normal calculations of government expenditure; that would be unthinkable for at least a generation. It has posed dilemmas of cost and strategy for British defence policy which have still not been properly resolved. The more immediate consequences were that, without doubt, Margaret Thatcher regained her political ground. Success in the 1983 general election was the reward for a party which, just one year earlier, had seemed doomed to defeat. The Tories collected a fractionally smaller share of the vote in 1983 than it had done in 1979 (in 1979 it was 43.9 per cent; in 1983 42.4 per cent). Labour's share dropped from 36.9

per cent to 27.6 per cent and the Liberal–SDP Alliance took 25.4 per cent, prompting much speculation on whether the mould of British politics had been broken. It had not, but that was not so clear at the time.

Rebuilding the economy: the politics of confrontation

The success of the government at the polls was achieved largely because of the disarray of the opposition parties, particularly the Labour Party, which went into the 1983 election with a policy of nuclear disarmament and the aim of withdrawing Britain from the EEC. The peculiarities of the British political system gave the Tories a huge parliamentary majority of 144. This was a firm basis upon which to carry out its political and economic mandate. That mandate justified further sales of council housing to encourage people to have an interest in their own property. It justified tax cuts to release initiative and enterprise. It involved tight controls over public spending to curb the power of Labour local authorities. It involved the privatization of nationalized industries to create a new class of small shareholders. Between 1979 and 1987 the proportion of the population owning shares increased from 7 per cent to 20 per cent (Leys 1989:118). The Tories brought in further legislation to control trades unions and a range of special measures to deal with still high levels of unemployment. It entailed firm policing of the inner cities. North Sea oil revenues and rising tax receipts from an expanding economy put the government in a strong position commanding the ideological high ground of society.

That success was bought, however, at a price. In the older industries in the north and west of the country there was rising unemployment. Between 1979 and 1983, 1.7 million jobs were lost in manufacturing industries. In 1985 official figures recorded that there were 3.18 million unemployed workers, and unemployment, as the Church of England report *Faith in the City* pointed out, 'has become a major cause of poverty in

Britain' (1985:197). The loss of jobs in manufacturing industry continued throughout the 1980s. Opportunities for young people were bleak and youth unemployment remained a serious problem, especially in the inner cities. Of the unemployed in 1985, 1.2 million were under the age of 25. Britain, through design, was becoming a much less equal society.

So far as the government and its supporters were concerned, this was not a problem. For those who experienced the pains of redundancy or of poverty amidst affluence, it was a different matter. The government's efforts radically to alter British industrial attitudes met with opposition on several fronts. The major political challenge came from the miners and it is to the 1984–5 miners' strike that we must turn. If the Falklands conflict crystallized a structure of feeling around one version of nationhood, the miners' strike illustrated clearly the persistence in British society of another structure of feeling rooted in class and the experience of workers in traditional working class communities.

Members of governments also have historical memories. The Thatcher government was determined to avoid the humiliation suffered by the Heath government of the early 1970s in the field of industrial relations, especially in the nationalized industries. The economic policies of the government were intended to reduce subsidies to public industries and restructure them to be responsive to market forces. Its energy policies were to promote nuclear power and diversify the energy economy. It was almost inevitable that these policies would combine to create conflict within the mining industry.

Two points are relevant here. The first is that the British coal industry had been run down by both Labour and Conservative governments. Between 1957 and 1971, 417,000 jobs had been lost in the pits. By 1984 the National Coal Board (NCB) controlled 170 collieries compared to the 958 pits at nationalization in 1948. In the same period the mining labour force had been reduced by 75 per cent (Winterton and Winterton 1989:22). With rising unemployment during the 1970s, miners were a threatened group of workers.

Secondly, the leadership of the National Union of Mine

Workers (NUM) was by the early 1980s a radical one. The national president, Arthur Scargill, was, and remains, a deeply committed political activist possessed of a clear Marxist analysis of how modern capitalism works. The policy of fighting pit closures, with which he is closely associated, was for him simultaneously a political struggle against the capitalist state itself. And he led a union whose ordinary members were drawn from communities with strong local ties and loyalties and clear images of themselves as the classic proletarians, who had always been in the vanguard of the British labour movement.

To Margaret Thatcher, still basking in the glory of the Falklands War, the miners represented an internal enemy who had to be overcome if her economic policies were to be successfully implemented. Unlike the government of Edward Heath, hers was well prepared for a confrontation. From 1981 onwards coal stocks had been built up. The import of foreign coal had increased. Many power stations were geared up to burn oil. Above all else, the law on industrial relations, especially secondary picketing, had been altered to the disadvantage of trades unions. The appointment of Ian MacGregor as chairman of the National Coal Board in 1983 was intended to stiffen the resolve of the Board to rationalize the industry and achieve pit closures.

The rest, as they say, is history. The attempt to close the Cortonwood colliery in Yorkshire forced the miners into strike action, and 55,000 Yorkshire miners came out on strike. That was 1 March. By 12 March a national strike began which was to last a full year. The miners' strike of 1984–5 turned out to be the greatest industrial struggle people in Britain had ever known. This is not the place to attempt to recapitulate its history. That will be continuously rewritten well into the next century and is already something of an industry in itself (for example, Adeney and Lloyd 1986; Beynon 1985; Winterton and Winterton 1989). But it is necessary to highlight features of the struggle which illustrate the persistence in Britain of a distinctive structure of feeling rooted in the experience and historical memory of the old working class.

It incorporates a strong historical sense of exploitation and struggle. Part of it is the belief that through struggle some of the finest values of the labour movement were born. These are the values of solidarity, justice and community. The iconography of that view is painted on the banners of miners' lodges in symbols of hope for a better world. With their brass bands and galas, mining folk celebrate those values in great acts of secular worship, secure in their knowledge that they have for a century maintained the best traditions of the British working class.

The strike tested those traditions severely and in the course of twelve hard months added new ones. The experience of battles with the police on picket lines are the ones that will be remembered. So, too, will be the work of miners' wives who, through their support groups, made a protracted struggle possible. The sympathy extended to miners by thousands of people outside the industry will be recalled with particular poignancy. Their sense of themselves as an embattled group let down in the end by fellow trades unionists and, as they still see it, by leaders of the Labour Party will take at least a generation to fade. That in defeat they could return to work with dignity, marching behind their banners, is for many what rescuued a sense of pride and purpose in what had become the most bitter experience of their lives.

To many outside the mining industry, the struggle of the miners became an opportunity to tackle Thatcher on a broad front for her policies on unemployment, nuclear energy, the police, social security and her whole broad vision of what values should govern Britain in the futre. Activists in the peace movement and the women's movement gave their support generously, for the miners' demands that their pits should stay open crystallized a whole range of political claims which struck at the heart of Thatcherism.

At the outset, however, there was no expectation of defeat. History, both recent and timeless, gave the miners courage and confidence. In his strike address to the Hatfield branch of the NUM in Yorkshire, David Douglass made a powerful and well-supported appeal to history to justify their actions in supporting the national leadership. The NCB and the mine owners of old were fused together as symbols of greed and exploitation:

If anyone needs reminding what the coalowners were, take a look around the graveyards in Durham, Northumberland, Barnsley and Wigan. The acres of monuments to our dead killed in their thousands. And the little kiddies, blown to kingdom come for the owners' greed. (Douglass 1986:5)

The struggle itself, played out on picket lines and relayed through television to virtually every home in the country, brought with it a range of emotions rarely felt in industrial disputes. A Yorkshire miner, B.B. Croucher, recalled a strong feeling of gratitude to the women of his village (Douglass 1986). He wrote of his feelings of comradeship and sympathy and of frustration at being turned back from police roadblocks as he attempted to join picket lines. He wrote of 'stark terror at dodging cavalry charges at Orgreave and Harworth', 'utter disblief at police activity' and 'disillusionment with certain aristocrats of the Labour and Trades Union movement'.

The strength of the norms of solidarity comes out clearly in the way miners expressed contempt for those who went back to work and who were known as 'scabs'. A popular badge from the strike asks, 'When is a miner not a miner? When he's a scab.' A young miner from Worsbrough said: 'Men have scabbed for many reasons, debt, mortgage, kids, but we don't see any excuse for scabbing' (Worsbrough Community Group [no date]). His friend, another young miner, added:

There's a bloke at our pit and he used to be with us on the picket lines all the time, his son was beaten up, arrested and put on a curfew, yet he scabs and goes into work with police help. I just don't know how he can do that. What is the point in just signing your life away and becoming a scab. Everyone knows what a scab is, people may not remember the 1926 strike, but they can still name the scabs and tell you what they were like. It is something you never forget and is passed on from generation to generation.

The historical imagery here extends far back beyond this man's lifetime and the words are of someone who knows his place in a community and wishes to keep it. They are not the words of a man prepared to 'get on his bike' (taking the advice of one of Margaret Thatcher's ministers, Norman Tebbit) and look for work elsewhere. This helps explain why there was so much resonance to the NUM slogan, 'Save our pits, save our communities.'

Mining communities have traditionally been dominated by men and mining culture places great value on manly qualities like toughness, hard drinking and the comradeship of the all-male peer group. What will surely stand out in histories of the dispute, however, is the central role played in it by women. That involvement contributed substantially to the maintenance of the strike. Through their work in support groups, in communal kitchens and on the picket lines, many women expressed their solidarity with their men and organized the means through which communities could sustain themselves without pay and under conditions of great stress.

In the course of that involvement, the lives of many women were transformed. They developed political skills they did not know they possessed and found support among other groups of women they could not have imagined possible. They linked their own struggles with the peace movement and with opposition to nuclear weapons. In a speech to the National Women's Rally on 12 May, Lorraine Bowler from Barnsley said: 'In this country we aren't just segregated as a class. We are separated as men and women . . . [but] They are now fighting men, women and families' (Barnsley Women Against Pit Closures 1984:22). Women from Worsbrough stressed that 'If women can get together like this, they know they're not on their own and it helps them keep the family going.' They were keen to have their role in the strike well documented for they felt strongly that 'There has not been enough emphasis on the struggle that is going on in the home (Worsbrough Community Group n.d.).'

In a considered review of the role of women in the strike in Yorkshire, the Wintertons summed it up like this:

The maintenance of the strike owed more to the emergence of the women's groups than to any other single factor. The women's groups destroyed the stereotype of families undermining the strike through their demands on strikers; they clothed and fed their communities and developed elaborate support networks. (1989:128)

Women activists from Barnsley were clear that their involvement had changed much in their lives: 'After the strike', they wrote, 'we shall have to find somewhere to channel our energy, most of us will never be able to sit at home again.' 'The women have changed', they said:

They have discovered a strength, a talent, a voice, an identity, that they never knew existed. The women who are involved in the miners' strike of 1984 will never be the same again. (Barnsley Women Against Pit Closures 1984:44)

Despite the support which the miners attracted throughout the labour movement, the strike failed. It is still a matter of debate why it did so and the divisions in the NUM which led to the splitting off of the Nottinghamshire miners from the national union remain an acrimonious issue.

After the Christmas holiday of 1984, it was difficult for the NUM to maintain the momentum of the strike, and as each week went by more men returned to work. In Yorkshire a distinction was drawn by striking miners between those driven back to work out of sheer financial necessity and those who returned unable any longer to support the strike. The first they called 'hunger scabs'; the latter were just scabs and were deeply despised by the strikers. The drift back to work, together with the 'back to work' campaign of the NCB, added to the enormous pressure of debt, increasing hardship and weariness to prompt an agreement to return to work in March. *The Guardian* ran a four-page feature on the strike describing it as 'the bitter battle that ended an era' (5 March 1985).

The strike left behind in the mining communities a residue of bitterness, humiliation and anger which will take years to subside or perhaps never will. Pit managers exercised their newly reinforced 'right to manage' ruthlessly. Sacked miners or those convicted during the strike for offences related to their strike activity were not allowed to return. Communities remain

divided. Men who went back to work remain vilified by those
who stuck it out. Those who supported the strike but who were
not active on picket lines returned to work with fears for the
security of their jobs.

The politics of the union itself became acrimonious and the
NCB pressed hard its programme of mine closures and of
increasing the productivity of pits. Thousands of men have since
left the industry and the run-down in the number of pits has
been just as Arthur Scargill, the miners' president, predicted.
Within two years twenty-seven pits were shut with several more
agreed to close; the numbers employed by the NCB dropped
from 234,000 when the strike began to 175,000. Forty-eight
thousand of those jobs were in the collieries (Adeney and Lloyd
1986:302). The Board's plans for productivity increases have in
some senses been achieved, but a study of the Yorkshire
coalfield attributed much of the productivity gain to the closure
programme (Richardson and Wood 1989). What these researchers also found was that attitudes underground were still, four
years on from the strike, resentful and without trust between
managers and men.

The effects of that strike are still felt in British industrial
relations. Success in the strike reinforced the government's
determination to remain firm with the unions. The failure of the
strike persuaded other trades unionists that, at least for the
foreseeable future, the strike weapon was likely to be an
ineffective bargaining tool. For the miners who lived through it,
there is little which was gained. Perhaps of greater importance
to them, or at least, to those who continued with the strike, is
the sense, now built into the way many of them report their
experience of it, that what they retained was their dignity and
their pride (for example, Worsbrough Community Group [no
date]). Memories and good feelings do not pay debts; but nor
can they be devalued like the currencies of a capitalist society.

And it is here that the long-term significance of the strike
should be assessed. Raymond Williams hinted at this in an essay
on the strike in which he analysed the way it challenged some of
the essential features of capitalist society itself and the principles
and rhetorics of its operation. By bringing into question such

ideological verities as 'the right to manage' or notions like 'the economic' or the meaning to be given to the idea of 'law and order', the strike opened up a debate which socialists, he argued, had a responsibility to follow through (1989). Of particular importance is the meaning to be attributed to the word 'community'. Rejecting what he called 'nomad capitalism', Williams underscored his main point:

> from the inner cities to the abandoned mining villages, real men and women know that they are facing an alien order of paper and money, which seems all powerful. It is to the lasting honour of the miners, and the women, and the old people, and all others in the defiant communities, that they have stood up against it, and challenged its power. (1989:124)

The miners, Williams argued, in seeking to defend their own interests, opened up the question of what the general interest of the whole society ought to consist of.

What Williams wrote, near the end of the strike, is itself part of an emerging historical memory, a way of rescuing something from what was, in fact, a well-orchestrated defeat of a major union by a determined government. It is a way of remembering which plays down the divisions within mining communities and the political incompetence of many features of the way in which the strike was conducted. He was, however, right. The strike did expose the degree to which a society, apparently united after the Falklands War around the symbols of its greatness, remained, nonetheless, a deeply divided one in which the ruthless logic of its economic organization could still erupt into bitter political confrontation, richly spiced with the rhetoric of class conflict. But it was class conflict of a well-contained kind, since it was confined to the older industrial areas of the country. The electoral geography of Margaret Thatcher's Britain left the older industrial heartlands in Labour control. Outside the coalfields, particularly in the more affluent parts of the country, daily life went on without serious interruption. It is to the contours of that life that I now turn.

Moral climates

There is no doubt that the defeat of the miners cleared the decks for the Thatcher government to press on with its policies to reform the economy. But in 1985, many still doubted the capacity of the government or, indeed, of any government to succeed in the task. In a final article with which to complete his stint as the London correspondent of the *New York Times*, R.W. Apple commented: 'Six years after Prime Minister Margaret Thatcher took office, proud old Britain – birthplace of the industrial revolution, master of a third of the world in the nineteenth century, a Great Power only four decades ago – remains a nation in decline' (1985:15). He quoted Michael Howard, Regius Professor of Modern History at Oxford, who had told him that 'The degree of national unity that we achieved under the leadership of Winston Churchill has been steadily eroded. The glorious flood tide that swept us all up together has ebbed, leaving a desolate foreshore littered with evil smelling detritus and decay.' And Brian Walden, former Labour MP turned right-wing political pundit, told him:

Every attempt in modern Britain by politicians to force cultural change founders because it is not rooted in popular sentiment. We are a radical people, but nobody knows how to harness our instincts. We need to abandon our passion for an ancient set of values that places great emphasis on continuity, security and sophistication, that exalts time-honoured good form in a sinking ship. We need to be a coarser, more vigorous, more hardnosed, more determined society. In other words we need to be in peace what we have always been in war. (Quoted Apple 1985:15)

These assessments of Britain's decline as a phenomenon with cultural and, indeed, moral roots were not new. Martin Wiener analysed the problem in this way claiming, along with Sir Keith Joseph, that bourgeois, capitalist values never struck deep roots in Britain (1981). What was distinctive about the Thatcher government was that it put questions of morality right at the centre of its political agenda. Margaret Thatcher herself looked back to Victorian values to help her guide the moral development of the country so that its economic fortunes would improve in a flourishing 'enterprise culture'. Norman Tebbit, chairman of the Conservative Party, in his Disraeli lecture in 1985, linked the troubles of British society in the mid 1980s to the way in which state collectivism undermined freedom and, through that, economic vitality (1985). He asked rhetorically whether, forty years ago, standing on Westminster Bridge, he would have predicted 'that after 40 years of housing policies there would still be a problem of homelessness; or that it would be more difficult to rent a house in England than a villa in Spain?' His point here was that state ownership and collectivism inevitably lead to economic failure. He drew a picture of Britain as a country which was overtaxed and underachieving; it was, he thought, a violent society and this he attributed directly to 'the era and attitudes of post-war funk which gave birth to the "Permissive society"' (1985:12). What was needed, he argued, was a return to traditional values and a defence of freedom and responsibility on the part of individuals.

Conservative ministers have returned again and again in their speeches to moral themes. In his Rivington lecture in November 1988, Kenneth Baker, the Education Secretary, dealt directly with right and wrong in describing how to re-establish 'all that has been best in our country and in our people' (1988:15). His target of attack was the liberalization of the 1960s, 'That great time', he said, 'of "do your own thing", "let it all hang out" and the four letter word' (1988:3). The social scientists of the period, he claimed, 'propagated excuses for the inexcusable' and values became relative. The result was escalating delinquency, political violence, attacks on free speech, rising divorce and illegitimacy, truancy in schools and vandalism.

In her speech to the General Assembly of the Church of Scotland in May 1988, the Prime Minister set out her understanding of the values she promoted as being rooted firmly in Christian tradition (1988). She drew on the scriptures to underscore her view that God gave man the power to choose between right and wrong; that responsibility comes with freedom and that 'We are told we must work and use our talents to create wealth' (1988:15). She argued that it was 'not the creation of wealth that is wrong but love of money for its own sake' (1988:17). The family, she said, 'was the nursery of civic virtue' and intervention by the state should not erode its responsibilities. In a final flourish in which she defended 'secular patriotism', she instructed the Church that its responsibilities lay in religion. 'Christianity', she said, 'is about spiritual redemption, not social reform.'

The moral outlook of the Thatcher government is therefore rooted in a particular interpretation of ideas like freedom, responsibility, choice and the market; it is hostile to 'permissiveness' and to 'collectivism'. Critics add, however, that behind the rhetoric of the free society, the Thatcher years have seen a strengthening of state power and considerable loss of autonomy by local government. In its education policies the government has seen fit to insist, through the 1988 Education Reform Act, on setting national standards in the curriculum of schools. In its higher education policies, the government has controlled tightly both the budgets of and the numbers of students in universities, polytechnics and colleges. Despite its declared aim of rolling back state power, the government has emasculated the autonomy of local government and constrained local expenditure in a tight financial straitjacket.

Because it has remained an overtly ideological government, a marked feature of the political argument of its ministers has been to attack its opponents and allocate responsibility for the country's troubles to almost anyone but themselves. The problems of the economy are then seen to be part of the failures of previous governments or of the trades unions. The problems of education are blamed on comprehensive education, the schools themselves and their system of management and accountability, as well as on the failure of teachers to insist on high standards of achievement and discipline. The inefficiency of local authorities – especially those controlled by opposition parties – are blamed for housing shortages or high levels of local taxation. Youth unemployment is attributed to the fact that young people's expectations of the wages they should earn have been too high. Problems in the Health Service are put down to the absence of market mechanisms in the allocation of health care.

Such a political stance has its roots in a Tory reading, not just of economics, but of morality and of history. Indeed, it is significant that, in its educational policies, the role of history teaching in schools has been given such prominence. Since 1984, when Sir Keith Joseph raised the issue in a lecture to the Historical Association, the discussion of what kind of history should be taught in schools has been an animated one. What Keith Joseph called for was a form of history teaching which underlined for pupils the 'shared values which are a distinctive feature of British society and culture' (1984:3). He linked the study of history to the development of a proper pride in the nation's institutions and declared that in British schools the emphasis ought to be on British history. Its role in the curriculum was that it prepared pupils for the responsibilities of citizenship 'as well as the demands of employment and the opportunities of leisure' (1984:3). The debate about history has since continued to reverberate through the teaching profession and the educational press. Through the National Curriculum Council set up by the Education Act, a history curriculum has been drawn up to give expression to many of the government's ideas on how the national past should be studied.

The government has not, however, firmly secured the moral or the ideological high ground. Without expressing its view in an overtly political way, the Church of England Board of Social Responsibility has questioned many of the values with which the Thatcher government is closely associated (1987). In its report, *Changing Britain: Social Diversity and Moral Unity*, the Board set out a view of individuality and community and the ethics of social responsibility clearly at odds with some of the central moral thrusts of contemporary Toryism. The Bishop of Durham, David Jenkins, became for many Tories a *bête noire* not only because of what were taken to be his controversial views on the resurrection of Christ, but also because of his criticisms of the morality of a society which seemed to place such emphasis on the pursuit of wealth and which could ignore the deprivation for many people which accompanied that pursuit.

Despite the emphasis the Thatcher government has placed on changing the values of British society and the moral outlook of people, there are strong grounds for claiming that the consequences of the government's own policies have been to underscore a set of values somewhat at odds with those the government claims to support. Critics of the government would develop their case in the following way. They would point out that the stress which the government places on the values of individual freedom and achievement is contradicted by many people's experience of disadvantage and inequality. The tolerance of differences becomes a sick joke in the face of racial threats and violence. The 'opportunity society' and the 'enterprise culture' stand in sharp contrast to high levels of unemployment and other structured inequalities in the labour market. That people should take more responsibility both for themselves and for others is something undermined by a fiscal system privileging tax cuts, and by the encouragement given to such high levels of personal consumption that they can only be financed through a quantity of borrowing never before known in the history of the country. Without the great good luck of the financial bonanza of the North Sea oil fields, the finances of Britain would have been in a serious state of crisis. Pride in the country's traditions and institutions is hardly credible when so many are effectively denied any opportunity to define what those institutions should be and when, after ten years of trying to improve it, the British economy still remains vulnerable to overseas competition, inflation and a weak external balance.

Critics differ, of course, both in their analysis of the problems of British society and in their views on the appropriate solutions to them. What is interesting, however, is that all critics seem to agree that the economic problems of modern Britain are simultaneously political, cultural, institutional and moral; that they are part of the kind of society Britain has become and are bound up with prevailing ideas about how people wish to lead their lives. Across the political spectrum there is also a pervasive sense that radical solutions are called for. The Thatcher government represents one form of that radicalism. Other forms have been defined on the Left (for example, S. Hall 1988; Hobsbawm

1989a, b, c; R. Williams 1989). The central, essentially liberal positions in British politics look for solutions in versions of the social market economy and reformed political institutions (Dahrendorf 1982; Marquand 1988).

The area of difficulty, however, for all the critics is essentially sociological. It concerns the relationship between values and experience, attitude and feeling, social and self perception among the diverse groups of a differentiated and, some would say, increasingly divided society.

But life goes on

The moral temper of a society is not something governments can control; how people construe their obligations to one another and define the values which matter to them is something related to their experience, interests, ambition and capacity to empathize with their fellow human beings. This last quality is related to how well people understand themselves and others and appreciate what is going on in the society around them.

British society is a variegated moral community. It is also a society which many social commentators regard as being markedly polarized (for example, Causer 1987). David Marquand has described it as being 'fragmented' and A.H. Halsey has commented that of the three great ideals of the nineteenth century – liberty, equality and fraternity – it is fraternity which has proved the most difficult to achieve (Marquand 1988:223; Halsey 1981). The problem to overcome is that of securing the optimal conditions of economic growth and improving living standards in a way which avoids the growth of inequalities of a kind which corrodes any collective sense of a common good or the will to realize it.

The pattern of social inequality in Britain during the 1980s has been one of growing differences between the rich and the poor. The measurable differences of wealth and income all indicate a widening of the gap between those who are well off and those who are poor (Halsey 1989; Walker and Walker

1987). The Church of England report, *Faith in the City*, drew attention to poverty and powerlessness in the inner cities of Britain and cautioned that 'we must not fall into the trap of letting economics suffocate morality by taking decisions for us: economic determinism is an insidious philosophy' (1985:209).

Whether economics has come to suffocate morality is a matter for political debate in Britain. The consequences of the social and ethnic divisions of the society are a little clearer. There is real social and political tension in some of Britain's inner cities. Rioting took place in 1985 in Birmingham and London. The Broadwater Farm Estate riot was particularly violent and led to the death of a policeman, PC Blakemore. Behind the riots was a seething resentment among young black people about their employment prospects, the way their communities were policed and the pervasive racism of the society around them.

That racism has led to increasing attacks on black people in this country is clear. Those who carry out the attacks are themselves the casualties of a society which has provided them with no other basis for their self respect than a distorted sense of their national identity. The effect of such violence is to drive communities further apart into ghettoes of fear, recrimination and mistrust. Sean Carey commented on the position of some of the young white people in Tower Hamlets, London, who openly admit to and take pride in 'Paki bashing' (1985). Their hatred, he claimed, is born of fear. They take out their frustrations about living in a decaying inner area by attacking Bengali residents. A Bengali community worker told Carey that 'Racial attacks are the most serious problem our community is facing in Tower Hamlets' (1985:124). In one year 200 Asian families reported 400 separate attacks. These attacks vary from arson attempts on their homes to jostling Asians in lifts, pulling women's saris, spitting and pissing through letter boxes. Frank, a member of the Teviot Street gang in Tower Hamlets, told Carey that he did not really know why he attacked Bengalis. 'Dunno', he said, 'I just don't like 'em . . . I just hate 'em, that's all' (1985:123).

Young people like Frank are a minority. But they are a

significant minority. They form the nucleus of an urban under-class without prospects in employment. They are the victims of decline. Their behaviour on the streets or on the football terrace has prompted forms of policing and crowd control which have led some sociologists to express fears about the growth of an authoritarian state (J.A. Hall 1987).

The case that Britain is a fragmented society cannot rest on observations about what happens in the inner cities between different ethnic groups. Even within inner cities, racial violence is exceptional behaviour. Most people live their lives in an entirely orderly way coping with the problems of ordinary daily life as best they can. Sandra Wallman's study of eight London families in the Battersea area underlined this point forcibly (1984). The families she studied did not raise the questions of ethnic relations as a serious issue in their lives; nor was their collective story 'a bleak tale of deprivation and disadvantage'. It was a story of the way ordinary families cope with everyday problems (1984:3).

It is also true that, although the differences between the top and bottom ends of the scales of income distribution have increased during the 1980s, there has been a steady increase in living standards for the majority of the employed population, bringing with it a sense of well-being. But it is a form of well-being which is calculated in terms of private rather than public achievements. The public realm is for most people an arena in which they can have little influence and even less control. A group of sociologists from the University of Essex have suggested that among British workers there is a strong sense of fatalism (Marshall et al., 1985). 'The economic well-being of the country', they write, 'is seen as being dependent on market forces' (1985:273). Such a perception has clear implications for the way in which workers think about politics. It results, so the Essex team argue,

not in a politics of protest but of quiet disillusion and cynicism, of which lack of partisanship, indifference to organized party politics, and a marked decline in support for altruistic social policies are the common features. It is not that people are unaware of inequalities. They simply judge them as unassailable. (1985:273)

It is in the private realm of their family life that people feel they can exert some control in their lives. It is understandable, therefore, that when people come to make judgements about public policies, they do so in the light of calculations about their own private interests.

Social survey evidence always indicates that people in Britain can be concerned about issues like inequality or poverty. But those same surveys also indicate that public concern for the disadvantaged is carefully qualified. Jowell and Airey, reporting on the results of the national attitude survey carried out by Social and Community Planning, noted in 1985 that most people felt the government should do more about the country's problems (1985). There was greater support for the view that unemployment benefits were too low than that they were too high. Increasing unemployment benefits was not, however, seen as a priority. Indeed, 65 per cent of those interviewed (a national sample of 1,761 people) believed large numbers of people falsely claimed benefit. The same survey organization found in 1989 a steady growth of support for increased taxation to pay for better social provision. Yet 61 per cent (of a national sample of 2,766) felt that they themselves were already overtaxed (Brook, Jowell and Witherspoon 1989).

Work done in the University of Kent on attitudes to welfare showed that people were satisfied with the services of the welfare state available to them (Taylor-Gooby 1983, 1986). But they expressed strongest support for improvements in areas where they themselves had a direct personal interest. Older people, for example, showed more concern about pensions or health care.

David Donnison, former chairman of the Supplementary Benefits Commission, has suggested an explanation for such attitudes (1982). Noting that survey evidence from the EEC indicates that people in Britain are much more likely than their counterparts in Europe to blame poverty on the poor themselves, he advanced the view that:

Public anxiety about anyone who seems to be better off out of work than in work is so acute that no government can be expected to raise social benefits above the political ceiling imposed by those anxieties. The living standards of the working poor are thus the fulcrum of social progress, determining what we can do for everyone else in poverty. (1982:4)

The solution, he argued, lay in the development of a new moral order in which a more humane, united and equal society would develop. The logic of his argument is that if economic decline were ever to reduce living standards, then such a moral order would not develop. The dilemma, of course, is that neither the rate nor the forms of growth in the British economy are adequate to sustain the kind of attitudes Donnison hopes for.

What is more, the sense of well-being which undoubtedly does exist among those in employment, especially in the more affluent regions of the country, is a precarious one. High levels of personal expenditure in the past few years have been achieved substantially through the expansion of credit. Consumer credit has risen sharply since 1981. Then it accounted for 8 per cent of annual disposable income. By 1988 that figure had increased to 14 per cent and outstanding credit stood at £40 billion (*Social Trends* 1989). Household saving as a percentage of disposable income was just above 2 per cent in 1979. It climbed to 4 per cent in 1981 but has since declined. By 1987 the figure was negative, 'indicating that the total of all households' annual expenditure exceeded their disposable income' (*Social Trends* 1989:111). Under such circumstances, those with debt to clear will look to governments to cut taxes and will reject policies aimed at the redistribution of wealth or incomes or which, through increased public expenditure, seek to improve the quality of publicly provided services.

But life goes on. People still marry, have children, buy and sell houses, go on holiday. They go to work and do their shopping. They eat out more than ever before in restaurants, travel increasingly by private car and build their pleasures around family and friends. Gardening and do-it-yourself work in the house consume an enormous amount of the time of ordinary families. They read the daily newspapers and watch their televisions. They name their babies and bury or cremate their dead. They pay their taxes, donate to charity and occasionally vote in elections. They sleep at night trusting the police will patrol the streets and in quiet moments dream their dreams of how it all might be improved.

What everyone experiences is change. How change is interpreted, however, varies according to experience and circumstances and all interpretations of it are embedded in feelings and evaluations. For many people in British society there is a dark undertow to change, a sense that some of the most valued qualities of social and community relationships have been lost. Regret and sadness become the predominant modes through which many people interpret the past. For others all is improvement; the future is something which can be anticipated with confidence. In between there is a zone of indifference or apathy, a feeling that both the past and the future are irrelevant to the needs of today.

Conclusion

During the 1980s successive Tory governments under Margaret Thatcher have attempted radical solutions to the widely acknowledged, long-term problems of the British economy. The strategies they have followed have been based on firm beliefs about how the society should be changed so that the economic goals they have pursued could be achieved. Thatcherism is therefore not just an economic philosophy; it is a moral programme. Conservative ministers have attempted to change the values governing how people behave. They and their supporters in well-organized and well-funded political think tanks have attacked what they understand as collectivism in the interests of what they understand as freedom. Theirs has been a programme to promote values like freedom of choice, individual responsibility and, above all, prosperity, a term which has come increasingly to mean private affluence. In short, they have attempted to change the whole moral climate of the society and erode further what was left by the mid 1970s of the post-war consensus about the role of government in the management of the economy.

It has been the aim of this chapter to show that such goals are not merely the programmes of one successful faction of British Toryism. They are that. But they reflect, too, the changes of the society which were set in train well before Margaret Thatcher got anywhere near the levers of power. They have arisen in the context of a weak economy and from the interests of social groups which have grown to prosperity and influence since the war. Thatcherism may well be the ideological reflex of a lower middle class concerned at inflation and its own loss of status. But the material interests to which it is an appeal are woven into the patterns of hope and ambition of successive post-war generations of working people. The promise of an ever-improving standard of living faltered in the 1970s, and radical solutions to the problem of the country's long-term economic decline as a world manufacturing power entered the political agenda.

The 'Iron Lady' – Margaret Thatcher – has not, however, or at least not yet, entered the soul of British society despite the way she straddles British politics. Had it not been for the victory over Argentina in the South Atlantic, Thatcher would have been a spent political force. But the war was won and her government was kept afloat on a tide of popular jingoism, echoing all the military achievements of a proud past. Her defeat of the miners in 1985 is a more ambiguous achievement, a political success which reinforced the social and political fragmentation of the country. Despite that, there is a widespread feeling, which has grown stronger since the end of the miners' strike, that Britain is on the mend.

This chapter has shown that such a feeling has been bought at a very high price, not only of growing inequalities in the society, but also of change in its moral climate. Changes in how people construe their obligations to one another and calculate their own interests are extremely difficult to describe. How people feel about themselves, about their neighbours and about what Ignatieff has called 'the needs of strangers' is something central to any evaluation of the moral order of any society (1984). There are too many signs that, despite the moral rhetoric of the government, Britain has become a divided, uncaring society shot through with narrow material hopes precariously poised on a mountain of debt.

Conclusion

The purpose of this book has not been a practical one. The issues with which it has been concerned, however, are of a kind for which people and governments have sought practical solutions. How to build a modern economy which grows without inflation; how to provide welfare and opportunity for all; how to create a more equal society in which people, irrespective of race, gender or class, are decently housed, fed, educated and looked after; how to arrange the defence of the country on a secure basis; how to build democratic institutions in which all groups in society can participate; how to discipline a labour force to higher levels of productivity; how to create a culture of enterprise: these are the questions which have dominated British political life since World War II and which have divided political opinion.

What has been shown is that these problems are not just given. History bequeaths them as problems to be solved and sets the constraints on what solutions are possible. These solutions are defined and then given priorities. Each one is entrenched in a way of thinking about society and in assumptions about how it functions, how it has changed and how the future should be ordered; each is embedded in feelings and attitudes which animate opinion and action. Those feelings – of hope and despair, pride and regret, ambition, fellow-feeling or resentment, love and hate, contentment or fear, indifference or determination – are shaped by experience. They translate into how people make sense of, and value, both themselves and their world.

The social and industrial policies of governments, if they are to be effective, cannot be indifferent to the underlying structures of feeling of the society. Which of thse becomes dominant and legitimate is something determined in the balance of the distribution of power in society. What new structures of feeling will emerge is also a matter of power and of the processes of acquiring it. But it is, too, a function of imagination and of purpose and of the determination of different groups to succeed and to achieve their goals. In this way, feelings are inseparable from values and therefore from the moral order of the society.

It amounts to this: how people feel is something related to how they are placed in society and where they stand in time. The social psychology of feeling is therefore inseparable from the changing social arrangements of a society. How those arrangements themselves alter is a matter of history and of the actions both of individuals and of groups to bring about change in themselves and in the world around them. None of this is new. Both the need for and value of an approach to the study of society which is simultaneously historical, sociological, and concerned to encompass the thoughts, feelings and actions of individuals, is something widely recognized (Abrams 1982; Giddens 1979; Mills 1959).

In a divided society, the conditions under which people make sense of their world and act to achieve their ambitions vary markedly. Similarly, the objective probability that a group of people will succeed in their aims is something which varies according to the control they have over the necessary resources of time, money, organization and imagination sufficient for their purpose. Class inequality of the kind built into the institutions of British society is for some a serious constraint, a limitation on what they can achieve in their lives; for others it is the foundation of their success. It is clear, therefore, that the pattern of distribution of power and resources in a community is something closely bound up with the social textures of sentiment and feeling.

The account which has been given here of social change underlines another important feature of this particular approach to historical sociology: it is that societies and individuals are in a constant process of simultaneous change, ensuring that the experience of one generation is qualitatively different to that of others; that experience itself is historically contingent and has to be examined against the unique circumstances of a given period of time. It follows that those who adopt this approach to the past have to be sensitive to the ways in which different groups of people come to terms with their own past experience and interpret it. Such an act of interpretation for many older people prompts feelings of regret and a sense of loss or anger. Others look on the past as a story of progress and improvement and feel confidently optimistic about the future. I hope this book has shown that such feelings are not random but that there is a structure to them which is intimately bound up with the social position and experience of different groups of people.

The main argument of the book has been about the decline of a particular kind of sentiment since World War II and the rise of another. What has declined is a structure of feeling which emphasized for people their common membership of a community in which sacrifice and a determination to defend values like justice, freedom and respect for human beings went hand in hand with a determination to build a better world, free of the miseries and the fear widely associated with the squalor and depression of pre-war days. What has grown up is a structure of feeling which attaches the greatest importance to rising living standards and high levels of private affluence. Individual goals and aspirations are, in this way of thinking and feeling, paramount. Public measures are judged in terms of private interests and public responsibilities do not extend very far beyond the clear boundaries of the private home.

Of course it is not as clear as that. In respect of the welfare state, for instance, Jose Harris has shown that any historian 'who surveys the wartime literature on reconstruction is soon struck by the fact that a common language of visionary patriotism and a common sense of national unity continued to mask an immense diversity of values and goals' (1986:239). The result, Harris has argued, is that the welfare state came into being without a clearly defined notion of welfare, or a coherent theory of the state. This has meant that the welfare state has been vulnerable to the ups and downs of the economy and to attacks from more rigorous intellectual opponents.

In respect of the argument about home-centred privatism and

materialism, it should not be forgotten that there is considerable support in British society for better public services. The value which is widely placed on the idea of community, and the extensive involvement of people in voluntary bodies, community centres, good neighbour schemes, community arts associations and churches, cannot be ignored. The sympathy extended to the families of striking miners during their great struggle in 1984–5 is evidence that, even when political opinion is sharply divided, there is a natural pool of compassion and understanding in British society for those who are in great need. One-off events like the Band Aid concert, which sought to raise funds for famine-stricken Africa, are testimony to a well of altruism and fellow feeling which extend beyond this society to embrace the whole world. Despite the fact that Tory governments under Margaret Thatcher have tried to capture the moral high ground in the name of individualism, the moral force of ideas which lay emphasis on collective goals and the caring community has not been dissipated.

Yet it would be misleading to claim that this is a society in which people are at ease with themselves. There have been many changes since the war in how people construe their obligations to one another and in the way the collective goals of the society are envisioned. Closer inspection reveals, too, that for many groups of people their daily lives are experienced as a series of traps and indignities, and their responses vary from quiet despair to enraged resentment. Trevor Blackwell and Jeremy Seabrook have summed up their feelings about living in Britain in the 1980s as follows: 'Rage, helplessness, a sense of redundancy; a feeling of being in exile, of disappointment and dividedness; loathing, contempt and fear, a dread of being suffocated; a disabling self-doubt' (1988:3).

They contrast their feelings now with the hopes they had in the 1940s, which their parents had won for them through the war. As young people they had, they say, 'absorbed a powerful sense of changed expectations' (1988:5). What they feel now is a terrible sense of loss at the way in which the possibilities of the early post-war world have not been realized. Blackwell and Seabrook are not unique. All the evidence points to what is perhaps the key underlying change of the past few decades, a change in the quality of hope.

Hope and everyday life

All societies must find a way to sustain for their members a credible version of the future in which the hopes of people stand some chance of realization. Not to do so increases the risks that the underlying claims about the legitimacy of the social order will no longer carry conviction or elicit respect. If the commitment people have to the prevailing social arrangements of their society is eroded, then they are faced with the choice either of sullen compliance or of action to change them. Both represent threats to the capacity of the institutions of a society to achieve their stated goals, and in this way bring into question the legitimacy of the social order as a whole.

Habermas has discussed this problem as an aspect of the 'motivation crisis' of advanced capitalism (1976). It is a crisis in which the prevailing motivational pattern of 'familial-vocational privatism' is no longer sustainable against the background of the structural changes taking place in the economic and political institutions of advanced capitalist society (1976:75). In this analysis, quite properly, the problem of how a society continues to legitimate its norms and values is linked directly to the ways in which people conceive of their hopes and expectations and measure whether the society around them offers any real prospect of their realization. Habermas offers no predictions about what will happen when the two fail to match up. What he claims, though, is that the legitimation crises of late capitalism are exemplified most clearly as growing demands for yet higher levels of personal consumption by citizens, who take no active part in the political life of the society. Their expectations are met, but at the expense of the poor and at a cost of chronic inflation.

The claim made here is that hope in British society now is increasingly individualistic in character, materialistic in content and short term; it is wrapped in a rhetoric of personal desires, expectations and ambition. The result is that hopes are chaotic and constantly refocused. It is a requirement of the consumer economy that hopes are literally unrealizable. The consequence is that hopelessness, the absence of hope, is a growing structure of feeling for some substantial groups of people in the society.

One way of exploring this is to consider the experience of young people, those without a personal memory of the early post-war period. In passing, it can be noted that, in any case, the number of people who do have such memories is declining. Less than half of those now living have memories stretching back to the war. But it is among the young that the character and textures of hope of any society can be detected.

A casual inspection of the position of young people in British society might suggest a group for whom the future, given the great changes of the past, looks particularly rosy. Without doubt, there have been profound changes this century, and particularly since the last war, in the position of young people in the society. Their earning power has increased; a steadily increasing proportion of them have had the opportunity of further education and the realm of their freedom from parental authority has widened considerably. Such changes have prompted David Marsland to conclude that 'far from being in a condition of exploitative deprivation', which is an image of young people often found in the sociological literature about them, 'they are the object of continuous, pampering idolatry' (1978:13). Marsland is not attempting here to paper over the obvious difficulties faced by young people in British society – unemployment, lack of housing, inadequate education and training etc.; far from it. His point is to argue that despite their affluence and freedom youth need help and support to savour both to full effect.

His attempt to locate the problems of youth as problems of the relationship between generations, rather than, for instance, as facets of the exploitation of the working class, is overstated but useful, for it sharpens up our perception of a paradox. The paradox is that despite achieving a higher standard of living than all previous generations a significant structure of feeling among young people, particularly but by no means exclusively among those most seriously disadvantaged in British society, is a deeply pessimistic outlook on the future. They have never had it so good but the future has never looked quite so bleak to them. All social change is achieved at some cost. What many young people have sensed is that the achievement of affluence – a necessary condition for the continued credibility of the economic and political institutions of modern capitalist society – is something being bought at the cost of undermining their future prospects of jobs and the erosion of their effective rights as citizens. Whereas many believe that individually they have little to fear for the future, there is a pervasive sense among those who think about it all that their collective futures will be bleak.

To explore this theme further I visited two inner city youth projects in two northern cities to talk to members and arranged for the fifth and sixth years of a large comprehensive school to write about their hopes for the future. Without claiming more for such data than that they can at best be only illustrative, there are grounds, nonetheless, for believing that what they illustrate is something real about the way young people in British society currently conceive of their own futures and the future of their world. Without doubt the prevailing mood is pessimistic; the 'voice' I heard was a deeply disturbing one.

The group of six in Newcastle were senior members of their club and their concern for the future was almost entirely about what they felt were the poor job prospects open to them. The two vocal members of the group had both been through Youth Training Schemes (YTS) and one stacked shelves in a suburban supermarket. The Youth Training Scheme they described as 'slave labour'. All agreed that they lived in a violent society and that it would get worse. All endorsed the view expressed by one of the oldest members of the group that there was 'nowt we can do' to change things. Some voiced the need for people to vote Labour, but there was agreement, too, when another member of the group said this would just as likely make matters worse because Labour would bankrupt the country.

There was great hilarity when the youngest member suggested an extraterrestrial solution to the country's problems by shipping all the criminals and all the pollution into outer space in rockets. My overwhelming impression, however, was that these young people thought little about the future and lived out their lives wholly in the present tense, solving their complex problems as best they could.

One young man lived in a hostel for the homeless and had to be out of the place between 9.00 a.m. and 5.00 p.m. each day. During the day he filled in his time 'grafting' and 'getting into trouble' in one of the north's largest and most opulent shopping precincts. The compelling pressures of the present were more than enough for this young man to treat talk of the future as a luxury he could not afford.

In Durham City a young unemployed man of twenty-one years told me:

I do think about the future. Will I be more stable? Will I get a decent job? It's frightening to think about. Do I have confidence? To grab hold of the future? Such a hard step. Will I ever get a job? I feel so mixed up I don't know what to do . . . You can't live without money. As you get older you want more. A lot of people steal; if you think what's right and wrong and stay on the straight and narrow you get so depressed . . . I always have the slightest glimmer of hope; if I did not I'd have committed suicide. *But there is always the greater doubt.* (My emphasis)

Suicide, of course, remains an option and it is one taken annually by about 400 people in the 15–24 age group. In this age group, it accounts for about 10 per cent of all deaths, having risen from 9.6 per cent in 1984 to 11.9 in 1987, and remains the third highest cause of death (calculated from *OPCS Monitors* 1984–7).

His friend, a seventeen year old on a YTS scheme he did not enjoy, made his point this way:

The future? Don't think that far ahead. Take one day at a time. Don't even want to think about. Don't want to hear about it.

This boy, homeless, excitable, out of touch with his parents, said nevertheless that he thought he would be all right in the future, but added darkly, 'The world, though, won't be.'

A schoolgirl from Peterlee, one of Durham's new towns, told me she hoped for a good job, which she defined as one with reasonable money, 'nice working environment and being with nice people'. She hoped the world would get better. That means, she explained, 'more jobs, less violence; you want to walk around without having someone jump on you.' 'You've got to be optimistic', she explained, 'but not too optimistic because you might be disappointed.' She went on to tell me that:

I don't think the world will get any better. You can't change it because of the people living in it. If there were more jobs there would be less violence and something for people to do. What is the world coming to? Watch the news! Bombings and that. Not something you should think about.

This particular young woman does not worry about nuclear weapons although she hopes they will one day disappear. She is worried about the natural environment but is confident that things here will improve 'because things are changing all the time and new things coming out'.

Her view of the future is demonstrably contradictory; it is based on a belief in the benign powers of scientific and technological progress, and her qualified confidence has little to do with her assessment of the capacities of her fellow human beings to bring about rational change. The greater availability of employment – 'jobs' – would in her view solve many problems, but there was little sense that this was something that could be rationally brought about. Jobs might come; but then they might not. This young woman was certain, however, that her personal hopes would be realized because she was determined to ensure that they would be.

The 'voice' of these young people is echoed in a wider literature on youth in modern British society. Frank Coffield and his collaborators detected, in the course of their discussions with young people in north-eastern towns, a growing sense of their marginality to the society around them:

During the course of our fieldwork, most of the young men and women in our sample changed from enthusiastic, optimistic school leavers into more level-headed and realistic young adults. We watched with interest as each one developed and matured but we also saw disillusionment and pessimism set in. (1986:197)

These researchers note that the contract between the young and the adult world had really broken down; many of the young people felt rejected and humiliated by the adult society around them, and when asked about politics their respondents on the whole, both women and men, 'slumped deeper in their chairs, rolled their eyes to convey utter boredom, groaned, and muttered at the very mention of the word politics' (1986:191). Though, with only a few exceptions, uninvolved in political life, these young people nonetheless held strong views, mostly of a kind the researchers in this study described as 'negative':

The attitudes of young adults that we have conveyed have been predominantly negative; we have shown them to be inward looking, resistant to change, racist and politically apathetic. (1986:202)

Ellis Cashmore summarized the results of his field work, carried out over a six-month period 'drifting' around the West Midlands talking to young people, in the following way. He says of those he met:

They have few ambitions, limited horizons, minimal prospects and no future. (1984:5)

He writes about the 'strangulating sense of futility' permeating the inner cities of British society and of people 'living in a void', of a generation suffering from a 'paralysis of ambition' and affected by a 'mood of fatalism', having no work and sensing no future (1984:6–8). In this analysis, despair and pessimism are presented as correlates of unemployment.

The studies mentioned so far were based on ethnographic research; it is difficult therefore to generalize their findings. A national sample survey of the attitudes of young people carried out by the Department of Education and Science in 1983 lends credence to their findings. 'When contemplating the future', the report noted, 'the young tended towards pessimism rather than optimism' (1983:26). The report went on:

Reasons for feeling optimistic about the future focused, in the main, on the perception that the present conditions were such that they could not fail to improve and that changes in unemployment and the economic conditions, as well as changes in government, were likely. (1983:26)

The pessimistic, on the other hand, fearing rising unemployment, government incompetence, the possibility of war, over-population, diminishing resources and deteriorating law and order.

For too many of them, the prospect of realizing for themselves the values of the consumer society is something remote. The pain of failure is difficult to bear because it is only as consumers that adult identities are constructed; failure to consume is therefore total failure. Since the consumer role is dependent on employment, the absence of regular employment, and unemployment in particular, is what propels some young people into retreatism, and this is then exemplified in heavy drinking, solvent abuse or a kind of aimless boredom.

Ellis Cashmore claims to have detected among young people a spreading feeling of fatalism, draining them of their sense of purpose (1984:102). He cites research into young unemployed people in Birmingham which claimed to demonstrate that they went through a period of despair and pessimism into resignation and apathy. Crime is one consequence, he believes; so, too, is the growing possibility of urban riots born of the hostility beneath the ostensible dull resignation. In the main, though, the predominant response is to 'look after number one', which is another way of saying that those young people most affected by unemployment are the least likely to look for collective solutions to it. Those economically marginalized become, simultaneously, depoliticized.

In these circumstances two often-noted responses of young people can be readily understood. Almost without exception the young people who set out for me their personal hopes placed getting a job high on their list. The other response is that of anger, frustration and resentment. Resentment at the way adult society treats them is not linked wholly to the experience of unemployment. Alan Sillitoe's novel, *The Loneliness of the*

Long Distance Runner (1959), explored this theme well before youth unemployment became an important public issue. It is something related to the way they experience some forms of the exercise of authority.

Anger is one way of coping with frustration and powerlessness. This particular theme has been very sensitively explored by the poet Tony Harrison in his poem *V*, which deals with the issue of vandalism and what this phenomenon tells us about the whole society (1985). Prompted by the vandalizing of his parents' grave in a Leeds cemetery, he has his imaginary unemployed skinhead who committed this act comment on his aspirations:

> *Aspirations, cunt! Folk on t'fucking dole*
> *'ave got about as much scope to aspire*
> *above the shit they're dumped in' cunt' as coal*
> *aspires to be chucked on t'fucking fire.*

In this poem the skinhead, in the end, evokes sympathy; he, too, is the victim of a violent, soulless and fractured society. His graffiti is an inarticulate and cynically violent expression of a deeply felt sense of despair.

The writers mentioned so far have been describing the marginalized young people of this society. The responses of the sixth formers I spoke to were different in only one major respect. These people looked forward with confidence to their own careers in university and in employment. Typical of most of their comments about what they hoped for was this one: 'Pass exams, drive, travel. Go to uni/college of my choice. Be happy, have a decent enjoyable job – which earns enough to be able to live relatively comfortably.' Asked about how they imagined their lives in middle age, the replies were conventional. One girl said she hoped to be 'happily married with several children – some still living at home. I hope that my husband will still bring me roses!' A young man looked ahead and saw himself 'Married, in good health, comfortable financially. Own a car and a house. No outstanding debts.'

Their hopes for themselves, however, were very different in

character to their expectations about the society around them. One student said he hoped the world would become 'less materialistic, less corrupt and less primitive. For man to have evolved beyond his primitive peasant state. For man's values to have changed for the better.' But he doubted this would happen. 'The world', he said, 'will not change dramatically. As for my own personal hopes, they will be achieved. I will make sure of that.'

Many of his friends drew the same distinction between themselves and their world. That distinction points to the need for another – that between hope and hopefulness. Both are social as much as they are psychological facts. Like needs, hopes are defined and given meaning in the context of a society. They are given expression in language. What Michael Ignatieff has written about the language of human needs seems to me to apply with equal force to the language of hope: 'Our needs are made of words; they come to us in speech, and they can die for lack of expression. Without a public language to help us find our words, our needs will dry up in silence' (1984:142).

Ignatieff is particularly concerned to develop a language adequate to the task of building a fraternal society, a society in which the needs of strangers can be identified, acknowledged and met. Nearly thirty years earlier, Richard Titmuss explored the same issue and drew attention to what happens when, ignoring the complex networks which bind people to an interdependence on one another, a society attaches the highest values to individual achievement (1958). Individuals under such circumstances become exposed to failure and, as he put it, to 'pain':

The corollary for any society which invests more of its values and virtues in the promotion of the individual is individual failure and individual consciousness of failure. (1958b:55)

The same point applies to hopes. A society which privileges the hopes of individuals, and fails to encourage the development of realizable hopes for the community as a whole, creates simultaneously the conditions of a sense of hopelessness in individuals and a sense of despair that improvement in the public sphere is possible. The only credible vision of the future which is then possible is one which continues to nurture the prospect of individual material success. For those who cannot succeed the options are limited; the abandonment of hope is the one which guarantees a life free of disappointments.

If the account of hope set out here has validity, then there are certainly grounds for hope for the future in British society. New structures of feeling can emerge to sustain new private hopes which have new implications for the society as a whole and which can only be realized in the context of broader social changes. The aspirations of those in the women's movement or the ecology movement are unrealizable without profound changes in public policy and in social structures. The governments of Margaret Thatcher have understood that their particular vision of a prosperous Britain is only realizable through deep alterations in prevailing social arrangements and moral values. It is not just a matter of altering some of the settings in the economic management of those parts of the economy governments can control.

The evidence of the past half century since the beginning of World War II is that social change can be brought about where there is commitment to do so. How that commitment is secured is, of course, a matter of politics. It is therefore something inextricably bound up with values and interests and convictions. All are held together by how people feel about themselves and others, and feelings change. Because this is so obviously the case, the grounds for both a hopeful and a despairing view of the future are clearly arguable. What is certain, however, is that there is no inevitability or necessity about the ways in which the future might unfold.

History and dialogue: endings and beginnings

This book began with the admission that it had its roots in personal biographical reflection. The changes it has described are changes in the world I grew up in. How I have come to understand those changes is a reflection of my own experience and reading. An obvious criticism of what I have written is that the account is therefore biased and that its subjectivity is misleading; that, at best, it is only one of several possible and very different accounts of post-war Britain. The strongest version of such an argument would rest on a claim that improving living standards have brought with them a well-being most people would never willingly give up. It would stress, too, that if more emphasis had been placed on those who have been successful in this society then a different, much more positive and optimistic range of emotional tones would have been detected.

Though the book deals with aspects of subjectivity, with feelings and sentiments, it is not a wholly subjective account. It is selective; there are many issues which I have not dealt with and no doubt many more which I have dealt with partially or, in the opinions of others with more direct experience of them, lightly or even inaccurately. Being white, male and now middle class imposes clear limitations on my ability to comment in a fully sympathetic way on the experience of other groups of people in this society. The social, intellectual and emotional boundaries of a divided society are difficult to overcome. And they will not be overcome by historians or social scientists who try to gloss their account of the world with a spurious objectivity, or by others who retreat into making claims about it based purely on personal experience. Experience alone is a poor guide to understanding.

All views of the world are partial. There is no transcendent historical truth which goes beyond the many partial interpretations of the past which make up human experience. At best there is dialogue and debate and the critical assessment and modification of different perspectives. In this sense history is an open and creative activity. If this book can be read in this light I will be gratified. For I wish to make no stronger claim for what it has achieved than that it is a contribution to a debate. My belief is that it is through open debate and the public testing out of arguments that our collective understanding of the past will be refined. The broader the debate, the more reliable the conclusion is likely to be.

There is, however, a discipline to historical and sociological discussions of this kind. There must be a respect for evidence. An effort must be made to understand that the past just does not reveal itself in the evidence it leaves behind; as Philip Abrams put it, the past 'can only be known in terms of some conscious effort to theorise it' (1982:329). There can be no historian-free history. Above all, it is vital to avoid simple and unhelpful abstractions such as 'the individual' or 'the market' or 'Britain'. At the point when sociological or historical terms come close to a description of the lives of persons, those who use them should acknowledge that complex interdependence which binds people to the societies of which they are a part. This is an approach to history which requires the use of what C. Wright Mills called 'the sociological imagination' (1959). It is a way of thinking which emphasizes that the private experience of individuals is something intricately woven into the structures of the society in which they lead their lives and that both change through time.

To write a book with strong autobiographical themes about feelings and sentiments brings with it an obligation to clarify where the author stands at its completion. Much of what I have written is critical of British society. I am not concerned that critics might feel that I have been less than fair in the way I have interpreted the actions of politicians or expressed controversial and debatable views about class structures or education or patriotism. I have, however, been critical of the values and attitudes which have come to dominate the lives of ordinary people – people like my parents and their neighbours and their friends and the children and grandchildren of those friends. That criticism requires comment, for that is not how I feel about them.

Brian Jackson was right to point out, as he did in 1968, that the habits of mutuality, of valuing people rather than abstractions and of directness of emotional response, are the best qualities of working class culture and that a civilized society would nurture and build on them (1968). Sid Chaplin captured for me much of what I feel, when he noted of himself that he was 'continuously fascinated, obsessed, appalled, amazed and delighted, by the infinite variety of human beings, and especially by their capacity for courage, nobility, and compassion' (1987:179). He saw his work as a novelist as an attempt, with parallels in theology and philosophy, 'to discover or impose a pattern on that very disordered thing we call life'. He was motivated by an unshakeable conviction that ordinary folk are also extraordinary – 'if you think they are shallow', he wrote, 'just talk to any ordinary Joe and find out just how deep an ordinary Joe can be.'

All the values Chaplin respected came, he said, 'from mining villages and mining folk', but what he knew only too well was that the future lay in the 'cities, great masses of roads and houses and factories, great masses of newly affluent people'. So the question, 'What will wither and die and what, on the other hand, will flower?' became the central question of his art.

Chaplin explored the question in fiction. My approach has been through social science. The question, though, is the same; so is the worry that what ordinary folk do and think is either ignored or manipulated. What they think about motor cars or washing machines or precooked food is not left to chance. A shameful press panders to the worst impulses of us all to create desires for, and a heightened awareness of, everything that is cheap, commercial and exploitable in the commercial culture of the modern economy. Political debate is reduced to the simplest formulae of prejudice and abuse that an ill-informed electorate can absorb. Human relations are presented in their most ruthless, exploitative forms as if that were the norm. But what people actually think and feel, how they struggle to understand the world in which they live with the inadequate resources given to them and what the answers are that they come up with, are features of working class life and culture largely ignored and certainly devalued in this society.

The result is for me a disturbing one. I remain convinced that the values which have been bequeathed to us through the struggles of working people to achieve a better life for themselves and their society – values like equality, justice, fairness, fraternity – remain the best hope for humanity in what is otherwise a crazy world. If those values could be made real and become part of how we ordered our affairs, both nationally and internationally, then the full promise of the potential in all human beings to enjoy and develop fully a creative and civilized life would be realized in abundance.

Such a world would be radically at odds with the narrow, individualistic, materialistic, authoritarian, indifferent, and environmentally myopic forms of society bred by the economic and political activities of those who dominate the modern capitalist economy. But there is the rub; it is no longer adequate to conjure up capitalists or Fascists to explain our plight. All of us with pension schemes and private homes are part of it, too. We are the problem. The political achievements of post-war social policy – the welfare state, decent homes, secondary education, pensions – have to be thought through again to assess clearly whether they actually do give expression to the values that once inspired them. The answer, I think, we know already; forty years of social research has provided us with it. Far from being a just and fraternal society, Britain is divided; the social frameworks of its society are damaging to the welfare of hundreds of thousands, indeed, millions of people.

What is even more distressing is that a sense of how the vision of a better society might be recovered has been lost. Many people are alienated from the political processes which govern their lives and even from one another. Britain has become a disconnected society. Many people have no access whatsoever to the ideas and skills with which to explore their world effectively and imagine alternatives to it. And at the point where an alternative vision became clear, which political movement could implement it?

That question, of course, is a political one; its answers are all debatable. But it is not at all a question of despair. There are no solutions to the complex problems of any modern society which lie outside the arenas of politics. Those arenas are themselves changing. At the beginning of the period with which this book has been concerned, Britain was very much a world power poised to lead a shattered Europe. Britain now is very much a

European power which looks to Europe and, perhaps, increasingly to Japan for leads for its own future development. Such changes bring new opportunities, new alignments as well as new dangers. The political movements of the future cannot merely re-enact the battles of an older generation, and indeed they do not. The peace movement, the women's movement and, more recently, the ecology movement have each demonstrated that what Raymond Williams called 'the resources of hope' are constantly renewed.

There is no need to despair either of the role this society could play in the modern world or of the ways in which it might itself be changed. The real danger is that through a failure to understand how this society really works we shall lose opportunities to utilize creatively, and in full, its vast resources of wealth, knowledge and technical ingenuity. What I hope to have shown in this book is that those resources are found ultimately in the ways in which people place a value on themselves and on others; that values are inseparable from sentiments and that it is feelings which shape convictions.

There are no doubt those who think that the real stuff of history is something else, that sentiment is something best left to psychologists or poets: that feelings are too insubstantial, fleeting and, above all, private, to be the concern of social science. The words of Lucien Febvre, the great French historian, can bring this book to an end where, in a way, it began (1973). To those who claim that a history of feeling and of sentiment is neither possible nor relevant, that such history – the history of hate, fear, cruelty, love; or, as in the case of this particular study, of belonging, hope, solidarity or despair – is just so much 'empty talk', Febvre, with telling irony, said this:

But the subject of such empty talk, which has so little to do with humanity, will tomorrow have finally made our universe into a stinking pit of corpses.

Bibliography

Abel-Smith, B. and Townsend, P. 1965: *The Poor and the Poorest* (Occasional papers in social administration No 17, Bell).

Abercrombie, N. and Warde, A. 1988: *Contemporary British Society* (Cambridge, Polity Press).

Abrams, P. 1982: *Historical Sociology* (London, Open Books).

Abrams, P. and Little, A. 1965: The Young Voter in British Politics. *British Journal of Sociology*, XVI, No 2, 95–109.

Addison, P. 1982: *The Road to 1945* (London, Quartet Books).

Addison, P. 1985: *Now the War is Over* (London, Cape).

Adeney, M. and Lloyd, J. 1986: *The Miners' Strike 1984–5: Loss Without Limit* (London, Routledge & Kegan Paul).

Ahier, J. and Flude, M. (eds) 1983: *Contemporary Education Policy* (London, Croom Helm).

Amis, K. 1963: What's Left for Patriotism? *Observer*, 20 January.

Apple, R.W. Jnr 1985: Embattled Britain. *Sunday Times*, 20 October.

Ashton, N. and Field, D. 1976: *Young Workers* (London, Hutchinson).

Baker, K. 1988: *Re-establishing Moral Values* (London, Conservative Central Office).

Balfour, M. 1979: *Propaganda in War 1939–1945: Organisations, Policies and Publics in Britain and Germany* (London, Routledge & Kegan Paul).

Banton, M. 1955: *The Coloured Quarter: Negro Immigrants in an English City* (London, Jonathan Cape).

Barker, R. 1972: *Education and Politics 1900–1951: A Study of the Labour Party* (Oxford, Clarendon Press).

Barnett, A. 1982: *Iron Britannia* (London, Allison & Busby).

Barnett, C. 1986: *The Audit of War* (London, Macmillan).

Barr, J. 1964: Pakistanis in Bradford. *New Society*, 19 November, 6.

Barnsley Women Against Pit Closures 1984: *Women Against Pit Closures* (Dodsworth, Barnsley).

Barraclough, G. 1967: *An Introduction to Contemporary History* (Harmondsworth, Pelican).

Bauman, Z. 1982: *Memories of Class* (London, Routledge & Kegan Paul).

Bechhofer, F., Elliot, B. and McCrone, D. 1983: Structure, Consciousness and Action: A Sociological Profile of the British Middle Class. In A. Stewart 1983a.

Beck, J. 1983: *Accountability, Industry and Education*. In Ahier and Flude 1983.

Berghahn, M. 1984: *German-Jewish Refugees in England: The Ambiguities of Assimilation* (London, Macmillan).

Beynon, H. 1984: *Working for Ford* (Harmondsworth, Penguin).

Beynon, H. (ed.) 1985: *Digging Deeper: Issues in the Miners' Strike* (London, Verso).

Beynon, H. and Wainwright, H. 1979: *The Workers' Report on Vickers* (London, Pluto).

Blackburn, R.M. and Prandy, K. 1965: White-Collar Unioniztion: A Conceptual Framework. *British Journal of Sociology*, XVI, No 2 (June), 111–22.

Blackwell, T. and Seabrook, J. 1985: *A World Still to Win: The Reconstruction of the Post-War Working Class* (London, Faber & Faber).

Blackwell, T. and Seabrook, J. 1988: *The Politics of Hope: Britain at the End of the Twentieth Century* (London, Faber & Faber).

Blythe, R. 1969: *Akenfield* (Harmondsworth, Penguin).

Bogdanor, V. and Skidelsky, R. 1970: *The Age of Affluence 1951–1964* (London, Macmillan).

Bommes, M. and Wright, P. 1982: 'Charms of Residence': The Public and the Past. In Centre for Contemporary Cultural Studies 1982.

Booker, C. 1970: *The Neophiliacs* (London, Fontana).

Bottomore, T. 1982: The Political Role of the Working Class in Western Europe. In A. Giddens and G. Mackenzie (eds), *Social Class and the Division of Labour* (London, Cambridge University Press).

Bourdieu, P. 1974: The School as a Conservative Force. In J. Eggleston (ed.), *Contemporary Research in the Sociology of Education* (London, Methuen).

Bragg, M. 1976: *Speak for England* (London, Secker & Warburg).

Briggs, A. 1983: *A Social History of England* (London, Book Club Associaties with Weidenfield & Nicolson).

Broady, M. 1956: The Organisation of Coronation Street Parties. *The Sociological Review*, 4, No 2 (Dec.), 223–43.

Brook, L., Jowell, R. and Witherspoon, S. 1989: Recent Trends in Social Attitudes. In *Social Trends 19* (London, HMSO).

Brown, R.K. 1978: Work. In P. Abrams (ed.), *Work, Urbanism and Unequality: UK Society Today* (London, Weidenfeld & Nicolson).

Brown, R.K. 1989: Work. In P. Abrams and R.K. Brown (eds), *UK Society, Work, Urbanism and Unequality* (London, Weidenfeld & Nicolson).

Bryan, B., Dadzie, S. and Scafe, S. 1985: *The Heart of the Race: Black Women's Lives in Britain* (London, Virago).

Bullock, A. 1967: *The Life and Times of Ernest Bevin. Vol II: Minister of Labour 1940–1945* (London, Heinemann).

Bullock, A. 1983: *Ernest Bevin, Foreign Secretary* (London, Heinemann).

Burke, P. (ed.) 1973: *A New Kind of History: from the Writings of Lucien Febvre* (London, Routledge & Kegan Paul).

Butler, Lord R. 1971: *The Art of the Possible: The Memoirs of Lord Butler* (London, Hamish Hamilton).

Calder, A. 1969: *The People's War: Britain 1939–1945* (London, Panther).

Calder, A. and Sheridan, D. 1985: *Speak for Yourself: A Mass Observation Anthology 1937–1949* (London, Oxford University Press). First edition 1984.

Calvocoressi, P. and Wint, G. 1974: *Total War* (Harmondsworth, Penguin).

Cannadine, D. 1983: The Context, Performance and Meaning of Ritual: The British Monarchy and the 'Invention of Tradition' 1820–1977. In E. Hobsbawn and T. Ranger (eds), *The Invention of Tradition* (Cambridge, Cambridge University Press).

Carey, S. 1985: 'I Just Hate 'Em, That's All'. *New Society*, 26 July, 123–6.

Carr, E.H. 1951: The Changing World. *The Listener*, 7 June, 914–18.

Carstairs, G.M. 1964: *This Island Now* (Harmondsworth, Penguin).

Cashmore, E.E. 1984: *No Future* (London, Heinemann).

Causer, G.A. (ed.) 1987: *Inside British Society: Continuity, Challenge and Change* (London, Wheatsheaf).

Cauter, T. and Downham, J.S. 1954: *The Communication of Ideas: A Study of*

Contemporary Influences on Urban Life (London, The Readers Digest Association).

Central Advisory Council for Education 1959: *15 to 18* [Crowther Report] (London, HMSO).

Central Advisory Council for Education 1963: *Half Our Future* [Newsom Report] (London, HMSO).

Central Advisory Council for Education 1967: *Children in their Primary Schools* [Plowden Report] (London, HMSO).

Centre for Contemporary Cultural Studies 1982: *Making Histories* (London, Hutchinson).

Chambers, P. and Landreth, A. (eds) 1955: *Called Up* (London, Allan Wingate).

Chaney, D. 1983: A Symbolic Mirror of Ourselves: Civic Ritual in Mass Society. *Media, Culture and Society*, 5, No 2, 119–35.

Chaplin, S. 1987: A Credo. In *In Blackberry Time*, eds Michael and Rene Chaplin (Newcastle-upon-Tyne, Bloodaxe Books).

Chappel, H. and King, S. 1981: The Wedding and the People. *New Society*, 30 July, 175–7.

Charlton, G. 1988: Gateshead Grammar. In N. Astley (ed.), *Poetry with an Edge* (Newcastle-upon-Tyne, Bloodaxe Books).

Cherry, D. and Potts, A. 1982: The Changing Images of War. *New Society*, 29 April, 172–4.

Church of England 1985: *Faith in the City: An Audit for the Local Church* (London, General Synod Board for Mission and Unity).

Church of England Board for Social Responsibility 1987: *Changing Britain: Social Diversity and Moral Unity* (London, Church House Publishing).

Coates, K. and Silburn, R. 1973: *Poverty: The Forgotten Englishmen* (Harmondsworth, Penguin).

Coffield, F., Borril, C. and Marshall, S. 1986: *Growing Up at the Margins* (Milton Keynes, Open University Press).

Cohen, G. 1972: *Folk Devils and Moral Panics* (London, MacGibbon & Kee).

Cole, G.D.H. 1955: *Studies in Class Structure* (London, Routledge & Kegan Paul).

Collins, S. 1955: The British – Born Coloured. *The Sociological Review* 3, No 1 (July), 77–92.

Committee on Higher Education 1963: *Higher Education* [Robbins report] (London, HMSO).

Connolly, C. 1944: Letter from a Civilian. *Horizon*, X, No 57, 151–3.

Cooper, D.E. 1970: Looking Back in Anger. In Bogdanor and Skidelsky 1970.

Cooper, S. 1964: Snoek Piquante. In Sissons and French 1964.

Cotgrove, S. 1976: Environmentalism and Utopia. *The Sociological Review*, 24, No 1, 23–43.

Cotgrove, S. and Duff, A. 1980: Environmentalism, Middle Class Radicalism and Politics. *The Sociological Review*, 28, No 2, 333–51.

Cox, C.B. and Boyson, R. 1975: *Black Paper 4* (London, Dent).

Cox, C.B. and Boyson, R. 1977: *Black Paper 5* (London, Temple Smith).

Cox, C.B. and Dyson, A.E. (eds) 1971: *Black Papers on Education* (London, Davis-Poynster).

Cox, M. 1984: Western Capitalism and the Cold War System. In M. Shaw (ed.), *War, State and Society* (London, Macmillan).

Crick, R. and Robson, W.A. (eds) 1970: *Protest and Discontent* (Harmondsworth, Penguin).

Cronin, J.E. 1984: *Labour and Society in Britain 1918–1979* (London, Batsford).

Crouch, C. 1970: *The Student Revolt* (London, Bodley Head).

Crosland, C.A.R. 1956: *The Future of Socialism* (London, Cape).

Crossman, R. 1976: The Role of the Volunteer in the Modern Social Service. In A.H. Halsey (ed.), *Traditions of Social Policy: Essays in Honour of Violet Butler* (Oxford, Basil Blackwell).

Cunningham, H. 1982: Who Speaks for Britain? *New Society*, 22 April, 130–2.

Dahrendorf, R. 1982: *On Britain* (London, British Broadcasting Corporation).

Dale, R. 1983: Thatcherism and Education. In Ahier and Flude 1983.

Dalton, H. 1962: *High Tide and After: Hugh Dalton Memoirs 1945–60* (London, Muller).

Darwin, J. 1988: *Britain and Decolonisation: The Retreat from Europe in the Post War World* (London, Macmillan).

Davies, A. 1989: *Where did the Forties Go? A Popular History. The Rise and Fall of the Hopes of a Decade* (London, Pluto).

Deacon, A. and Bradshaw, J. 1983: *Reserved for the Poor: The Means Test in British Social Policy* (Oxford, Basil Blackwell).

Deakin, N. 1970: *Colour, Citizenship and British Society* (London, Panther).

Demaine, J. 1981: *Contemporary Theories in the Sociology of Education* (London, Macmillan).

Dennehy, C. and Sullivan, J. 1977: Poverty and Unemployment in Liverpool. In F. Field (ed.), *The Conscript Army: A Study of Britain's Unemployed* (London, Routledge & Kegan Paul).

Dennis, N. 1958: The Popularity of the Neighbourhood Community Idea. *The Sociological Review* 6, No 2, 191–207.

Dennis, N. 1972: *Public Participation and Planner's Blight* (London, Faber & Faber).

Dennis, N., Henriques, F. and Slaughter, C. 1956: *Coal is Our Life* (London, Eyre & Spottiswoode).

Department of Education and Science 1983: *Young People in the 1980s: A Survey* (London, HMSO).

Donnison, D. 1982: We Compel the Poor to Make Intolerable Choices. *The Listener*, 25 March, 2–4.

Douglass, D.J. (ed.) 1986: *A Year of Our Lives: A Colliery Community in the Great Coal Strike 1984/5* (Doncaster, Hooligan Press).

Dunleavy, P. 1981: *The Politics of Mass Housing in Britain 1945–1975: A Study of Corporate Power and Political Influence in the Welfare State* (Oxford, Clarendon Press).

Eccleshall, R. 1977: English Conservatism as Ideology. *Political Studies*, XXV, No 1 (March), 62–84.

Edgar, D. 1976: *Destiny* (London, Methuen).

Edwards, E.G. 1982: *Higher Education for Everyone* (London, Spokesman).

Eglin, J. 1987: Women and Peace. In R. Taylor and Young 1987b.

Elias, N. and Scotson, J.L. 1965: *The Established and the Outsiders* (London, Frank Cass & Co. Ltd).

Eliot, T.S. 1944: The Man of Letters and the Future of Europe. *Horizon*, X, No 60, 382–90.

Eliot, T.S. 1948: *Notes Towards a Definition of Culture* (London, Faber & Faber).

Elliot, B. 1984: Cities in the Eighties: The Growth of Unequality. In P. Abrams and R. Brown (eds), *UK Society, Work, Urbanism and Unequality* (London, Weidenfeld & Nicolson).

Falls, C. 1952: A Window on the World: British Youth under the Lens. *Illustrated London News*, 19 January, 88.

Febvre, L. 1973: Sensibility and History. In Burke 1973.

Fisk, T. 1970: The Nature and Courses of Student Unrest. In Crick and Robson 1970.

Fletcher, R. 1962: *Britain in the Sixties: The Family and Marriage* (Harmondsworth, Penguin).

Flude, M. and Ahier, J. (eds) 1974: *Educability, Schools and Ideology* (London, Croom Helm).

Foot, M. 1982: *Aneurin Bevan 1897–1945* (London, Paladin).

Fox, A. 1966: *Industrial Sociology and Industrial Relations*. Research Paper No 3, Royal Commission on Trades Unions and Employers' Associations (London, HMSO).

Frayn, M. 1964: Festival. In Sissons and French 1964.

Fryer, P. 1984: *Staying Power: The Story of Black People in Britain* (London, Pluto).

Fyvel, T.R. 1968: *Intellectuals Today: Problems in a Changing Society* (London, Chatto & Windus).

Gamble, A. 1979: *The Conservative Nation* (London, Routledge & Kegan Paul).

Gamble, A. 1981: *Britain in Decline* (London, Macmillan).

Gavron, H. 1983: *The Captive Wife: Conflicts of Housebound Mothers* (London, Routledge & Kegan Paul). First edition 1966.

Gerth, H. and Mills, C. Wright 1970: *Character and Social Structure: The Psychology of Social Institutions* (London, Routledge & Kegan Paul). First edition 1954.

Giddens, A. 1979: *Central Problems in Social Theory* (London, Macmillan).

Glasgow Media Group 1980: *More Bad News* (London, Routledge & Kegan Paul).

Glass, D. (ed.) 1954: *Social Mobility in Britain* (London, Routledge & Kegan Paul).

Goldsworthy, D. 1971: *Colonial Issues in British Politics 1945–1961* (Oxford, Clarendon Press).

Goldthorpe, J.H. 1977: Industrial Relations in Great Britain: A Critique of Reformism. Reported in T. Clarke and L. Clements, *Trade Unions Under Capitalism* (London, Fontana).

Goldthorpe, J.H., Llewellyn, C. and Payne, C. 1980: *Social Mobility and Class Structure in Modern Britain* (Oxford, Oxford University Press).

Goldthorpe, J.H. and Lockwood, D. 1963: Affluence and the British Class Structure. *The Sociological Review* 11, No 2 (July), 133–65.

Goldthorpe, J.H., Lockwood, D., Bechhofer, F. and Platt, J. 1971: *The Affluent Worker in the Class Structure* (Cambridge, Cambridge University Press).

Gordon, S.L. 1981: The Sociology of Sentiments and Emotion. In M. Rosenberg and R.H. Turner (eds), *Social Psychology: Sociological Perspectives* (New York, Basic Books).

Gosling, R. 1972: Winston's Wake. In P. Barker (ed.), *One for Sorrow, Two for Joy* (London, George Allen & Unwin).

Gough, I. 1983: Thatcherism and the Welfare State. In S. Hall and Jacques 1983.

Granzow, B. 1964: *A Mirror of Nazism: British Opinion and the Emergence of Hitler 1929–1933* (London, Gollancz).

Guttsman, W.L. 1963: *The British Political Elite* (London, MacGibbon & Kee).

Habermas, J. 1968: Student Protest in the Federal Republic of Germany. In

J. Habermas (ed.), *Towards a Rational Society* (London, Heinemann).

Habermas, J. 1976. *The Legitimation Crisis* (London, Heinemann).

Hall, J.A. 1987: *The State*. In Causer 1987.

Hall, S. 1988: *The Hard Road to Renewal: Thatcherism and the Crisis of the Left* (London, Verso).

Hall, S. and Jacques, M. 1983: *The Politics of Thatcherism* (London, Lawrence & Wishart).

Halmos, P. 1967: The Personal Service Society. *The British Journal of Sociology* XVIII, No 1 (March), 13–27.

Halsey, A.H. 1954: Social Mobility in Britain – A Review. *The Sociological Review*, 2, No 2, 169–79.

Halsey, A.H. 1972a: *Educational Priority – EPA Patterns and Policies* (London, HMSO).

Halsey, A.H. (ed.) 1972b: *Trends in British Society Since 1900* (London, Macmillan).

Halsey, A.H. 1981: *Change in British Society* (Oxford, Oxford University Press).

Halsey, A.H. 1989: Social Trends Since World War 2. In L. McDowell, P. Sarre and C. Hamnet (eds), *Divided Nation: Social and Cultural Changes in Britain* (Milton Keynes, The Open University).

Halsey, A.H., Health, A.F. and Ridge, J. 1980: *Origins and Destinations: Family, Class and Education in Modern Britain* (Oxford, Oxford University Press).

Halsey, A.H. and Trow, M. 1971: *The British Academic* (London, Faber & Faber).

Hargreaves, D.H. 1967: *Social Relations in a Secondary School* (London, Routledge & Kegan Paul).

Harker, D. 1980: *One for the Money: Politics and Popular Song* (London, Hutchinson).

Harris, J. 1986: Political Ideas and the Debate on State Welfare 1940–45. In H.L. Smith 1986.

Harris, L. 1985: British Capital: Manufacturing, Finance and Multi-National Corporations. In D. Coates, G. Johnston and R. Bush (eds), *A Socialist Anatomy of Britain* (Cambridge, Polity Press).

Harrison, J. (ed.) 1973: *Condemned, A Shelter Report on Housing and Poverty*. Reproduced in J. Raynor and J. Harden (eds), *Cities, Communities and the Young* [Readings in Urban Education Vol. 1] (London, Open University Press).

Harrison, P. 1983: *Inside the Inner City: Life Under the Cutting Edge* (Harmondsworth, Penguin).

Harrison, T. 1984: *Selected Poems* (Harmondsworth, Penguin).

Harrison, T. 1985: *V* (Newcastle-upon-Tyne, Bloodaxe Books).

Hayek, F. 1944: *The Road to Serfdom* (London, Routledge).

Heineman, B.W. 1972: *The Politics of the Powerless: A Study of the Campaign Against Racial Discrimination* (London, Oxford University Press).

Hennessy, P. 1986: *The Great and the Good: An Enquiry into the British Establishment* (London, Policy Studies Institute Research Report No 654).

Heron, L. (ed.) 1985: *Truth, Dare or Promise: Girls Growing Up in the Fifties* (London, Virago).

Hewison, R. 1986: *Too Much: Art and Society in the Sixties, 1960–75* (London, Methuen).

Hewison, R. 1987: *The Heritage Industry: Britain in a Climate of Decline* (London, Methuen).

Hewison, R. 1988: *In Anger: Culture in the Cold War 1945–1960* (London, Methuen). First edition 1981.

Hill, D. (ed.) 1977: *Tribune 40: The First Forty Years of a Socialist Newspaper* (London, Quartet).

Hindess, B. 1971: *The Decline of Working Class Politics* (London, Paladin).

History Workshop 1979: *History Workshop: A Journal of Socialist Historians*, 7 (Spring).

Hobsbawm, E. 1989a: Falklands Fallout. In E. Hobsbawm (ed.), *Politics for a Rational Left* (London, Verso).

Hobsbawm, E. 1989b: The Forward March of Labour Halted. In E. Hobsbawm (ed.), *Politics for a Rational Left* (London, Verso).

Hobsbawm, E. 1989c: The Verdict of the 1979 Election. In E. Hobsbawm (ed.), *Politics for a Rational Left* (London, Verso).

Hoffman, J.D. 1964: *The Conservative Party in Opposition 1945–51* (London, MacGibbon & Kee).

Hoggart, R. 1957: *The Uses of Literacy* (Harmondsworth, Penguin).

Home Office 1981: *The Brixton Disorders 10–12 April 1981* [The Scarman Report: Cmnd 8427] (London, HMSO).

Howard, M. 1964: We Are the Masters Now. In Sissons and French 1964.

Hunt, P. 1980: *Gender and Class Consciousness* (London, Macmillan).

Ignatieff, M. 1984: *The Needs of Strangers* (London, Chatto & Windus/The Hogarth Press).

Ingham, M. 1981: *Now We Are Thirty* (London, Methuen).

Irving, C., Hall, R. and Wallington, J. 1963: *Scandal '63: A Study of the Profumo Affair* (London, Heinemann).

Jackson, B. 1968: *Working Class Community* (Harmondsworth, Penguin).

Jackson, B. and Marsden, D. 1986: *Education and the Working Class* (London, Ark Paperbacks).

Jennings, H. 1962: *Societies in the Making: A Study of Development and Redevelopment within a County Borough* (London, Routledge & Kegan Paul).

Johnson, B.S. (ed.) 1973: *All Bull: The National Servicemen* (London, Quartet).

Joseph, Sir Keith 1984: Why Teach History? (Lecture to the Historical Association Conference, 10 February, University of London).

Joseph, Sir Keith 1986: Solving the Union Problem is the Key to Britain's Recovery. (Centre for Policy Studies.) In D. Coates and J. Hullard (eds), *The Economic Decline of Modern Britain* (London, Harvester Press).

Jowell, R. and Airey, C. 1985: British Social Attitudes, In *Social Trends 15* (London, HMSO).

Kelsall, R.K., Poole, A. and Kuhn, A. 1972: *Graduates: The Sociology of an Elite* (London, Methuen).

King, R. 1969: *Values and Involvement in a Grammar School* (London, Routledge & Kegan Paul).

Koestler, A. 1963: When the Daydream Had to Stop. *Observer*, 10 February.

Kogan, M. 1971: *The Politics of Education* (Harmondsworth, Penguin).

Kumar, K. 1983. The Social and Cultural Setting. In B. Ford (ed.), *The New Pelican Guide to English Literature: The Present* (Harmondsworth, Penguin).

Kumar, K. 1988: *The Rise of Modern Society: Aspects of the Social and Political Development of the West* (Oxford, Basil Blackwell).

Kuper, L. (ed.) 1953: *Living in Towns: Selected Research Papers in Urban Sociology* (London, The Cresset Press).

Lacey, C. 1970: *Hightown Grammar: The School as a Social System* (Manchester, Manchester University Press).

Laing, R.D. 1967: *The Politics of Experience* (Harmondsworth, Penguin).

Laqueur, W. 1982: *Europe Since Hitler* (Harmondsworth, Penguin).

Larkin, P. 1974: *High Windows* (London, Faber & Faber).

Layton-Henry, Z. 1980: Immigration. In Z. Layton-Henry (ed.), *Conservative Party Politics* (London, Macmillan).

Lebzelter, G.C. 1978: *Political Anti-Semitism in England 1918–1939* (London, Macmillan).

Lee, L. 1951: An Obstinate Exile. *The Listener*, 13 September, 418–19.

Leigh, D. 1980: *The Frontiers of Secrecy: Closed Government in Britain* (London, Junction Books).

Leitch, D. 1964: Explosion at the King David Hotel. In Sissons and French 1964.

Lewis, R. and Maude, A. 1949: *The English Middle Classes* (Harmondsworth, Penguin).

Leys, C. 1989: *Politics in Britain: From Labourism to Thatcherism* (London, Verso).

Little, K. 1948: *Negroes in Britain – A Study of Racial Relations in English Society* (London, Routledge & Kegan Paul).

Lloyd, T.O. 1979: *Empire to Welfare State: English History 1906–1978* (London, Oxford University Press).

Longmate, N. 1971: *How We Lived Then. A History of Everyday Life During The Second World War* (London, Arrow Books).

Lupton, T. and Wilson, C.S. 1973: The Social Background and Connections of 'Top Decision-Makers'. In J. Urry and J. Wakeford (eds), *Power in Britain* (London, Heinemann).

MacIntyre, A. 1956: Manchester: The Modern Universities and the English Tradition. *The Twentieth Century*, February, 123–9.

MacKenzie, J.M. (ed.) 1986: *Imperialism and Popular Culture* (Manchester, Manchester University Press).

Macleod, I. and Powell, J.E. 1949: *The Social Services – Needs and Means* (London, Conservative Political Centre).

MacRae, D. 1958: Class Relationships and Ideology. *The Sociological Review*, 6, No 2 (Dec), 261–72.

Mallalieu, J.P.W. 1963: *Very Ordinary Seaman* (London, Panther).

Marquand, D. 1988: *The Unprincipled Society: New Demands and Old Politics* (London, Fontana).

Marsden, D. 1982: *Workless* (London, Croom Helm).

Marshall, G., Rose, D., Vogler, C. and Newby, H. 1985: Class, Citizenship and Distributional Conflict in Modern Britain. *British Journal of Sociology*, 36 (No 2), 259–84.

Marshall, T.H. 1950: *Citizenship and Social Class* (London, Cambridge University Press).

Marshall, T.H. 1965: *Social Policy* (London, Hutchinson).

Marsland, D. 1978: *Sociological Explorations in the Service of Youth* (Leicester, National Youth Bureau).

Martin, B. 1981: *A Sociology of Contemporary Cultural Change* (Oxford, Basil Blackwell).

Marwick, A. 1968: *Britain in a Century of Total War* (Harmondsworth, Penguin).

Marwick, A. 1980: *Class: Image and Reality in Britain, France and the USA Since 1930* (London, Collins).
Marwick A. 1982: *British Society Since 1945* (Harmondsworth, Penguin).
Maschler, T. (ed.) 1958: *Declaration* (London, MacGibbon & Kee). First edition 1957.
Mass Observation 1943: *War Factory: A Report* (London, Gollancz).
Mass Observation 1945a: *File Report 2258: Twenty-Five Year Cycle* (June).
Mass Observation 1945b: *File Report 2278B: Feelings about the Peace* (August).
Mass Observation 1945c: *File Report 2301: Attitudes to Russia* (November).
Mass Observation 1946a: *File Report 2370: World Organisation and the Future* (March).
Mass Observation 1946b: *File Report 2441: Report on Anti-Semitism and Free Speech* (July).
Mass Observation 1946c: *File Report 2431: The Squatters* (November).
Mass Observation 1947a: *File Report 2463: Mass Observation Panel on the Jews* (March).
Mass Observation 1947b: *File Report 2466: Undergraduate Opinion in Oxford* (April).
Mass Observation 1947c: *File Report 2477: Usage and Abusage* (May).
Mass Observation 1947d: *File Report 2490: Aspects of Britain* (May).
Mass Observation 1947e: *File Report 2454: Anti-Americanism* (June).
Mass Observation 1947f: *File Report 2507: Voluntary Services* (August).
Mass Observation 1947g: *File Report 2508: Aspects of Charity* (August).
Mass Observation 1948: *File Report 3073: Middle Class: Why?* (December).
Mass Observation 1949: *File Report 3140: Report on the Health Service* (July).
McCallum, R.B. and Readman, R. 1947: *The British General Election of 1945* (London, Oxford University Press).
McKenzie, R.T. and Silver, A. 1968: *Angels in Marble: Working Class Conservatives in Urban England* (London, Heinemann).
Melly, G. 1965: *Owning Up* (London, Futura Publications).
Middleton, N. and Weitzman, S. 1976: *A Place for Everyone* (London, Gollancz).
Midwinter, E. 1972: *Priority Education: An Account of the Liverpool Project* (Harmondsworth, Penguin).
Miliband, R. 1961: *Parliamentary Socialism: A Study in the Politics of Labour* (London, Allen & Unwin).
Miliband, R. 1969: *The State in Capitalist Society* (London, Weidenfeld & Nicolson).
Mills, C. Wright 1959: *The Sociological Imagination* (New York, Oxford University Press).
Mishra, R. 1984: *The Welfare State in Crisis: Social Thought and Social Change* (London, Harvester Press).
Mitchell, J. 1971: *Women's Estate* (Harmondsworth, Penguin).
Mitford, N. 1955: The English Aristocracy. *Encounter*, 24 September, 5–12.
Mogey, J.M. 1956: *Family and Neighbourhood: Two Studies in Oxford* (Oxford, Oxford University Press).
Moore, R. 1975: *Racism and Black Resistance in Britain* (London, Pluto).
Morgan, J. (ed.) 1981: *The Backbench Diaries of Richard Crossman* (London, Hamish Hamilton & Jonathan Cape).
Morgan, K.O. 1985: *Labour in Power 1945–1951* (London, Oxford University Press). First edition 1984.
Morris, J. 1979: *Farewell the Trumpets: An Imperial Retreat* (Harmondsworth, Penguin).

Morse, M. 1965: *The Unattached* (Harmondsworth, Pelican).

Mortimer, J. 1982: *Clinging to the Wreckage* (Harmondsworth, Penguin).

Mount, F. 1982: *The Subversive Family* (London, Jonathan Cape).

Mumford, E.M. 1959: Social Behaviour in Small Work Groups. *The Sociological Review*, 7, No 2, 137–59.

Musgrove, F. 1967: Social Class and Levels of Aspiration in a Technological University. *The Sociological Review*, 15, No 3, 311–22.

Nairn, T. 1981: *The Break-up of Britain* (London, Verso).

Namier, Sir L. 1955: Human Nature in Politics. In L. Namier (ed.), *Personalities and Powers* (London, Hamish Hamilton).

Nemzer, L. 1949: The Soviet Friendship Societies. *Public Opinion Quarterly*, 13 (Summer), 265–84.

Newby, H. 1977: *The Deferential Worker* (Harmondsworth, Penguin).

Nichols, T. 1969: *Ownership, Control and Ideology: An Enquiry into Certain Aspects of Modern Business Ideology* (London, George Allen & Unwin).

Nichols, T. and Beynon, H. 1977: *Living with Capitalism: Class Relations and the Modern Factory* (London, Routledge & Kegan Paul).

Nicolson, H. 1968: *Diaries and Letters 1945–1962* (London, Collins).

Nordlinger, E. 1967: *The Working Class Tories* (London, MacGibbon & Kee).

Oakley, A. 1981: *Subject Women* (Oxford, Basil Blackwell).

Oakley, A. 1984: *Taking it Like a Woman* (London, Flamingo).

Orlans, H. 1952: *Stevenage: A Sociological Study of a New Town* (London, Routledge & Kegan Paul).

Orwell, G. 1945: London Letter. *Partisan Review*, 12, 77–82.

Orwell, G. 1947: Towards European Unity. *Partisan Review*, 14, 346–51.

Orwell, G. 1962: England Your England. In George Orwell, *Inside the Whale and Other Essays* (Harmondsworth, Penguin).

Osborne, J. 1956: *Look Back in Anger* (London, Faber & Faber).

Osborne, J. 1958: They Call it Cricket. In Maschler 1958.

Osmond, J. 1988: *The Divided Kingdom* (London, Constable).

Pahl, R. 1984: *Divisions of Labour* (Oxford, Basil Blackwell).

Paneth, M. 1944: *Branch Street: A Sociological Study* (London, George Allen & Unwin).

Parkin, F. 1968: *Middle Class Radicalism: The Social Bases of the British Campaign for Nuclear Disarmament* (Manchester, Manchester University Press).

Patterson, S. 1963: *Dark Strangers: A Sociological Study of Absorption of a Recent West Indian Migrant Group in Brixton, South London* (London, Tavistock Publications).

Pear, T.H. 1955: *English Social Differences* (London, George Allen & Unwin).

Phillips, A. (ed.) 1979: *A Newnham Anthology* (Cambridge, Cambridge University Press).

Pimlott, B. 1985: *Hugh Dalton* (London, Jonathan Cape).

Pimlott, B. and Cook, C. 1986: *Trades Unions in British Politics* (London, Longman).

Rankin, W. 1973: What Dunkirk Spirit? *New Society*, 15 November, 396–8.

Rees, A.M. 1985: *T.H. Marshall's Social Policy* (London, Hutchinson).

Rex, J. and Moore, R. 1967: *Race, Community, and Conflict* (London, Oxford University Press).

Rex, J. and Tomlinson, S. 1979: *Colonial Immigrants in a British City: A Class Analysis* (London, Routledge & Kegan Paul).

Richardson, R. and Wood, S. 1989: Productivity Changes in the Coal Industry and the new Industrial Relations. *British Journal of Industrial Relations*, 1 (March), 33–57.

Richmond, A.H. 1954: *Colour Prejudice in Britain: A Study of West Indian Workers in Liverpool 1941–1951* (London, Routledge & Kegan Paul).

Robb, J.H. 1954: *Working Class Anti-Semite: A Psychological Study in a London Borough* (London, Tavistock Publications).

Robins, D. 1984: *We Hate Humans* (Harmondsworth, Penguin).

Rock, P. and Cohen, S. 1970: The Teddy Boy. In Bogdanor and Skidelsky 1970.

Rollet, C. 1972: Housing. In Halsey 1972b.

Rose, J. and Ziman, J. 1964: *Camford Observed: An Investigation of the Ancient Universities in the Modern World* (London, Gollancz).

Ross, A.S.C. 1955: 'U' and 'Non-U': An Essay in Sociological Linguistics. *Encounter*, 25 October, 11–20.

Rowbotham, S., Segal, L. and Wainwright, H. 1979: *Beyond the Fragments: Feminism and the Making of Socialism* (London, Merlin Press).

Rowntree, S. and Lavers, G.R. 1951: *Poverty and the Welfare State* (London, Longman).

Rowntree, S. and Lavers, G.R. 1952: *English Life and Leisure* (London, Longman).

Royle, T. 1986: *The Best Years of Their Lives: The National Service Experience 1945–63* (London, Michael Joseph).

Runciman, W.G. 1964: 'Embourgeoisement', Self-Related Class and Party Preference. *The Sociological Review* 12, No 2 (July), 137–54.

Russell, Lord B. 1951: Present Perplexities. *The Listener*, 17 May, 787–8.

St Clair Drake 1955: The 'Colour Problem' in Britain: A Study in Social Definitions. *The Sociological Review*, 3, No 2 (Dec.), 197–217.

Sarsby, J. 1983: *Romantic Love and Society: Its Place in the Modern World* (Harmondsworth, Penguin).

Scott, J. 1982: *The Upper Classes: Property and Privilege in Britain* (London, Macmillan).

Seabrook, J. 1975: Blackburn, Summer 1969. In C. Lambert and D. Weir (eds), *Cities in Modern Britain* (London, Fontana).

Seabrook, J. 1978: *What Went Wrong?* (London, Gollancz).

Seabrook, J. 1982: *Unemployment* (London, Quartet Books).

Seabrook, J. 1986: *Unemployment* (London, Quartet Books).

Seaton, J. 1986: Trades Unions and the Media. In Pimlott and Cook 1986.

Segal, L. (ed.) 1983: *What is To Be Done About the Family?* (Harmondsworth, Penguin).

Selbourne, D. 1982: Wolverhampton on Ice. *New Society*, 21 January, 94–6.

Seldon, A. 1963: Beveridge: 20 years After. *New Society*, 20 November, 9–12.

Sennet, R. 1978: *The Fall of Public Man* (London, Cambridge University Press).

Sennet, R. and Cobb, J. 1972: *The Hidden Injuries of Class* (London, Cambridge University Press).

Sharf, A. 1964: *The British Press and Jews Under Nazi Rule* (London, Oxford University Press).

Sharpe, S. 1976: *Just Like a Girl: How Girls Learn to be Women* (Harmondsworth, Penguin).

Sharpe, S. 1984: *Double Identity: The Lives of Working Mothers* (Harmondsworth, Penguin).

Shils, E. and Young, M. 1953: The Meaning of the Coronation. *The Sociological Review*, 1, No 2, 63–81.

Sillitoe, A. 1959: *The Loneliness of the Long Distance Runner* (London, Panther).

Simey, T.S. 1956: The Problem of Social Change – The Docks Industry: A Case Study. *The Sociological Review*, 4, No 2, 157–67.

Sissons, M. and French, P. 1964: *Age of Austerity 1945–1951* (Harmondsworth, Penguin). First edition 1963.

Sked, A. and Cook, C. 1979: *Post-War Britain: A Political History* (Harmondsworth, Penguin).

Slaughter, C. 1958: The Strike of Yorkshire Mineworkers. *The Sociological Review*, 6, No 2, 241–61.

Smith, H.L. (ed.) 1986: *War and Social Change: British Society in the Second World War* (Manchester, Manchester University Press).

Smith, K. 1984: *The British Economic Crisis* (Harmondsworth, Penguin).

Social Trends (updated annually): (London, HMSO).

Spence, M. 1983: British Imperialism and the Falklands. *Monthly Review*, 34, No 11, 20–8.

Spender, S. 1945: Comment. *Horizon*, XII, No 67, 5–10.

Stewart, A. (ed.) 1983a: *Contemporary Britain* (London, Routledge & Kegan Paul).

Stewart, A. 1983b: The Social Determination of Life Changes in Contemporary Britain. In A. Stewart 1983a.

Stewart, N.K. 1988: *South Atlantic Conflict of 1982: A Case Study in Military Cohesion* (US Army, Research Institute for the Behavioural and Social Sciences, Virginia).

Summerfield, P. 1985: *Women Workers and the Second World War* (London, Croom Helm).

Taylor, R. 1978: *The Fifth Estate: Britain's Unions in the Modern World* (London, Pan).

Taylor, R. 1981: The Born-Again CND. *New Society*, 10 September, 424–6.

Taylor, R. and Young, N. 1987a: Britain and the International Peace Movements in the 1980s. In R. Taylor and Young 1987b.

Taylor, R. and Young N. (eds) 1987b: *Campaign for Peace: British Peace Movements in the Twentieth Century* (Manchester, Manchester University Press).

Taylor, W. 1963: *The Secondary Modern School* (London, Faber & Faber).

Taylor-Gooby, P. 1983: Legitimation, Deficit, Public Opinion and the Welfare State. *Sociology*, 17, No 2, 165–84.

Taylor-Gooby, P. 1986: Privatisation, Power and the Welfare State. *Sociology*, 20, No 2, 228–46.

Tawney, R.H. 1964: *Equality* (London, Unwin Books).

Tawney, R.H. 1981: The War and Social Policy. In R.H. Tawney, *The Attack and Other Papers* (London, Spokesman).

Tebbit, N. 1985: Old Values that will Bolster a New Freedom. (Disraeli Lecture) *The Guardian*, 15 November, 12.

Thatcher, M.H. 1988: Speech to the General Assembly of the Church of Scotland, Saturday 21 May (London, Press Office, Prime Minister's Office).

Thompson, B. and Finlayson, A. 1963: Married Woman Who Work in Early Motherhood. *British Journal of Sociology*, XIV, No 2, 150–68.

Thompson, D. (ed.) 1964: *Discrimination and Popular Culture* (Harmondsworth, Penguin).

Thompson, E.P. 1975: Europe Debate. *Sunday Times*, 27 April, 32.

Thompson, E.P. 1978: Outside the Whale. In E.P. Thompson, *The Poverty of Theory and Other Essays* (London, Merlin Press).

Thompson, E.P. 1980: The Doomsday Consensus. In E.P. Thompson (ed.),

Writing By Candlelight (London, Merlin Press).

Thompson, E.P. 1984: Mr Attlee and the Gadarene Swine. *The Guardian*, 3 March, 9.

Thomson, K. 1988: *Under Siege: Racial Violence in Britain Today* (Harmondsworth, Penguin).

Titmuss, R. 1950: *Problems of Social Policy* [History of the Second World War United Kingdom Civil Series] (London, HMSO).

Titmuss, R. 1958a: *Essays on the Welfare State* (London, Allen & Unwin).

Titmuss, R. 1958b: The Social Division of Welfare. In Titmuss 1958a.

Titmuss, R. 1960: *The Irresponsible Society* [Fabian Tract 32] (London, The Fabian Society).

Titmuss, R. 1962: *Income Distribution and Social Change: A Study in Criticism* (London, George Allen & Unwin).

Titmuss, R. 1968: *Commitment to Welfare* (London, George Allen & Unwin).

Townsend, P. 1962: *The Last Refuge: A Survey of Residential Institutions and Homes for the Aged in England and Wales* (London, Routledge & Kegan Paul).

Townsend, P. 1963: *The Family Life of Old People: An Inquiry in East London* (Harmondsworth, Pelican).

Townsend, P. 1979: *Poverty in the United Kingdom* (Harmondsworth, Penguin).

University of Liverpool Department of Social Science 1951: *Social Aspects of a Town Development Plan: A Study of the County Borough of Dudley* (Liverpool, The University Press of Liverpool).

Utley, T.E. 1968: *Enoch Powell: The Man and his Thinking* (London, William Kimber).

Vereker, C., Mays, J.B., Gittus, E. and Broady, M. 1961: *Urban Redevelopment and Social Change: A Study of Social Conditions in Central Liverpool 1955–56* (Liverpool, Liverpool University Press).

Wainwright, H. 1984: Women and the Division of Labour. In P. Abrams and R. Brown (eds), *UK Society, Work, Urbanism and Unequality* (London, Weidenfeld & Nicolson, 1984).

Wakeford, J. 1969: *The Cloistered Elite: A Sociological Analysis of the English Public Boarding Schools* (London, Macmillan).

Walker, A. and Walker, C. 1987: *The Growing Divide: A Social Audit 1979–1987* (London, Child Poverty Action Group).

Walkerdine, V. 1985: Dreams from an Ordinary Childhood. In Heron 1985.

Wallace, W. 1970: World Status without Tears. In Bogdanor and Skidelsky 1970.

Wallman, S. 1984: *Eight London Households* (London, Tavistock).

Ward, R. 1983: Race Relations in Britain. In A. Stewart 1983a.

Warde, A. 1982: *Consensus and Beyond: The Development of Labour Party Strategy since the Second World War* (Manchester, Manchester University Press).

Watt, D.C. 1965: *Britain Looks to Germany: British Opinion and Policy Towards Germany Since 1945* (London, Oswald Wolff).

Waugh, E. 1984: *Unconditional Surrender* (Harmondsworth, Penguin).

Wiener, M.J. 1981: *English Culture and the Decline of the Industrial Spirit 1850–1980* (London, Cambridge University Press).

Westergaard, J.H. 1972: The Myth of Classlessness. In R. Blackburn (ed.), *Ideology in Social Science* (London, Fontana).

Westergaard, J.H. and Little, A.N. 1964: Educational Opportunity and Social Selection in England and Wales: Trends and Policy Implications. *British*

Journal of Sociology, 15, No 4 (Dec.), 301–16.

Westergaard, J. and Resler, H. 1975: *Class in a Capitalist Society* (London, Heinemann).

White, L.E. 1951: *New Towns: Their Challenge and Opportunity* (London, The National Council of Social Service).

Whitehead, P. 1986: *The Writing on the Wall: Britain in the Seventies* (London, Michael Joseph).

Williams, P.M. (ed.) 1983: *The Diary of Hugh Gaitskell 1945–56* (London, Jonathan Cape).

Williams, R. 1958: *Culture and Society: 1780–1950* (Harmondsworth, Penguin).

Williams, R. 1965: *The Long Revolution* (Harmondsworth, Penguin).

Williams, R. 1977: *Marxism and Literature* (London, Oxford University Press).

Williams, R. 1983: *Towards 2000* (Harmondsworth, Penguin).

Williams, R. 1985: *The Country and the City* (London, The Hogarth Press).

Williams, R. 1989: Missing the Meaning: Key Words in the Miners' Strike. In R. Gable (ed.), *Resources of Hope: Culture, Democracy, Socialism* (London, Verso).

Williams, W.M. 1956: *The Sociology of an English Village* (London, Routledge & Kegan Paul).

Williamson, B. 1981: Class Bias. In D. Warren Piper (ed.), *Is Higher Education Fair?* (London, Society for Research into Higher Education).

Williamson, B. 1982: *Class, Culture and Community: A Biographical Study of Social Change in Mining* (London, Routledge & Kegan Paul).

Williamson, B. 1983: The Peripheralisation of Youth in the Labour Market: Problems, Analyses and Opportunities: Britain and the Federal Republic of Germany. In Ahier and Flude 1983.

Williamson, B. 1984: Students, Higher Education and Social Change. *European Journal of Education*, 19, No 3, 253–67.

Williamson, J.W. (unpublished): *Recollections: 1930–1945.* (Private papers: consultation by request to author).

Willis, P. 1977: *Leaning to Labour* (London, Saxa House).

Willmott, P. 1963: *The Evolution of a Community* (London, Routledge & Kegan Paul).

Wilson, E. 1980: *Only Half Way to Paradise* (London, Tavistock Publications).

Wilson, E. 1982: *Mirror Writing* (London, Virago).

Wilson, H. 1964: *Poverty in Britain Today* (London, Society of Friends Home Service Committee).

Wilson, H. and Herbert, G.W. 1978: *Parents and Children in the Inner City* (London, Routledge & Kegan Paul).

Winterton, J. and Winterton, R. 1989: *The 1984–85 Miners' Strike in Yorkshire* (Manchester, Manchester University Press).

Woolton, The Rt. Hon. the Earl 1959: *The Memoirs of the Rt. Hon. the Earl of Woolton* (London, Cassell).

Worsbrough Community Group (no date): *The Heart and Soul of It* (Barnsley, Worsbrough Community Group).

Worsthorne, P. 1956: The New Unequality. *Encounter*, 28 November, 24–34.

Wright, P. 1985: *On Living in an Old Country: The National Past in Contemporary Britain* (London, Verso).

Yass, M. 1983: *Home Front Propaganda in the Second World War* (London, Public Records Office: HMSO).

Young, M. and Willmott, P. 1957: *Family and Kinship in East London* (Harmondsworth, Penguin).

Zeldin, T. 1978: *France 1848–1945* (London, Oxford University Press).

Zweig, F. 1948: *Labour, Life and Poverty* (London, Gollancz).

Zweig, F. 1963: *The Student in the Age of Anxiety* (London, Heinemann).

Index